The Limits of Concept Formation
in Natural Science

Heinrich Rickert (1863–1936) was one of the leading neo-Kantian philosophers in Germany and a crucial figure in discussions of the foundations of the social sciences in the early years of this century. His views were extremely influential, most significantly on Max Weber.

The Limits of Concept Formation in Natural Science, Rickert's most important work, is here translated into English for the first time. In attempting to answer the question of how historical knowledge of contingent and individual phenomena is possible, it develops a systematic theory of knowledge and philosophy of science. Rickert provides an account of the limits of concept formation in natural science, a criterion to demarcate the natural and the human sciences, and an account of objective value, which underpins the objectivity of historical knowledge.

Rickert's views, which he works out in contrast to those of Dilthey, the positivists, Idealists, and early phenomenologists, are of great intrinsic interest and considerable historical importance. Working from the fifth German edition, Professor Oakes has prepared an abridgment that effectively brings out those arguments and displays their significance. He has also provided his translation with an illuminating introduction to the content and context of the work.

TEXTS IN GERMAN PHILOSOPHY

General Editor: CHARLES TAYLOR

Advisory Board: RÜDIGER BUBNER, RAYMOND GEUSS, PETER HEATH,
GARBIS KORTIAN, WILHELM VOSSENKUHL, MARX WARTOFSKY

The purpose of this series is to make available, in English, central works of German philosophy from Kant to the present. Although there is rapidly growing interest in the English-speaking world in different aspects of the German philosophical tradition as an extremely fertile source of study and inspiration, many of its crucial texts are not available in English or exist only in inadequate or dated translations. The series is intended to remedy that situation, and the translations where appropriate will be accompanied by historical and philosophical introductions and notes. Single works, selections from a single author, and anthologies will all be represented.

Friedrich Nietzsche *Daybreak*

J. G. Fichte *The Science of Knowledge*

Lawrence S. Stepelevich (ed.) *The Young Hegelians: an anthology*

Wilhelm von Humboldt *On language*

Heinrich Rickert *The limits of concept formation in natural science*

HEINRICH RICKERT

The Limits of Concept Formation in Natural Science

A Logical Introduction to the Historical Sciences
(abridged edition)

Edited and Translated by
Guy Oakes

MONMOUTH COLLEGE AND NEW SCHOOL
FOR SOCIAL RESEARCH

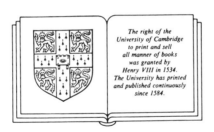

The right of the
University of Cambridge
to print and sell
all manner of books
was granted by
Henry VIII in 1534.
The University has printed
and published continuously
since 1584.

Cambridge University Press

Cambridge

London   New York   New Rochelle
Melbourne   Sydney

Published by the Press Syndicate of the University of Cambridge
The Pitt Building, Trumpington Street, Cambridge CB2 1RP
32 East 57th Street, New York, NY 10022, USA
10 Stamford Road, Oakleigh, Melbourne 3166, Australia

English translation © Cambridge University Press 1986

First published 1986

Printed in the United States of America

Library of Congress Cataloging in Publication Data
Rickert, Heinrich, 1863–1936.
The limits of concept formation in natural science.
(Texts in German philosophy)
Translation of Die Grenzen der naturwissenschaftlichen
Begriffsbildung.
Includes bibliographical references and index.
1. History – Philosophy.   2. Science – Philosophy.
I. Title.   II. Series.
D16.8.R53213   1986   901   85-22369

British Library Cataloguing in Publication Data
Rickert, Heinrich
The limits of concept formation in natural
science: a logical introduction to the historical
sciences. – Abridged ed. – (Texts in German
philosophy)
1. History – Philosophy   2. Science – Philosophy
I. Title   II. Oakes, Guy   III. Die Grenzen der
naturwissenschaftlichen Begriffsbildung. *English*
IV. Series
901   D16.8

ISBN 0 521 25139 7 hard covers
ISBN 0 521 31015 6 paperback

Contents

v

Introduction: Rickert's Theory
of Historical Knowledge

"I have just finished Rickert," Max Weber wrote to his wife from Florence in the spring of 1902. "He is *very* good."[1] This referred, of course, to the philosopher Heinrich Rickert, Weber's friend from his Freiburg period,[2] and the book Weber had just finished was to become the major work of Rickert's career: *Die Grenzen der naturwissenschaftlichen Begriffsbildung*, an attempt to develop a philosophy of history independent of both positivism and neo-Hegelian idealism along lines already sketched by his teacher Wilhelm Windelband in the 1890s. In a note of uncharacteristic modesty, Rickert admits that the main thesis of *Die Grenzen* had already been clearly articulated by Windelband in "History and Natural Science," his famous inaugural lecture as rector of Strassburg University in 1894. Rickert even suggests that the reader who had thought his way through the consequences of Windelband's lecture may find parts of his own

For advice on this work, thanks are due to Thomas Burger, Wolfgang Schluchter, and Gerhard Wagner. Support was provided by a grant from Monmouth College, New Jersey.

[1] Marianne Weber, *Max Weber: A Biography*, trans. Harry Zohn (New York: Wiley, 1975), p. 260.

[2] Rickert (1863–1936) and Weber (1864–1920) had been colleagues since the time of Weber's professorship at Freiburg (1894–7), where Rickert was a privatdocent in philosophy. Rickert completed his doctoral studies under Wilhelm Windelband in 1888 with a monograph on the logic of definition (*Zur Lehre der Definition*). He then moved to Freiburg for his *Habilitation*, the work that qualified him for university teaching. Completed in 1891, this was a general introduction to the problems of the theory of knowledge from a neo-Kantian perspective (*Der Gegenstand der Erkenntnis*). When a professorship in philosophy at Freiburg fell vacant upon Alois Riehl's departure for Kiel, Weber successfully supported Rickert's candidacy. In the year that followed this letter to his wife, Weber characterized his first and most ambitious methodological study as, in part, an attempt to test the value of Rickert's ideas for his own methodological purposes. See Max Weber, *Roscher and Knies: The Logical Problems of Historical Economics*, trans. Guy Oakes (New York: Free Press, 1975), p. 213 n. 9. For the influence of Rickert on Weber's methodology, see Thomas Burger, *Max Weber's Theory of Concept Formation* (Durham, N.C.: Duke University Press, 1976).

treatise superfluous.[3] During the twenty years of his Strassburg period, Windelband became the leader of the Baden, or Southwest German, school of neo-Kantianism, thus named because its leading figures held appointments at southwest German universities: Windelband at Strassburg and later at Heidelberg; Rickert at Freiburg and then at Heidelberg; and Emil Lask – Rickert's student at Freiburg and subsequently Windelband's postdoctoral student at Heidelberg – at Heidelberg as well.

The principal philosophical contribution of the Southwest German school lies in its development of a theory of historical knowledge or an epistemology of the cultural sciences. Its basic outlines may be sketched as follows. First, Windelband formulated the ideal of a historical science the distinctive interest of which lies in knowledge of individual or concrete reality. This is the methodological ideal of idiographic knowledge, which Rickert later analyzes more precisely as knowledge of the historical individual. Second, Lask's account of the analytic and emanationist theories of concept formation and his discussion of the *hiatus irrationalis* between concept and reality provide an analysis of the conditions under which knowledge of the historical individual is possible. Third, Rickert's theory of historical knowledge provides an account of the conceptualization of individual entities that undertakes to show how the problem of the *hiatus irrationalis* can be solved – not by surmounting the gap between concept and reality, however, but rather by employing it as an essential premise for the development of a theory of historical concept formation. Rickert's account, therefore, can be conceived as an attempt to show that the

---

[3]Heinrich Rickert, *Die Grenzen der naturwissenschaftlichen Begriffsbildung* (Tübingen: Mohr, 1902), p. 302. Windelband (1848–1915) received his doctorate in philosophy at Berlin in 1870 and completed his *Habilitation* at Leipzig in 1873. Studies with Kuno Fischer at Jena and Rudolf Hermann Lotze at Göttingen were the principal influences on his conception of the aims and limits of philosophy. For an account of the genesis of the neo-Kantian movement that focuses on the development from Kant through Fichte and Lotze to the immediate prehistory of neo-Kantianism in the 1850s and 1860s, see Gerhard Lehmann, "Kant im Spätidealismus und die Anfänge der neukantischen Bewegung," *Zeitschrift für philosophische Forschung* 10 (1963): 438–56. Hans-Ludwig Ollig provides a good general account of the two main tendencies of the movement, the Marburg school and the Southwest German school. See his introduction, pp. 5–52 in Hans-Ludwig Ollig, ed., *Neukantianismus* (Stuttgart: Reclam, 1982). One of the best recent accounts of neo-Kantianism is contained in the introductory materials with which Werner Flach and Helmut Holzhey preface their anthology on neo-Kantian logic and epistemology, *Erkenntnistheorie und Logik im Neukantianismus* (Hildesheim: Gerstenberg, 1980). See especially pp. 10–13 and 35–9. For a general account of the neo-Kantian movement in English, see Thomas E. Willey, *Back to Kant* (Detroit: Wayne State University Press, 1978).

conditions for the possibility of knowledge of the historical individual are satisfied.[4]

WINDELBAND: THE METHODOLOGICAL IDEAL OF IDIOGRAPHIC KNOWLEDGE

In one of his last critical appreciations of Kant's importance for modern philosophy, Windelband introduces some observations on Kant's conception of historical knowledge and thereby reaffirms one of the main doctrines of his own philosophical program: To understand Kant is to go beyond him.[5] Kant conceived the scope of science as limited to the enterprise of Newtonian natural philosophy: the attempt to discover the necessary and universally valid laws that account for the properties of the phenomenal world. Historical claims to knowledge, on the other hand, are particular and contingent. In the final analysis, history has an inferior cognitive status because it fails to qualify as a science according to the criteria for scientific knowledge that Kant elaborates in his *Critique of Pure Reason*: Historical propositions lack the necessity and general validity that would qualify them as possible objects of scientific knowledge. Windelband argues that this is the point on which the Kantian theory of knowledge is most in need of revision.[6] Arguing against Kant thirteen years earlier in "History and Natural Science," Windelband held that the possibility of history as a science rests on three premises: an individualistic conception of value, a nomological or nomothetic conception of the limits of natural science, and an individualistic or idiographic conception of historical science.

Windelband claimed that values can be ascribed only to phenomena that are unique and incomparable in their individuality. This thesis is ultimately grounded in the individualistic conception of value introduced by Christian theology in its polemic against the axiological universalism of Greek philosophy. The Christian idea that values can be ascribed only to individual phenomena has its origins in the conception of the Creation, the Fall, and the events of the life of Christ as unique events endowed with unprecedented significance.

4Since the basic elements of Rickert's theory of historical knowledge were in place long before Lask's dissertation, the above analysis is obviously not a genetic account of how the philosophy of history of the Southwest German school was in fact developed. It is rather a reconstruction of the logic on which its solution to the problem of historical knowledge is based.

5"Ueber die gegenwärtige Lage und Aufgabe der Philosophie," in *Präludien: Aufsätze und Reden zur Philosophie und ihrer Geschichte*, 2 vol. II, 9th ed. (Tübingen: Mohr, 1924), vol. II, pp. 1–23.

6*Präludien*, vol. II, pp. 13–14.

Windelband argued that this idea represents the first powerful insight into what he called the inalienable metaphysical right of historiography: its interest in reality as unique and unrepeatable.[7] According to this conception of value, we lose interest in an object if we discover that it is nothing more than a representative case of a general phenomenon. Consider the horror produced by the idea of the *Doppelgänger*, the revulsion inspired by the idea of the eternal recurrence of all things, and the inability of an object to engage our emotions if it is merely one among innumerable others of the same sort. According to Windelband, these considerations all confirm the individuality of values: The attribution of values must always have a concrete and singular referent. The source of our interest in knowledge of individual phenomena lies in this basic fact of philosophical anthropology: that we ascribe values exclusively to individuals.

This theoretical interest cannot be satisfied by natural science, which abstracts from the unique and qualitatively distinctive properties of real phenomena in order to disclose the laws on which they depend. This is the sense in which natural science is nomothetic. It has no intrinsic interest in the individual events of concrete reality. On the contrary, the individual datum is relevant to natural science only to the extent that it can be represented as a type, an instance of a generic concept, or a case that can be subsumed under a general law. This is a consequence of the ultimate theoretical purpose of natural science, which is to produce a system of maximally abstract and general laws, nomological regularities that govern all events. Nomothetic knowledge, therefore, represents the triumph of abstract thought over our perception of concrete reality.

The interest of historical science, on the other hand, is idiographic. Here the purpose of knowledge is to comprehend the distinctive properties of the unique event itself. History is interested in a phenomenon not because of what it shares with other phenomena but, rather, because of its own definitive qualities. Unlike the natural scientist, the historian attempts to establish knowledge of the concrete and singular features of reality. Therefore, it is historical science that will realize the theoretical ideal generated by our interest in knowledge of individual phenomena.

Windelband stressed the purely formal or logical character of this theoretical ideal. The criterion for the distinction between natural science and historical science lies in the "formal property of the theoretical or cognitive objectives of the science in question."[8] Because

---

[7]"History and Natural Science," trans. Guy Oakes, *History and Theory* xix (1980): 182.
[8]Ibid., p. 175.

Windelband did not investigate the properties of history as a mode of existence, he did not inquire into the conditions that would have to be satisfied by the kind of being to which a historical existence can be ascribed. On the contrary, his purpose was to raise the question of the "subjective" conditions for the possibility of a certain kind of knowledge. This is the respect in which he saw his own investigation as following the transcendental and critical method of Kant, even if it did not agree with Kant's assumptions about historical knowledge and his conclusions about the possibility of history as a science. Windelband's analysis is an attempt to identify the conditions that must be satisfied by the historical subject, the agent of historical knowledge, which he conceived as a transcendental or epistemological consciousness. Windelband called it a normative consciousness (*Normalbewusstsein*) because its norms constitute conditions under which knowledge is possible. Thus Windelband's problem concerns the subjective presuppositions on which a certain kind of science is based rather than the subject matter or object of that science.

Windelband's taxonomy of the sciences classifies scientific disciplines on the basis of their theoretical purposes or cognitive interests. He identified three consequences that the formal character of this methodological taxonomy entails for his philosophy of history. First, we should not expect this taxonomy to conform to the division of labor between the different fields of science as they actually exist in university faculties or academies of science. In these cases, the classification is governed not by methodological criteria but by practical pedagogical considerations and extrascientific historical contingencies. Second, it is clear that the same object can be a datum of both natural science and historical science. Because Windelband's distinction between the nomothetic and the idiographic characterizes different forms of knowledge or modes of investigation and not the subject matter or content of knowledge, it follows that no phenomenon lies essentially or intrinsically within the domain of either nature or history. Finally, there is a sense in which the distinction between the nomothetic and the idiographic is ultimately relative. From the perspective of the natural science of biology, for example, the domain of organisms is conceived as a part of nature, and thus as a field governed by the operation of general laws. From the perspective of natural history, on the other hand, this same domain of organisms is conceived as a unique process of evolutionary history. The same phenomenon represented nomothetically by natural science may also be represented idiographically by historical science. There is, of course, another sense in which Windelband's taxonomy is not relative. Because the nomothetic/idiographic dichotomy marks an absolute distinction between mutually exclusive modes of investigation, the same inquiry cannot qualify as both nomothetic and idiographic. But this consideration does not entail that the same datum cannot be investigated by both nomothetic and idiographic disciplines.

In view of this relativity of the distinction between the nomothetic and the idiographic and the fact that no datum necessarily falls into the domain of either nature or history, it is clear that Windelband's dichotomy of natural science and historical science cannot be ontologically grounded. In other words, it cannot be established by making a substantive distinction between two mutually exclusive domains of reality such as nature and mind, a distinction that implies that cognitive access to nature is based on observation or external perception and cognitive access to the mind is grounded in a special faculty of intuition or inner perception. In addition, Windelband rejected an ontological solution to the problem of the possibility of historical knowledge on three other grounds. First, there is no reason to suppose that knowledge of historical facts is possible solely on the basis of a faculty of inner perception. Second, the legitimacy of this alleged faculty of inner perception is in doubt. It is not clear that an inner and purely private mode of intuition, understanding, or empathy can qualify as knowledge.[9] Finally, psychology is an anomaly and an embarrassment for the ontological solution because it cannot be unambiguously classified as either a natural science or a historical science. As regards its subject matter, it falls in the former domain. As regards its method of investigation, however, it falls in the latter.[10]

The main theses of "History and Natural Science" – the individualistic conception of value, the nomothetic conception of the limits of natural science, the methodological ideal of idiographic knowledge, the formal strategy by which the distinction between natural science and historical science is drawn, and the rejection of the ontological

---

[9]On this point, the neo-Kantian attack by Windelband, Rickert, and Weber on the private cognitive faculties postulated by Dilthey, *Lebensphilosophie*, and early phenomenology anticipates Wittgenstein's more radical critique of private knowledge in the 1930s and 1940s. See especially Wittgenstein's *Philosophical Investigations*, trans. G. E. M. Anscombe (New York: Macmillan, 1953), part I. In addition to the texts by Windelband and Rickert discussed in this essay, see Weber's *Roscher and Knies*.

[10]For the neo-Kantians the most important advocate of the ontological solution was Wilhelm Dilthey, who had become a whipping boy for Windelband and Rickert by the mid-1890s. Gregor Schöllgen makes a case for minimizing the differences between Dilthey's conception of human science [*Geisteswissenschaft*] and Rickert's conception of cultural science [*Kulturwissenschaft*]. See his *Handlungsfreiheit und Zweckrationalität: Max Weber und die Tradition praktischer Philosophie* (Tübingen: Mohr, 1984), pp. 48–55.

solution – are also major doctrines in Rickert's philosophy of history. In addition, the basic problem generated by the arguments of "History and Natural Science" also becomes the fundamental question Rickert attempts to solve in *Die Grenzen*.[11]

Windelband alluded to this problem in the final paragraphs of the lecture. The occurrence of individual events cannot be explained by general laws. Put another way, there is no set of nomological statements, regardless of how exhaustive and precise, from which any description of an individual event can be deduced. This is why our theoretical interest in individual phenomena cannot be satisfied by natural science. As Windelband claimed, nomothetic and idiographic cognitive interests are independent and juxtaposed to one another: The law and the event remain as the "ultimate, incommensurable entities of our world view."[12] But if natural science cannot establish knowledge of individual phenomena, how is such knowledge possible? In response to this problem, Windelband offered nothing more than a few obscure metaphorical suggestions.[13] At the end of the lecture, we are left with the conclusion that the individual historical datum represents a "residuum of incomprehensible, brute fact." It is an "inexpressible and indefinable phenomenon."[14]

[11]Rickert adopted certain other positions from Windelband that can be characterized as the definitive doctrines of the Southwest German school: the rejection of epistemological realism and the correspondence theory of truth; the distinction between the genetic method of the empirical sciences, which are concerned with the causation of phenomena, and the critical method of philosophy, which is concerned with the validity of values; the consequent rejection of any epistemological naturalism, such as psychologism or historicism, which reduces philosophical questions to empirical problems; the transcendental turn in philosophical thought, which includes both the use of transcendental modes of argumentation and the crucial status ascribed to a transcendental subjectivity or a normative epistemological consciousness; the axiological turn in philosophical thought, in which this normative consciousness is defined by objective or generally valid values that are necessary presuppositions of theoretical, practical, and aesthetic judgments; and the doctrine that in the final analysis, going back to Kant requires going beyond Kant. Under these circumstances, it is not surprising that the exigencies of Rickert's career required that he stress the differences between his own position and Windelband's in order to make a case for his own philosophical originality. For a recent account of the relationship between Windelband and Rickert, see Herbert Schnädelbach, *Geschichtsphilosophie nach Hegel: Die Probleme des Historismus* (Freiburg/Munich: Karl Alber, 1974), pp. 137–59, and also his *Philosophy in Germany 1831–1933*, trans. Eric Matthews (Cambridge: Cambridge University Press, 1984), pp. 58, 129–34, 180–5.

[12]"History and Natural Science," p. 185.

[13]For example, we are told that the historian breathes new life into the past. In this respect, history is said to resemble the creativity of the fine arts. See "History and Natural Science," p. 178.

[14]Ibid., p. 184.

LASK'S ANALYSIS OF CONCEPT FORMATION AND
THE IRRATIONALITY OF CONCRETE REALITY

Although the purpose of historical science is knowledge of individual
phenomena, such phenomena are incomprehensible. In the work of
the Southwest German school, the most careful and exhaustive
exposition of the issues this problem poses for the theory of historical
knowledge is set out in Emil Lask's precociously brilliant doctoral
dissertation on Fichte's philosophy of history.[15]

For the Southwest German school, epistemological questions are
concerned with the formation of concepts. The conditions for the
possiblity of knowledge of an object are conditions for the possibility
of forming concepts of that object. An item becomes an object of
knowledge when it is brought under concepts, or when concepts are
formed that represent the item. Valid concept formation, therefore,
constitutes knowledge. It follows that the problem of historical
knowledge is the problem of individual concept formation: the
question of the conditions under which concrete reality can be
conceptualized, or represented by means of concepts. This relationship between knowledge and concept formation in the epistemology
of the Southwest German school explains why Lask attacks the
problem of historical knowledge by analyzing theories of concept
formation.

Lask claims that all theories of the concept fall into one of two main
groups. One theory, typified by the work of Kant, he calls an analytic
logic of concepts. The other, consummated by Hegel, he calls an
emanationist logic.

The analytic theory holds that the concrete object of immediate
experience is the sole reality, the basis from which all concept
formation begins. Reality itself, however, cannot be conceptualized.
Individual existence, which is unique and unfathomable, marks the
limit of concept formation. The concept itself is an artificially abstracted part or aspect of reality, produced by analyzing elements that
actually exist together in a diffuse or inchoate fashion. Because of its
abstract character, the concept is general, articulating what is common
to a plurality of phenomena. This is the sense in which concept
formation qualifies as an analysis of what is immediately given. The
concept recasts the reality it represents in such a way that this reality
is conceived as an instance of the application of the concept itself. As

[15]*Fichtes Idealismus und die Geschichte*, in *Gesammelte Schriften*, vol. I (Tübingen: Mohr,
1923). Lask (1875–1915) studied with Rickert in Freiburg (1894–6, 1898–1901)
and with Windelband in Strassburg (1896–8). *Fichtes Idealismus* was completed
under Rickert's supervision in 1901.

a result, the relationship between the concept and its object is not one of real dependence. It is a purely logical relationship, established by thought and with no ontological foundation. Because the concept is an artificial intellectual construct, reality is ontologically richer than the concept. Indeed, the more abstract and general the concept, the more remote from reality it becomes. Thus even though concrete reality falls under concepts, it cannot be derived from them. This is because concepts – as ontologically empty products of intellectual abstraction – cannot contain reality itself. Because concrete reality cannot be conceptualized, it is "irrational"; that is, it is not a possible object of knowledge.

The definitive theses of the analytic theory of concept formation can be summarized as follows: (1) Concept formation represents an analytic abstraction from reality. (2) This is responsible for the substantive poverty or the ontological emptiness of the concept. (3) As a result, there is a dualism of concept and reality. The concept is what can be comprehended or known, even though it has no ontological status. Individual existence, on the other hand, is not a possible object of conceptualization, even though it is the sole reality. (4) Thus reality is irrational in the sense that it is inaccessible to conceptualization.[16]

The emanationist theory rejects each of these theses. The concept is not an abstracted aspect or part of reality. On the contrary, individual existence realizes or embodies the content of the concept, from which it emanates. It follows that concrete events can be deduced from concepts, which are ontologically richer than these events and in this sense represent a "higher reality." As a result, not only does individual existence fall under concepts, but its content is also included in the content of concepts. Thus the purely logical relation between concept and reality maintained by the analytic theory becomes an ontological relationship in the emanationist theory. The dialectical or logical process of thought becomes a *Weltprozess*, a universal or cosmic process of real events. This means that "logic is also a metaphysics and an ontology."[17] Because the concept is fully real and individuality, which emanates from the concept, is fully rational, the dualism of concept and reality collapses. Thus the irrationality of reality is nullified as well. Because the content of individual reality can be exhaustively derived from concepts, what is real is rational and what is rational is real.

Although Lask admits that the logic of the emanationist theory is sound, he cannot accept the main premises that generate the theory:

---

[16]*Fichtes Idealismus*, pp. 30–1, 43–4.
[17]Ibid., p. 67. See also pp. 30, 66, 72. 88.

Hegel's account of the concept and the Hegelian thesis that concepts are more real than individual existence.[18] As a student of Rickert and Windelband, Lask also regards concepts as artificial intellectual constructs that abstract from reality. This means that in returning to Kant in order to confront the problem of historical knowledge, the Southwest German school is committed to the analytic theory. And yet this theory entails a consequence that seems to preclude conceptualization of the individual: the dualism of concept and reality and the irrationality of individual existence.

Borrowing an expression from Fichte, Lask claims that the contingent, arbitrary, and anomic character of individual existence represents a *hiatus irrationalis* between thought and reality. This is a result of the absolute dualism of concept and reality.[19] There is a hiatus because reality cannot be derived from concepts. And it is irrational because reality can be rationalized only by conceptualizing it, which according to the analytic theory is impossible. Thus, as Windelband notes in the conclusion of his lecture, concrete reality simply must be accepted as an incomprehensible brute fact. Even though individual existence falls under laws, it cannot be deduced from them; and even though it follows laws, it does not follow from them. Therefore, the law and reality, or concepts and reality, are "incommensurable quantities."[20]

In summary, Lask's analysis of theories of concept formation entails that historical knowledge is possible only if the problem of the *hiatus irrationalis* can be solved, either by surmounting the *hiatus irrationalis* and closing the gap between concept and reality or by developing a strategy that will show that historical knowledge is possible in spite of – or perhaps even because of – the *hiatus irrationalis*. Hegel and the partisans of the emanationist theory take the former course. Rickert takes the latter. By employing the *hiatus irrationalis* as a premise of his philosophy of history, he attempts to show how historical knowledge depends on the irrationality of reality. In Rickert's thought, therefore, the *hiatus irrationalis* is not a radical problem or an obstacle that seems to preclude historical knowledge. It is, rather, an essential condition for the possibility of historical knowledge.

RICKERT'S PROJECT

Rickert's main purpose in *Die Grenzen* is to solve the problem posed by the *hiatus irrationalis*. There are five links in the chain of reasoning

[18] Ibid., p. 72.
[19] Ibid., pp. 63, 117–18, 144–5.
[20] Ibid., pp. 173–4.

that leads him to a solution: a phenomenology of reality, a critique of epistemological realism, a theory of cognitive interests and a theory of concepts, an analysis of the limits of concept formation in natural science, and a demarcation criterion for distinguishing natural science from historical or cultural science.

The Phenomenology of Reality. Reality as an object of experience is an infinite manifold of single events and processes that has no identifiable temporal beginning or end and no discernible spatial limits. Moreover, it appears in an infinite number of combinations. There are two respects in which reality as a whole is infinite. It is *unendlich*, or endless in the sense that it cannot be exhaustively incorporated into experience. And it is *unübersehbar*, or without limits in the sense that it is impossible to survey reality in toto. Rickert calls this the extensive infinity of reality. In addition, each event and process within this extensively infinite manifold of experience is also infinitely complex in two respects: First, the number of parts into which any event can be divided or analyzed, or the number of elements that compose it, is also unlimited in principle. Second, every such event and its parts can be said to possess an infinite number of aspects. Put another way, every event can be described in terms of properties each of which exhibits an indeterminate number of aspects. Rickert calls this the intensive infinity of reality. Thus reality as a whole is irrational in the sense that there is no criterion that can specify what would qualify as knowledge of this totality. And every element of reality is irrational in the sense that there is no criterion that can specify what would constitute a complete description of its aspects.

Rickert stresses that this conception of the irrationality of reality is not a thesis about the nature of existence itself but, rather, a statement of fact about our experience of what exists. In other words, it is a phenomenological claim, not an ontological doctrine. In Rickert's view, therefore, it would be a mistake to suggest that his solution to the problem of historical knowledge rests on an ontology according to which reality is ultimately irrational.[21]

The Critique of Epistemological Realism. The second link in Rickert's reasoning is the inference he draws from this phenomenology of reality: a refutation of epistemological realism. The idea of epistemological realism is employed quite informally in *Die Grenzen*, and Rickert never subjects it to a careful analysis. But his remarks on the

[21]*Die Grenzen der naturwissenschaftlichen Begriffsbildung*, 5th ed. rev. and enlarged (Tübingen: Mohr, 1929), chapter 1, section I.

idea indicate that he conceives it as a thesis concerning the nature of both knowledge and truth. According to this view, the purpose of knowledge is to reproduce reality as we actually experience it. A proposition qualifies as a valid cognitive claim insofar as it faithfully reproduces the properties of its object. Such a theory of knowledge requires a correspondence theory of truth. A proposition is true if it corresponds to the facts it represents – in other words, insofar as it reproduces these facts. It is false to the extent that it constitutes a defective reproduction.

In light of the irrationality of reality and the impossibility of cognitively reproducing not only reality as a whole but also any of its aspects, it is not surprising that Rickert finds epistemological realism unacceptable. Reality as we experience it cannot be reproduced in any sense, either extensively or intensively.

The rejection of epistemological realism is required by two constitutents of Rickert's theory of knowledge. First, he defends a theory of concept formation that holds that knowledge cannot qualify as a reproduction. Thus the only purpose of concept formation can be knowledge of reality based on a criterion of what is deemed important or essential. Such a criterion amounts to a principle of "selection" that makes possible the conceptualization, but not the reproduction, of selected aspects of reality from the standpoint of specific cognitive interests.[22] Second, Rickert defends a theory of truth that holds that the idea of a correspondence between any set of propositions and reality is incoherent. A proposition is not true because it corresponds with reality. On the contrary, it is true because what is asserted by the proposition – its "ideal," "unreal" theoretical content or import – holds validly for reality. The Southwest German school conceives truth as a value. The domain of values is not existence but validity. Therefore, existence or nonexistence cannot be ascribed to values; only validity or invalidity can. This is because values are ideal, not real: unreal (*unwirklich*) or nonreal (*irreal*). Because the properties of what is real cannot be ascribed to values, there can be no relation of correspondence between values and reality. This means that what is true cannot be said to exist. It can only be said to hold validly. Thus a true proposition does not reproduce the properties of its object. Because it does not have the properties of what exists but rather the properties of what holds validly, truth cannot constitute a relationship of correspondence between knowledge and reality.[23]

[22]Ibid., pp. 214–15.
[23]Ibid., pp. 214–16.

Rickert's Epistemology: A Theory of Cognitive Interests and a Theory of Concepts. Is there an adequate theory of knowledge that can take the place of epistemological realism? Rickert's answer to this question has two parts. First, he provides an account of the essential aims of knowledge, or an analysis of cognitive interests. This account might also be called a teleology of cognitive discourse, which in the face of the infinite complexity of reality, identifies specific aspects of reality that fall under our cognitive interests. Second, in light of the essential values we expect knowledge to realize, Rickert provides an account of the indispensable means, instruments, or methods for establishing the type of knowledge in question. This account might be called a methodology of cognitive discourse. "Concepts" is the name Rickert reserves for these essential instruments of knowledge. Given the irrationality of reality, knowledge is possible only by means of concepts that simplify, recast, and transform reality on the basis of the interests these concepts are intended to fulfill. Rickert calls the product of the conceptualization of some aspect of reality a representation (*Darstellung*) of that aspect. Rickertian concepts are not mere ideas or facts of mental life. On the contrary, they are logical constructs that realize a certain cognitive purpose. The question of methodology is the problem of how concepts are to be formed in order to realize the cognitive interests they are expected to serve. Rickert's theory of method, therefore, is a theory of concept formation.[24]

[24]Rickert makes a distinction between methodology and epistemology. This is based on a distinction between constitutive and methodological forms. Constitutive forms are the general categories necessary to define a given material as objective reality or as an object of knowledge in general. Methodological forms are more specialized and are required for the analysis of reality as the data of a specific kind of scientific knowledge. Causality, for example, is a constitutive form because a material cannot be represented as objective reality without this category. Nomological regularity or the concept of a law of science, on the other hand, is a methodological form: Although it is required for the analysis of reality by natural science, it is not necessarily essential to any other kind of scientific knowledge. Constitutive and methodological forms are distinguished by reference to both generality and logical priority. The former are more general than the latter. In addition, the analysis of material by means of methodological forms presupposes that it is defined as reality on the basis of constitutive forms. The development and systematization of constitutive forms are the domain of epistemology or the theory of knowledge in general [*Erkenntnistheorie*]. The development and systematization of methodological forms are the domain of methodology or the theory of scientific knowledge [*Wissenschaftslehre*]. See Rickert, *Der Gegenstand der Erkenntnis*, 3rd ed. (Tübingen: Mohr, 1915), pp. 403–36.

The Limits of Concept Formation in Natural Science. Following Windelband, Rickert claims that our interest in most facts of reality is determined by what they have in common with others. From the perspective of this interest, phenomena are conceptualized as nature: Reality insofar as what we want to know about it is exhausted by its general properties, those it shares with other phenomena. The definitive theoretical purpose of knowledge of nature, or natural science, is to establish laws of nature: general propositions that identify features common to phenomena that otherwise may be quite different. This is the fourth link in the reasoning that leads Rickert to a solution to the problem of the *hiatus irrationalis*: his theory of natural science and its limits.

Natural science solves the problem of both the extensive and the intensive infinity of reality by means of its distinctive conceptual instrument, the law of nature. A natural law does not designate entities that have a unique spatiotemporal location. Rather it holds validly for all members of a certain class of such entities. Nor does the law of nature constitute a representation of the perceptual manifold of reality. This is why Rickert emphasizes that concepts in natural science should not be confused with those of classical Greek philosophy, for example, the forms in Plato's theory of ideas. Concepts in natural science are not ideas of things or images of reality. On the contrary, they recast and transform reality in such a way that its complexity is reduced and simplified in the interest of systematic comprehensibility. This holds true both for the spatiotemporal limits of reality, or its extensive complexity, and for the elements that compose it, or its intensive complexity. Knowledge of reality as nature is possible because what Rickert calls *die Anschaulichkeit der Wirklichkeit* – the concrete perceptuality of reality, the distinctive feature of reality that is responsible for its irrationality – is irrelevant to natural science. The concepts of natural science are not attempts to reproduce the concrete perceptuality of reality. On the contrary, they are attempts to abstract universal features from its perceptual qualities. Precisely because they are universal, these features are not perceptual; and because they are not perceptual, they are not real.[25]

Abstraction from the perceptuality of reality is a condition for the possibility of natural science.[26] Indeed, the progress of natural science is defined by this process of abstraction. As laws of nature become more general, explanations become more powerful, and thus natural science advances. But as laws become more general, their concepts

---

[25] *Die Grenzen*, chapter 1, section vi.
[26] Ibid., pp. 192, 196.

also become more abstract. This means that they also become increasingly devoid of perceptual content and therefore increasingly remote from reality.

The perceptual properties of a real entity, however, are also its individual properties: the properties of the entity as we experience it, its spatiotemporally unique and nonrepeatable qualities that differentiate it from every other real entity. Thus the same reasoning that holds for the perceptual properties of reality also applies to its individual properties. By means of abstraction, concept formation in natural science brackets the unique and nonrepeatable properties of reality as well.[27] Since reality is constituted by its perceptual and individual qualities, Rickert's conclusion is hardly surprising. It is reality itself that disappears from the conceptual abstractions of natural science. These considerations establish that there is a limit to concept formation in natural science, and they also show what that limit is: empirical reality itself as defined by its individual and perceptual qualities.[28]

This reasoning shows why it is systematically necessary for Rickert to refute epistemological realism. Put another way, it shows why the rejection of this thesis is essential to his own theory of knowledge. If epistemological realism were sound, then Rickert's thesis concerning the limits of natural science would be false. These limits would not be defined by the individual and perceptual properties of reality. On the contrary, the purpose of natural science would be the reproduction of these properties.[29]

The Demarcation Criterion. There is another reason why Rickert is obliged to disavow epistemological realism. One of the main objectives of his philosophical project is to develop a taxonomy of the sciences that differentiates natural science from historical or cultural science in such a way that an independent province of theoretical discourse can be staked out for the latter. In other words, one of his basic intentions is to refute a positivist theory of historical knowledge. Following Karl Popper, this kind of issue is generally called a demarcation problem.[30]

Rickert sees that epistemological realism entails a solution of the demarcation problem that he cannot accept. One consequence of epistemological realism is a doctrine that might be called methodolog-

[27]Ibid., pp. 197–8.
[28]Ibid., pp. 199–200.
[29]Ibid., p. 214.
[30]Karl R. Popper, *The Logic of Scientific Discovery* (New York: Basic Books, 1959), chapter 1.

ical monism: If the reproduction of reality is the aim of science, ultimately only one such reproduction can qualify as knowledge. In that case, there can be only one scientifically valid conceptualization of reality. This, of course, rules out the solution of the demarcation problem Rickert proposed to defend, a solution that establishes a distinctive domain of inquiry for historical science. Thus Rickert's solution of the demarcation problem depends on a refutation of epistemological realism.

Rickert's criterion for demarcating natural science from historical science is the fifth and final link in the chain of reasoning that leads him to a solution of the problem of historical knowledge. This demarcation criterion is not ontological. In other words, Rickert does not follow Wilhelm Dilthey in arguing that the difference between natural science and historical science is ultimately grounded in differences between two kinds of material or modes of existence. Rickert does not deny that such differences can be identified. He claims only that they are irrelevant for a valid taxonomy of the sciences. The criterion is rather determined by Rickert's theory of cognitive interests and his methodology, or theory of concept formation. In the final analysis, it can be said that the criterion is axiological: Natural science and historical science are differentiated on the basis of two irreducibly different theoretical values that require corresponding differences in the conceptualization of reality.

Natural science conceptualizes reality on the basis of an interest in abstract generalizations that become increasingly remote from the individual and perceptual qualities of reality. Put another way, natural science is anchored not in an interest in reality itself but in an interest in the general laws that hold validly for reality. It is our interest in the individual and perceptual qualities of reality, the value we ascribe to knowledge of its distinctive features, that differentiates natural science from historical science.[31]

In consequence, natural science is a *Begriffswissenschaft*, a science of concepts in the sense that its goal is knowledge of the conceptual relations that govern reality. History, on the other hand, is a *Wirklichkeitswissenschaft*, a science of reality in the sense that its goal is knowledge of reality itself. The distinction between *Begriffswissenschaft* and *Wirklichkeitswissenschaft* is borrowed from Georg Simmel's theory of historical knowledge.[32] It is based on two considerations. First,

[31]See *Die Grenzen*, pp. 218, 222, 224–5, 227.
[32]The distinction originally appears in Georg Simmel, *Die Probleme der Geschichtsphilosophie* (Leipzig: Duncker & Humblot, 1892), p. 34. For an English translation of the second edition (1905) of this book, see *The Problems of the Philosophy of History*, trans. Guy Oakes (New York: Free Press, 1977).

although both kinds of science employ concepts, the validity of concepts in natural science depends on the extent to which they abstract from reality. This does not hold true for historical science, in which there is a more proximate relationship between concept and reality. Second, natural science is interested in the validity of concepts, not in the existence of the concrete entities to which these concepts ultimately refer. Historical science, on the other hand, is interested in the real existence of individual entities.

THE PROBLEM OF CONCEPT FORMATION IN HISTORY

In light of the *hiatus irrationalis* between concept and reality, Rickert's demarcation criterion clearly poses serious problems for the possibility of historical science. The doctrine of the irrationality of reality entails that the reproduction of its individual and perceptual content is not a possible ideal for any science. Thus the historical interest in reality cannot be satisfied by knowledge of reality itself, for this sort of knowledge is impossible. If reality as such is irrational, it is not a possible object of knowledge in any sense. Rickert claims, however, that "individuality" also designates the irrational content of reality. Thus it seems that the doctrine of the *hiatus irrationalis*, together with Rickert's demarcation criterion, entails that the interest in knowledge of the individual content of reality cannot be satisfied. Historical knowledge as Rickert conceives it appears to be impossible. Or is there some sense in which the apparently absurd undertaking of conceptualizing the irrationality of reality is possible? Can reality be rationalized in such a way that its individuality remains a possible object of knowledge? In view of the *hiatus irrationalis*, is there any strategy by means of which knowledge of the individual content of reality is possible?

The answers to these questions lie in Rickert's theory of individual or historical concept formation. This theory is generated by the following problem: Given the *hiatus irrationalis* and our interest in knowledge of the individuality of reality, is it possible to distinguish the concrete perceptuality of reality from its individuality in such a way that the latter can be defined as an object of historical knowledge? Like natural science, historical science is unable to reproduce the concrete perceptuality of reality. Therefore, it also requires what Rickert calls a principle of selection on the basis of which the essential aspects of reality – those that matter to us because knowledge of these aspects satisfies our theoretical interests – can be distinguished from its inessential aspects. Unlike natural science, the theoretical interest of historical science is anchored in the value we ascribe to the individual.

It follows that this principle of selection must identify some sense in which the individuality of reality can become a possible object of knowledge. It must discriminate or select certain individually defined aspects of reality that qualify as important in relation to our values. The search for this principle is the primary objective of Rickert's philosophy of history and the main issue of *Die Grenzen*. He calls it the problem of historical concept formation.

The reasoning that leads Rickert to a solution begins with the attempt to establish the sort of distinction he needs. The concrete perceptuality of reality can be distinguished from its individuality by differentiating two kinds of individuality. The premises crucial to Rickert's reasoning can be outlined as follows: (1) Individuals in the most general sense – discrete, independently identifiable phenomena – are all unique. (2) However, we do not regard all such phenomena as irreplaceable. On the contrary, if their uniqueness is of no interest to us, they become objects of knowledge only because they fall under some general concept. This is the sense of individuality in which concrete perceptuality is equivalent to individuality, and all reality qualifies as individual. (3) There is another kind of individuality that cannot be ascribed to a phenomenon simply because it is unique in this most general sense. Rickert calls it "in-dividuality," and the objects to which it is ascribed are called "in-dividuals." A phenomenon qualifies as an in-dividual when it is constituted by a coherence and an indivisibility that it possesses in virtue of its uniqueness. (4) This individuality, however, is not defined by reference to all the properties of the phenomenon. Because of the intensive infinity of reality, this is obviously impossible. It obtains only by virtue of specific properties that we regard as indispensable because we see them as responsible for the coherence and indivisibility of the phenomenon. (5) Precisely for this reason – because we regard phenomena constituted in this way as irreplaceable – their uniqueness is of interest to us.

How is the distinction between individuality and in-dividuality made? How does the in-dividuality of a diamond differ from the individuality of a lump of coal? Clearly, the coherence and indivisibility characteristic of the uniqueness of the former have a significance for us that the latter lacks, a meaning that is determined by the values we attach to it. In other words, the in-dividuality of a phenomenon is due to the value we ascribe to the singular coherence and indivisibility that are responsible for its uniqueness.

The ultimate basis of Rickert's individuality–in-dividuality dichotomy is neither metaphysical nor epistemological. On the contrary, it is grounded in a general fact about human experience that lies within what might be called the universal pragmatics of human life. Human beings establish certain values, act on them, and attempt to realize them. It is impossible, however, for everything in the domain of human experience to have the status of an in-dividual. This is because action is possible only on the basis of an orientation to generalizations or general rules of experience.[33] The possibility of ascribing values to certain objects presupposes other objects for which this is not possible. Or, to employ Rickert's language, the possibility of in-dividuals presupposes individuals, entities that fall within the domain of our experience and interest us only as instances of general concepts. Thus the praxeology of human life entails that experience cannot exclusively comprise in-dividuals. On the other hand, the fact that we ascribe values to individuals by virtue of their distinctive properties shows that there must be some individuals. If all individuals were nothing more than representative cases of general concepts, we would have no basis for differentiating one such case from any other, and thus no basis for an interest in any given individual. Therefore, it is because human beings ascribe values to certain things that some individuals become in-dividuals.

The in-dividual is constituted as a historical individual, and thus as a possible object of historical science, by reference to what Rickert calls the purely theoretical value relation (*Wertbeziehung*). Put another way, an in-dividual can be conceptualized as a historical individual only if it falls under some value relation. Because of the connection between value relations and the constitution of historical individuals, Rickert claims that the elimination of value relations from historical science would also eliminate the object of cognitive interest in history, and thus the possibility of historical knowledge as well. The doctrine of value relevance is Rickert's solution to the problem of individual or historical concept formation.

This doctrine is constituted by four theses, each of which places constraints on the values that define historical individuals. In other words, each thesis states certain conditions that must be satisfied by the values to which historical individuals are related. The first thesis holds that a commitment on these values must be made by the historical actors whose conduct is the ultimate datum of a historical investigation, and thus the ultimate object of historical concept formation. In Rickert's language, the "historical centers" of a historical investigation must take a position on these values. The second thesis holds that these values cannot be purely personal or private. They must express the general concerns of a culture. In Rickert's

---

[33] *Die Grenzen*, p. 319.

language, they must be "cultural values." The third thesis holds that these values must be objective in the sense that an unconditionally general validity can be ascribed to them. They are not merely empirical values to which all the members of a society are in fact committed. Nor are they merely normatively valid values commitment to which is required by a social norm that all the members of a society in fact acknowledge. On the contrary, they are unconditionally general values: Their validity or binding force represents a categorical commitment that is independent of both empirical maxims and hypothetical imperatives. The fourth thesis holds that the historical investigation itself cannot take a position on these values. Rather, it must relate them to the historical individual in a purely theoretical fashion.

The first thesis rests on the distinction between the investigator's values and the values of the historical actor, or between the values of the historian and those of the historical center. In Rickert's terminology, this is also the distinction between the values of the historical subject and those of the historical object. This thesis is explained in Rickert's discussion of the concept of the historical center in Chapter 4, sections 7–9. The second thesis rests on the distinction between personal, or private, values and general cultural values. It is explained in Rickert's discussion of culture as the content of the concept of history in Chapter 4 sections 8 and 9. The third thesis rests on the distinction between subjective and objective values and is explained in Rickert's various attempts in Chapter 5 to prove that the objectivity of historical science is not inferior to that of natural science.

The fourth thesis rests on the distinction between a valuation, or value judgment, and a purely theoretical value relation. Rickert claims that "insofar as the value perspective is decisive for history, this concept of the 'value relation' – in opposition to 'valuation' – is actually *the* essential criterion for history as a pure science."[34] In his attempt to clarify the importance of this distinction, Rickert considers the methodological status of a history of religion that is based on confessional assumptions. Such a history, he claims, is not grounded in a purely theoretical value relation. For this reason it cannot possess scientific objectivity. Why is this so?

Consider two different confessional biographies of Martin Luther, a Roman Catholic account and a Protestant account. Because they are committed to rival subjective valuations, Rickert claims that it is impossible to resolve the conflicts between them. Historical accounts of this sort can never be regarded as purely scientific, because their

[34]Ibid., p. 329.

valuations will never be valid for all scientists. According to Rickert, this is one sense in which the domain of values is irrational: There is no principle by means of which the conflicts between such rival valuations can be resolved. It follows that if the domain of values were exhausted by valuations, historical science would be impossible. The purpose of the value/valuation dichotomy is to avoid this consequence by showing that there is a sphere of purely theoretical value relations that is independent of valuations.

Suppose the two biographies of Luther are not grounded in the confessional commitments of Protestantism and Roman Catholicism. Suppose the historian simply defines Luther's individuality by reference to religious values in general and does not take any stand on their validity. In that case, the issue of value irrationality – the question of whether there is a principle on the basis of which conflicts between value judgments can be resolved – does not arise. If the conceptualization of Luther's individuality is based exclusively on such value relations, the problem of historical knowledge of Luther can be solved, or so Rickert claims. Because the purely theoretical value relation that defines religious values will be valid for both Roman Catholics and Protestants, the same aspects of the individual that we identify as "Luther" will also prove essential for historians of both persuasions. Thus these aspects will be synthesized to form the same historical concept. In other words, they will constitute the historical individual "Luther" as an object of historical knowledge in the same way. As a result, the value/valuation dichotomy preserves the objectivity of historical knowledge from the consequences of the irrationality of subjective valuations.

In summary, the doctrine of value relevance may be formulated in the following terms. Consider an entity, I, that is an in-dividual and a value, V, that satisfies the following conditions: V is a general cultural value on which the historical actors of a given society take a position, and it is also unconditionally valid. If V is linked to I in a purely theoretical fashion, I qualifies as a historical individual and thus an object of historical concept formation. To link I to V in this fashion is to conceptualize it historically, as a result of which it becomes an object of historical knowledge. It should be noted that the doctrine of value relevance does not attempt to solve the problem of conceptualizing the individual by surmounting the *hiatus irrationalis*, or closing the gap between concept and reality. On the contrary, the dualism of concept and reality is presupposed by this solution. If reality could be exhaustively derived from concepts, there would be no grounds for the claim that any one individual aspect of reality is more significant than another. In that case, the ultimate basis for the doctrine of value relevance – the distinction between individuals and in-dividuals – would collapse.

A NOTE ON THE ABRIDGMENT

The text employed for this translation is *Die Grenzen der natur-wissenschaftlichen Begriffsbildung: eine logische Einleitung in die historischen Wissenschaften*, fifth edition, revised and enlarged (Tübingen: Mohr, 1929). Breaks in the translation produced by deleting material from the German text are noted by means of ellipses (. . .).

The material translated from the prefaces is taken from *Die Grenzen*, pages vii–viii, ix, and xix–xxvi. The material translated from the Introduction is taken from pages 1–25. The material translated from Chapter 3 is taken from pages 188–92, 196–203, 214–34, and 237. The material translated from Chapter 4 is taken from pages 277–87, 292–302, 303–6, 308–9, 314–25, 328–41, 342–7, 357–62, 364–6, 432–3, 438–9, 442–3, 473–5, 479–83, 503–23, 533–44, 544–6, 548–67, 572–3, 574–8, 588–91, and 610–11. The material translated from Chapter 5 is taken from pages 623–67 and 673–96.

Die Grenzen was originally published in two installments. The first three chapters ("Conceptual Knowledge of the Corporeal World," "Nature and Spirit," and "Nature and History"), consisting of more than three hundred pages, appeared in 1896. Rickert completed Chapters 4 and 5 in 1901; and the entire first edition, comprising all five chapters, was published in 1902. A second edition followed in 1913 and a third and fourth in 1921.

Rickert attempts to clarify his language in each successive edition. He also tries to sharpen the focus of his arguments, which are frequently quite lengthy and somewhat muddled in their purpose. These efforts, however, are sometimes compromised by the introduction of digressions, which are often quite peripheral to Rickert's primary intentions. Except for the incorporation of a few illuminating notes, the only significant addition of new material is the long ninth section of Chapter 4, which first appeared in the edition of 1921. This represents a systematic attempt to confront the problem of the ontological basis for a theory of historical understanding. Put another way, it is Rickert's most serious attempt to come to terms with the problematic of Dilthey's philosophy of history.

The present abridgment of Rickert's text of more than seven hundred pages to less than half this length is based on three criteria: coherence, which calls for deletions that do not destroy the intelligibility and structural integrity of the text; originality, which calls for the deletion of material that was part of the philosophical stock-intrade of Rickert's time; and relevance, which calls for the deletion of Rickert's discussions of philosophical positions that have a limited bearing on his main objectives. From the perspective of these criteria, Chapters 4 and 5 are clearly the most important parts of *Die Grenzen*, and Chapter 4 is crucial text in the articulation of Rickert's philosophy of history. As Rickert himself notes, the first three chapters stand as an independent text that has the negative purpose of establishing that the problem of historical concept formation cannot be solved by natural science. Rickert's own solution to this problem is set out in Chapter 4, and its consequences for the objectivity of historical science are developed in Chapter 5. Material from Chapter 3 is included only insofar as it is essential for the understanding of Chapters 4 and 5. Chapters 1 and 2 are omitted in toto.³⁵

These remarks on the principles governing the abridgment are not meant to suggest that everything of philosophical importance in *Die Grenzen* has been retained. Rickert's philosophy of natural science and his analysis of the relationship between concepts and judgments (Chapter 1), his philosophy of mind (Chapter 2), the details of his critique of an ontologically grounded taxonomy of the sciences (Chapter 3), his discussion of the concept of historical development (Chapter 4), and part of his account of the relationship between the theory of historical knowledge and the theory of value (Chapter 5) – all these and more have been deleted.

Rickert writes in the tiresome and didactic style of the university lecturer who, faced with unimaginative and obtuse students, takes refuge in pedantry and repetition in the hope that some of his main ideas will be grasped. For this reason, there is a temptation to relieve the tedium by deleting apparently redundant sections of substantial portions of text that cover a single problem. On the whole, this temptation has been resisted. Sometimes there is a point to Rickert's prolixity. In addition, the reader of the English abridgment should have an opportunity to get a sense of the way the book was written and a feel for Rickert's style, which occasionally approaches unendurable verbosity. Finally, yielding to this temptation would produce a highly fragmented text of doubtful coherence.

Since Rickert is an advocate of "scientific" philosophy as a legitimate academic discipline with valid standards and objective methods, it is not surprising that the language of precision and rigor is an impor-

---

³⁵The foregoing reconstruction of the reasoning that leads Rickert to a solution to the problem of historical concept formation traces the links between Chapters 1 through 3 and Chapter 4. In providing the background necessary for an understanding of *Die Grenzen*, it also represents an attempt to fill some of the lacunae created by the abridgment.

tant component of his philosophical rhetoric. In fact, Rickert tries hard to be clear and methodical, and by the standards of those he regards as his peers, these efforts are largely successful. In the main, this group comprises academic philosophers in the German university system from the beginning of the Wilhelmian period to the later years of the Weimar Republic, such as Wilhelm Dilthey, Wilhelm Windelband, Alois Riehl, Edmund Husserl, Georg Simmel, Paul Natorp, Emil Lask, Max Scheler, Nicolai Hartmann, Jonas Cohn, and Bruno Bauch. Regrettably, it does not include G. E. Moore, Bertrand Russell, or even Gottlob Frege. Neither on the basis of our own standards nor even by the best philosophical standards of his own time, does Rickert ever manage to state a thesis or develop an argument with tolerable precision. The introduction and institution-alization of more exacting standards of philosophical clarity are perhaps the most significant permanent legacy of the linguistic revolution in philosophy begun by Moore, Russell, and Wittgenstein and consummated by the Vienna Circle, Ryle, Austin, and their successors. One of its consequences is that considerable patience is required when postrevolutionary readers take up prerevolutionary philosophical texts.

GUY OAKES

Glossary

In *Die Grenzen*, Rickert employs certain terms in a technical or quasi-technical fashion. Because of their importance or frequent appearance in the text, they are translated uniformly throughout, even where this results in an English style that is somewhat awkward and unidiomatic. A list of these terms and their English translations follows:

anschaulich	perceptual
Anschaulichkeit	concrete actuality or perceptuality
Anschauung	perception
Begriffsbildung	concept formation
Begriffswissenschaft	science of concepts
Besonderheit	distinctiveness
Darstellung	representation
Einmaligkeit	uniqueness
Einzigkeit	singularity
Gebild	construct
Geist	spirit or mind (depending on context)
Geisteswissenschaft	human science
geistig	spiritual
In-dividuum	in-dividual
Individuum	individual
irreal	nonreal
Körper	body
körperlich	corporeal
lebendig	vital

leitend	governing (for example, *leitende Werte* is translated as governing values)
Materie	matter
nacherleben	reexperience
Psyche	psyche
psychisch	psychic
Realität	reality
Realwissenschaft	science of reality
sachlich	substantive
Seele	mind
seelisch	mental
Stellungnehmen	taking a position
Stoff	material
unwirklich	unreal
wertbeziehend	value relevant
Wertbeziehung	value relevance or relation to values
wertend	valuing
Wirklichkeit	reality or actuality
Wirklichkeitswissenschaft	science of reality
Wissenschaftslehre	theory of science
wollend	volitional or willing (referring to a being that wills or has volition)
Zusammengehörigkeit	coherence
Zusammenhang	nexus

The Limits of Concept Formation
in Natural Science

HEINRICH RICKERT

From the Preface to the First Edition

I have been working on a theory of scientific concept formation since my doctoral dissertation, *Zur Lehre der Definition* (1888). Even then I opposed the idea of a universal method based on natural science, and I tried to demonstrate the emptiness of the doctrine according to which the common elements of things are the same as the essential features of concepts. It had become clear to me both that we always need a specific purpose with reference to which the essential features are distinguished from the inessential, and also that methodology is obliged to identify the diversity of these purposes in order to understand the variety of scientific methods and do justice to it. In my book *Der Gegenstand der Erkenntnis* (1892), I attempted to establish both a general epistemological "standpoint" for my further work and a theoretical basis for the primacy of practical reason. Thereafter I returned to methodological investigations. Very soon, however, I saw that the attempt to develop a theory of concept formation embracing all the sciences posed incalculable difficulties owing to the immense body of specialized scientific knowledge that would be required. So I tried to limit myself, above all attempting to understand the nature of *historical* concept formation – first, because this is the area to which logic has thus far contributed least; in addition, because an insight into the fundamental difference between historical thought and thought in the natural sciences proved to be the most important point for understanding all specialized scientific activity; and finally, because it also seemed to me that this insight was an essential condition for the treatment of most philosophical problems or questions of weltanschauung. Here logical theory is employed to oppose naturalism and also to ground a historically oriented philosophical idealism.

My view of the relationship between the concept and empirical reality in general, the view that is decisive for the whole of the subsequent train of thought, was first published in an essay, "Zur Theorie der naturwissenschaftlichen Begriffsbildung," in *Avenarius' Vierteljahresschrift* for 1894. Two years later, the first three chapters of this book appeared. Above all, their aim was to show that the method of natural science is *not* applicable to history. As the *negative* part of the work, they form a self-contained whole. In the subsequent lecture *Kulturwissenschaft und Naturwissenschaft* (1899), I attempted to sketch, as simply as possible, the basic outlines of a *positive* account of the logical nature of history. . . .

. . . At the time I planned my work, the theme of historical method was not an important issue at all in the discipline of history itself. Nor could one have any reason to expect that quite soon specialists would return to the discussion of this question. In those days, however, I would have considered it the least plausible of all possibilities that even in historical circles, the old idea of the "elevation of history to the status of a science" by means of the method of natural science would reappear so soon and prove itself capable of attracting attention; for at that time, the belief in Buckle and related thinkers seemed to be thoroughly discredited in the province of history and retained a role only in naturalistic philosophy. Today, nevertheless, the old speculations of the Enlightenment are treated as the most novel and important achievements of history. For this reason, I thought it necessary to demonstrate the conceptual confusions that lie at the basis of these views, and especially to clear up the ambiguity of the shibboleths with which these basically antiquated theories are again defended in our own time. . . .

At this point, a brief word about my mode of exposition: On the basis of the limits of concept formation in natural science, I try to understand the nature of history as it actually exists. I do not, for example, draw up plans for sciences of the future. At the same time, however, it is far from my intention simply to *analyze* or describe history as it is. On the contrary, I want to discover the inner logical structure of all historical concept formation. For this reason, I am obliged to begin with quite general concepts that contain very little of what is usually called history. Gradually, I add one element after another to these concepts. As a result, the concept that conforms to the sciences that are conventionally called historical is not identified until the conclusion of the fourth chapter. The consequence of this *synthetic* procedure is not only the disagreeable fact that one must read the entire book to know what I think. It is also necessary to suspend judgment concerning the soundness of my position until the conclusion. Nevertheless, even with the best intentions, I could not make any changes in this regard.

Freiburg i.B., January 1902

From the Preface to the
Third and Fourth Editions

. . . As regards the use of the words "actuality" (*Wirklichkeit*) and "reality" (*Realität*), they have the same meaning in this work. Moreover, they are used to refer to both physical and psychic being as it exists in its pure facticity, independent both of its conceptual transformation by science and also of every meaning and value with which it is linked. Perhaps what is merely real or what is merely actual never directly presents itself to us with this sort of purity. But we have to try to identify it, and thus form a concept of it, if we want to achieve clarity concerning the nature of the sciences of reality (*Realwissenschaften*). In the ensuing, therefore, I designate as actual or real the methodologically unanalyzed and value-free material of individual research. Perhaps it will be said that my concept of reality, which follows from this definition, is positivist. It may also be claimed that because this concept was developed at a time when positivist trends prevailed, my terminology makes a concession to positivism. As regards these claims, one should not fail to see how far removed my views are from any form of positivism, given that I try to show that even the immediately given world cannot be comprehended as purely real in the positivistic sense. Of course, everyone is free to reject the term "real" as designating the scientifically unanalyzed material of the sciences of reality and to reserve it instead for formations concerning which the following is believed. Their actually existing content corresponds precisely to the content of our *concepts* of the real. Anyone committed to this sort of *conceptual realism* must deny genuine reality to what I call the real. But anyone who takes this view is obliged to apply it consistently. In that case, peculiar consequences follow. For example, the paper on which this book is printed, just as we see it, cannot be called real. Nor is it any more legitimate to apply this term to our psychic acts of perception. If we ascribe reality not only to formations of this sort but also to the content of our concepts of them, we will never arrive at a clear and consistent way of expressing ourselves. At this point we confront an absolute alternative that we cannot escape. Since I am aware of no scholarly or scientific work in which the repudiation of the positivist concept of reality is carried out with complete terminological rigor, I will retain the positivist *terminology*. That is, I will call "real" the same thing that positivism designates as real. This is the surest way of avoiding every form of positivist conceptual nominalism as well as every form of metaphysical conceptual realism.

But the foregoing account does not seem sufficient to understand the language used here. In addition to the concept of reality employed by conceptual realism, there is another more comprehensive concept, of which the concept considered earlier forms a special case. In general, it can be called the concept of *value realism*. It is expressed in a thesis of Hegel's: The rational is the real, and the real is the rational. Obviously Hegel did not intend to apply the term "rational" to objects such as this piece of paper, which we all call real. As a consistent conceptual realist, he would have to deny that such an object qualifies as genuine reality. But he did mean that, even in our ordinary view, a purely *contingent existence* does not deserve the emphatic name of "reality"! This word by itself already shows that both reason and reality, although admittedly they did not signify a norm or a prescriptive standard for Hegel, nevertheless certainly did designate a *value*; for only concerning the meaningful or what has the status of a value can it be said that it deserves an emphatic name. No sort of emphasis can be ascribed to what is value free. The famous Hegelian thesis, therefore, has the following consequence: Only what has meaning or value – which, in this book, is called the nonreal – is acknowledged as "real." Or, at most, actual entities insofar as meaning or value can be ascribed to them qualify as real. Assuming that such a terminology could be consistently employed, there is nothing objectionable about it. Not even Hegel himself, however, – not to mention other value realists – managed to do this. Thus in opposition not only to conceptual realism but also to every form of value realism, I remain terminologically committed to the positivist concept of reality. In consequence, I try to make an absolute distinction between reality itself and all "emphatic" meanings, in conformity with the nature of the empirical sciences of reality, the sciences of physical and psychic being. Of course, this also leads to formulations that some will find paradoxical. But there is no terminology that fails to conflict with ordinary language in the use of the expressions "actual" and "real." For this reason, it is a question of choosing the lesser evil. From this perspective and in opposition to Hegel's usage, I stipulate the following thesis as governing the use of these concepts in this book: *The rational is not restricted to the real, and what is only real is not yet rational.* Those who observe this rule will at least know what I mean by the actual or the real.

Finally, my position on the question of "rationalism," so much discussed today, is also closely related to the concept of reality. In publishing the first chapters of this book twenty-five years ago, I tried to prove that the real is the limit of all scientific concept formation. At that time, I was attacked because of my *irrationalism.* More recently – and especially since the appearance of my book on *Lebensphilosophie,*[1] the basic ideas of which had already appeared in the journal *Logos* ten years before – I am chided as a rationalist. *Tempora mutantur.* For myself, I believe that I have not altered my position on rationalism and that I am neither a rationalist nor an irrationalist. From my perspective, of course, anything that is merely real bears an irrational stamp. But the name "irrationalism" is not appropriate for my philosophical standpoint. This is because I am very far from identifying the world in its totality with the purely real and irrational world. I do not doubt that there are eminently rational formations such as concepts. Although the entire content of reality itself can never be subsumed under them, they are theoretically or rationally valid for reality. In particular, I hold that science is possible only on the basis of concepts and, in this sense, only on the basis of *ratio.* On the other hand, this circumstance does not justify calling my view rationalistic. Quite irrespective of the real, I hold that theoretical or rational formulations of meaning are not the only entities to which validity can be ascribed. For this reason, I try to show that philosophy – if it proposes to become truly universal – must also take extratheoretical or irrational values into account. Accordingly, I discern the irrational not only in the real but also in the domain of the nonreal or that which holds validly, and I reject every position to which the name of rationalism is appropriate. In this respect, I might be called an *antirationalist.* But it remains true that slogans such as rationalism and irrationalism have nothing at all to say that bears on my position. My endeavor is always to do justice to both the irrational and the rational components of the world. This also holds for my book on *Lebensphilosophie;* even though, in the polemic against fashionable movements of irrationality, the significance of the rational belonged in the foreground. Of course, it seems to me that the irrational is *scientifically* admissible in one way only: by forming *concepts* of it. This is because whatever we have not somehow conceived and whatever we are unable to designate by means of rationally comprehensible words cannot be spoken of in science at all, regardless of how suprarational

---

[1] [*Die Philosophie des Lebens*) (Tübingen: Mohr, 1920).]

the content may be of that from which we form our concepts. To this
extent, all scientific theorists must decisively commit themselves to the
clarity and penetrating force of rational thought, especially in opposition to the romantic excesses and insipid aestheticism of our own
time, in Germany largely the outcome of an exhausted and purely
imitative idolization of Nietzsche. If this qualifies as rationalism, there
is no science that does not proceed rationalistically.

Although rational factors can make up only a small part of the
world, the exclusive task of science is to reach the conceptual clarity of
theoretical insight, and in this sense to master its subject matter by
means of *ratio*. Quite early, this conviction linked me spiritually with
the man to whose memory the new edition of this book is dedicated.
Since the dedication is not intended merely as an expression of
personal friendship, I should like to say a few words about this too.

My more intimate relationship with Max Weber goes back to the
time in Freiburg when we were both at the beginning of our academic
careers. Weber always remained not only a man of science but also a
political man. An ardent patriotism and a powerful temperament did
not make it easy for him to separate the theoretically justifiable factors
from the impact of the suprarational powers of life in the historically
oriented economic theory on which he lectured. Weber's intellect was
no less powerful than his will, and the need to attain clarity, especially
concerning what in history qualifies as "science" in the strict sense, was
all the more intensive in his case. As young men, the common interest
in this question, which I had attacked from a different and purely
theoretical aspect, brought us together intellectually. At first, of
course, there is a certain sense in which we quickly came into conflict.
Windelband's lecture on history and natural science, which appeared
at that time, provoked Weber's opposition. The "idiographic"
method, in his view, would amount to aestheticism. Even after
reading the first three chapters of this book and seeing that what I
required for history were not the "configurations" of Windelband
but, rather, individual *concepts*, he still took the view that my attempt
to develop a logic of history was not *feasible*. Often he told me that I
would never complete this work. In Weber's view, although the
material set out in the first three chapters was sound, it posed an
irresolvable problem for me because history cannot be understood as
a pure science. It was not until 1902, long after he had left Freiburg
and when I gave him the two final chapters, on historical concept
formation and historical objectivity, that he became one of the first to
be convinced that on the basis of my concept of the theoretical value
relationship, the conceptual method of the science of history can
correctly be characterized as that of an individualizing science of

culture. Shortly thereafter, he developed the consequences of this insight for his own science in methodological works, which, to me, remain the most splendid result of my efforts to reach enlightenment concerning the logical nature of all history. Thus, for me, there was a powerful desire to link this book to the name of Weber, in grateful recollection of the unforgettable Freiburg period of the development of my ideas. When I wrote it, I learned much from his objections.

Nevertheless, the relations between Weber's work and mine extend farther than this. It seems to me that Weber – assuming that one undertakes to classify this altogether incomparable man – was one of the great historians. At the same time, however, he was motivated by a powerful drive for systematic construction, which is seldom found in historians. Especially in later years, this led him to develop the same material of his historical research in the direction of generalizations and, in this sense, ahistorically. Eventually he came to describe his last works as "sociology," thereby ascribing a new significance to the name that, since Comte, has been much used and abused. A harsh fate, the oppressive meaninglessness of which made it difficult to bear, tore him from the midst of his most intensive and extensive original work in this new sphere of activity. Thus the work of this scholar – as a whole man, capable as few are of forming a whole work – inevitably remained a fragment, as if the infirmity of our time could no longer endure anything whole. Nevertheless, the extraordinarily intense productivity of his last period created enough for us to see the outlines of the imposing system. Especially for the theory of science as I pursue it, there is little that would be more instructive than this powerful torso. Here we can see how a body of material – almost superabundant and in part completely irrational – can be rationally dominated by the power of the human mind. If we want to characterize Weber in a scientific or scholarly fashion, we should not call him a philosopher. That word applies to him only in a very vague sense. As Weber himself often stressed, it was not his intention to work in academic philosophy. Finally, we cannot do justice to the significance of this unique man by numbering him, as even Troeltsch does, among the neo-Kantians, going so far as to refer to him, along with Windelband and myself, as "the third chief figure" of the Southwest German "school." We could take pride in this if it were true. Intellectually, however, Weber was not a member, to use Goethe's expression, of any guild. On the contrary, his scientific greatness consists in the fact that he created a *cultural science* that – in the connection it establishes between *history* and *systematics* – will not fit any of the usual methodological schemata. Precisely in this way, *specialized research* is directed along new paths. I wanted to stress this in the preface to a book in which I try to exhibit the profusion of the *different* forms in which the scientific life can develop. Whenever I want to call to mind a dramatic example of the scope of which the human intellect is capable, even when it is most rigorously limited to what can be conceptually grasped within the confines of a specialized discipline, I can never do better than to consider the work of Max Weber.

I can no longer submit my work to my friend's scholarly and personal interest, which was always lively. I can only dedicate it to his memory. There is another special reason why this is profoundly painful to me. While he was still alive and I was writing the first part of my *System der Philosophie*, there was no reader I wanted more than him. Weber had formed a rather one-sided view of philosophy as a science and its contemporary possibilities. Put another way, he really believed only in "logic." Thus he was also "skeptical" about my plan for a universal and scientific theory of weltanschauung based on a comprehensive system of values, an undertaking of which my theory of science forms only a part – just as, earlier in Freiburg, he had been skeptical about my plan for a logic of history. However, it goes without saying that he was very far removed from every sort of relativism to which the weaklings of modern philosophy are committed. He also had a pronounced and quite justified aversion to everything he regarded as *Gartenlaube*, in other words, all scientific or scholarly feuilletonism.[2] This made him suspicious of a philosophy of art, religion, or even love grounded on a theory of values. Weber's personality, however, towered so high not least because he was capable of such an astonishing and impersonal objectivity, and he had never shown himself to be unteachable. In his last letter to me, he expressed an intense interest in the development of my system. It is no longer possible for me to convince him through my completed work that today even a philosophy proceeding in a strictly scientific fashion need not restrict itself to "logic."

Concerning what his loss means to me *personally*, I will remain silent. Anyone who has ever felt merely a touch of the spirit of this man,

[2][The literal meaning is "arbor," but in this context it refers to the weekly family magazine of the same name. Founded as a popular literary, political, and scientific journal with liberal pretensions in 1852, and inspired by the unsuccessful attempt four years earlier in Frankfurt am Main to found a German parliament on liberal and democratic principles, within ten years *Die Gartenlaube* reached a circulation of 100,000. After 1900, however, the magazine became increasingly sentimental and traditional, unabashed in its advocacy of the most reactionary German cultural values. In its appeal to sensibilities Weber regarded as flaccid and hypocritical, it represented the sort of false intellectual, emotional, and moral seriousness that offended his own standards of honesty, conscience, and what he ironically called good taste.]

equally great in his goodness of heart and in his acuteness of understanding, will surmise what my scholarly and personal relationship to Weber – extending, as it did, through nearly an entire lifetime, frequently interrupted by external fate, but never inwardly troubled – has meant to me. In that case, he must also understand that it is not easy to speak about it with the requisite propriety.

Heidelberg, October, 1921

Introduction

Historical investigations occupy an important place in the scientific and scholarly life of our time. Does history also receive the attention it deserves in *philosophy*? This has been claimed. In a widely read work, a book that – not only on the basis of its content but also because of its external success – is quite characteristic of recent philosophical interests and views, especially in Germany, *history* is mentioned as one of the *directions* in which philosophy seems to be moving. This tendency is even described as a distinctive feature that stamps the entire character of nineteenth-century philosophy, in contrast to the immediately preceding period, which emphasized mathematics and natural science.[1] To what extent can this characteristic really be identified in the philosophy of the nineteenth century *as a whole*? Moreover, to what extent is it identifiable in contemporary philosophy? Above all, has there been an attempt to understand the nature of history *philosophically* – in other words, in such a way that its significance also becomes evident for the problems of a comprehensive theory of weltanschauung? Or does this claim represent more of a wish than a matter of fact?

During the early decades of the nineteenth century, there were, of course, some thinkers who had begun to come to terms with history philosophically. Indeed, there never was a weltanschauung so historically oriented as German idealism. But can the same be maintained for subsequent philosophy? In France too, about the same time that Hegel expounded his philosophy of history, Comte was developing ideas intended both to assign the historical sciences their proper place in the totality of knowledge and to define their proper mode of investigation. But in spite of beginnings that were promising in certain respects, has this not remained a matter of mere intentions? At least it cannot be claimed that the impact of Comte's ideas tended to

[1]Paulsen, *Einleitung in die Philosophie*, 1892, preface, p. xi. In three decades, thirty-five editions of this book have appeared, and it is probably still read even today.

strengthen the historical turn in *opposition* to the preceding natural scientific period. When Comte proposed to turn historical science into "sociology," he demanded that it proceed as a natural science. Thus in the second half of the nineteenth century, his direct influence – even in Germany – could only encourage a repetition of the suppression of the grand historical character exhibited by the philosophy of German idealism. This holds true even more for his indirect influence, which was chiefly mediated by English authors. It was only historical research that took possession of this idealist heritage and experienced a powerful surge of development. Philosophy, however – to the extent it retained any significance at all for spiritual life in general – came completely under the influence of the natural sciences. The words of more farsighted thinkers faded away without being heard.

And what about contemporary philosophy? If proof were needed for the unhistorical character of the philosophical spirit that predominates today, it would be sufficient to point to the following fact: Among the German philosophers of the last decades, it is above all Schopenhauer and the thinkers who more or less follow him who have been read and taken seriously. Of course, Schopenhauer – like few other thinkers of the modern period – quite early perceived and clearly formulated the philosophically decisive and logically fundamental difference between natural science and history – at least from one aspect – with the acute penetration of hatred. In spite of this, his incomprehension of historical life can hardly be exaggerated. Because history cannot proceed as a natural science, Schopenhauer denied it the status of a *science*; and in fact, a *philosophical* interest in historical life is incompatible with his weltanschauung. The paralysis of the historical sense in philosophy, on the one hand, and the preference for natural science, or for its jargon, on the other, were necessary conditions for the belated success of Schopenhauer. He gained a hearing for the ideas of German idealism only by translating them into a physiological language that was as unfortunate as it was agreeable to the taste of the time. And above all, the success achieved by the fanciful and mystical elements of Schopenhauer's philosophy should not deceive us concerning the true situation. As Fichte rightly observed, "All fanaticism [*Schwärmerei*] is and necessarily becomes a philosophy of *nature*."[2]

Among Schopenhauer's successors whose work is in fashion, there is also little in the way of a historical tendency to be observed. One

[2]*Die Grundzüge des gegenwärtigen Zeitalters.* Lecture 8: On the manner in which such an age reacts against itself by erecting the incomprehensible as an ultimate principle. *Collected Works*, VII, p. 111. [*Characteristics of the Present Age*, trans. W. Smith (Frederick, Md.: University Publications of America, 1978).]

only needs to consider Nietzsche, or indeed Spengler.[3] It is especially striking that even Bergson is quite remote from historical science, although in some respects he has discerned the limits of natural science with a clarity that is rarely matched.

Thus, regardless of whether one finds it a source of lament or satisfaction, the fact itself is undeniable: The influence of the historical sciences on the most recent philosophy has been quite modest. With only a few exceptions, very little can be seen in the way of a historical tendency – in contrast to a natural scientific interest – in the contemporary philosophical consciousness. On the contrary, the idea that all authentic science is fundamentally natural science, the belief in a "natural scientific weltanschauung," is once again the general view, and it dominates even those thinkers who are not explicitly aware of it. It should be noted, however, that in opposition to the preceding period of philosophy, in which the stress was on mathematics and natural science, more biologistic and psychologistic tendencies have moved into the foreground. But in principle, the failure of biologism and psychologism to understand historical thought is necessarily just as great as that of mechanism.

To be sure, the most unreflective form a philosophy essentially influenced by natural scientific interests can assume, the metaphysics of materialism, can probably be regarded as an episode of recent intellectual history that already has been surpassed. Today, at any rate, the idea that the world is purely corporeal and that all mental life is only a special form of corporeal change has practically no currency in circles seriously concerned with philosophical problems. On the contrary, ideas on the relationship between psychic and corporeal processes are dominated by a dualism no less rigorous than the position developed by Descartes. The refutation of this dualism by modern Spinozism is apparent. The distinctiveness of mental life is acknowledged. Indeed, today the radical differences between physical and psychic processes – and especially the impossibility of reducing the psychic to the physical – are practically regarded as self-evident. Even materialists shun the name and call themselves "monists," without being able to say why.

Despite this, the belief in the unconditional and exclusive domination of natural science remains unshaken by the recognition of an *uncorporeal* reality, and it is also not clear how it could be shaken by this consideration alone. Regardless of how firmly materialistic speculations are rejected, there is still a strict commitment to the *method* of

---

[3]*Der Untergang des Abendlandes*, 1918. In the ensuing, we will see how unhistorical the idea of a "morphology of history" is. [*The Decline of the West*, trans. Charles Francis (Atkinson, N.Y.: Knopf, 1961).]

natural science. The scientific results achieved by its means in the domain of corporeal nature seem to guarantee that the investigation of the uncorporeal – in other words, the mental – can and should proceed in a natural scientific fashion as well. A natural science of "spiritual" life, a psychology that follows the method of natural science, is regarded by many as the only psychology that qualifies as scientific. This view also determines the conception of the character of history as a science. Reality, insofar as it is accessible to experience, seems to be exhausted by the division into corporeal and mental processes. Because psychology has become a natural science, it is believed that we can have good grounds to assert that there could be no method for the empirical sciences other than that of natural science. If history is to become a genuine science, it too will ultimately have to employ the method that has been proved in the natural sciences, above all in biology; and a scientific treatment of historical life – which is, after all, mental life – must succeed all the more certainly the more advanced the investigation of the human psyche according to the method of natural science becomes.

With reference to this view, we can make the following judgment. Suppose we take the position that in a natural science of biology or psychology, we possess the infallible means for elevating history to the rank of an "exact" science. In that case, an investigation of historical life has perhaps never been undertaken with greater *confidence* than in our own day. Yet this confidence reigns only because of the belief that history itself can become a natural science, just as biology is. The question of whether the existence of such convictions deserves to be called an historical orientation of philosophy is, at the very least, problematic. From a philosophical standpoint, those who see history and natural science as polar antitheses will regard these considerations as demonstrating as clearly as possible that contemporary thought is unhistorical, even where there seems to be a lively interest in the investigation of historical life; or they will take it that, philosophically, the nature of historical science is thoroughly misunderstood.

In any case, it is not necessary to provide a more exact characterization of the contemporary mode of thought. For those who want to reach clarity concerning philosophical problems, there is usually little to be gained by considering which of the philosophical tendencies of their time dominates the consciousness of the wider public. Thus it is also superfluous to venture hypotheses concerning whether this trend is on the rise or whether it has already passed its peak. What will happen depends on what scientists will do. The belief in a general "zeitgeist," for which the individual is nothing more than a subordinate "instrument," can arise only on the basis of a one-sided natural scientific conception of reality. This is one of the propositions that the ensuing account attempts to establish. Therefore, those who understand these matters should not hesitate to express their views, even if they believe that the "general" – in other words, the most prevalent – spiritual tendency of the time is only modestly receptive to these views.

Nevertheless, there is one respect in which they can also be influenced by this tendency, especially when they undertake to write down their thoughts for others. What they have to say will easily take the form of a polemic against prevailing views. Or they may at least make such a polemic the *starting point* of their investigations. Above all, their task will be to establish the *limits* of the scientific strategy that can tolerate nothing but itself. As a result, there is a certain sense in which they will open up the field for what is really important. If they are successful, they will have the best chance of finding a hearing for the ideas to which they are committed. Thus, in our case, even those who believe that there is more to scientific life than natural science and its method, and that philosophy also has to consider and understand these other matters, will first discuss natural science and its method.

The form of the ensuing analyses is based on these considerations. They developed from the conviction that a lack of philosophical understanding of the nature of the historical sciences is one of the most serious defects in the philosophy of our time. The best way to communicate this conviction to others seemed to be an attempt to demonstrate the one-sided character of thought in natural science. At the outset, this involves pointing out the lacunae that even an ideally complete natural science, comprehending both corporeal and mental nature, must necessarily leave in the totality of the empirical sciences. Only if this happens will it be possible to destroy the belief that we could reach clarity concerning what we are accustomed to call – employing an expression that is not very happy, but one that is difficult to dispense with – our weltanschauung with a philosophy *exclusively* oriented to the natural sciences.

In other words, our task is to understand the *diversity* of the methods of the empirical sciences before we take up the problems of philosophy as a science. Perhaps there is a shorter way to arrive at a comprehensive theory of weltanschauung.[4] Given the present dispo-

---

[4] I have tried to do this in the "Allgemeine Grundlegung der Philosophie," which forms the first part of my *System der Philosophie* (1921). In this book as well, however, there are detailed discussions devoted to the relationship of philosophy to history. See especially chapter 6 on philosophy and historical culture.

sition of things, however, it seems that the course adopted here is the most certain. For this reason, we undertake an investigation of the *limits of natural science* in order to achieve clarity concerning the nature and the philosophical significance of the historical sciences.

Today, however, such an undertaking is open to misunderstandings from several directions. At the outset, it seems necessary to counter them.

First, there is no sense in which it is my intention to disparage the importance of modern natural science. Our own age especially has experienced such impressive success in this area that any reservation could only produce an impression of idiotic grumbling. Perhaps natural science owes its popularity more to extraneous products of technology than to its purely scientific content. Nevertheless, irrespective of all practical achievements, there remains quite enough that cannot be too highly esteemed. However, the claim of natural science – even if we take this term in the most comprehensive sense imaginable, a sense we shall have to fix more precisely in the ensuing – to be regarded as the *only* science is completely independent of this immense significance. We can follow the accomplishments of modern natural scientists with an astonished admiration, we can even assess their significance for philosophy very favorably, and still hold that the view of scientific life in general as exhausted by natural scientific investigations with the inclusion of psychology – the view that in *all* questions, natural science has the decisive word – will inevitably lead to a lamentable impoverishment of intellectual life. Thus our investigation is directed not against the natural sciences but only against their *exclusive domination*, and ultimately against the attempt to construct a philosophy as a theory of weltanschauung on their basis.

A second misunderstanding lies in another direction. In our time, there is much talk about the "limits of knowledge of nature," and discussions under this heading coming from the natural sciences themselves have become popular. For this reason we should say at the outset that the ensuing has practically nothing in common with inquiries of this sort. In the context of natural scientific investigations, or so it has been held, there are problems that arise with an inescapable necessity and can be shown to be necessarily irresolvable for all time. Thus the human mind would be better off abstaining from speculation about them. As regards genuine problems, prudent reflection can hardly be expected to conclude that they are irresolvable. From our perspective, the much-discussed phenomenon of *Ignorabimus* is the product of a false problematic. It is a result of the one-sided natural scientific mode of thought that cannot comprehend that where it sees limits to the knowledge of nature, and thus the limits of knowledge in general, for a more farsighted view, problems of a quite different sort can be identified. Nevertheless, it will suffice if we stress that our intention, at least, is not to confirm that there are irresolvable problems. On the contrary, our concern is *not that too many questions are asked, but rather too few*. We propose to identify problems that cannot arise in the context of natural scientific investigations. Only those who have freed themselves from the constraints of a one-sided form of natural scientific thought will be able to see these problems and regard them as worth solving. Our objection to natural science is that it fails to recognize these problems, not to mention its inability to contribute anything to their solution. In consequence, it illegitimately restricts the domain of human inquiry, and thus it is completely unsuitable as the foundation for a genuinely comprehensive theory of weltanschauung. This is our objection, to natural science. This is the perspective from which we speak of its limits.

Finally, one further supposition should be averted precisely on this point. Those who defend the legitimacy and the distinctiveness of history, and moreover those who point to its importance for questions of weltanschauung, easily bring themselves under the suspicion of being committed to *historicism*. This trend is also quite remote from our position. Indeed, we are most resolute in our opposition to the view that philosophy needs to be based *only* on the historical sciences, or even that it should be reduced to historical thought. There are limits to history just as there are limits to natural science. It is only because of the ubiquitous contemporary overestimation of natural science that we begin with its limits. In particular, there is no more a "historical weltanschauung" than there can be a natural scientific weltanschauung. Here at the outset, we will only defend the legitimacy and distinctiveness of history as an *empirical science*. We propose to show that a natural scientific treatment of history is repugnant to its character and destroys its sense. Philosophy itself can employ neither the method of natural science nor that of history. It must, rather, maintain its autonomy vis-à-vis *all* the individual sciences.

For philosophy, historicism is even more dangerous than naturalism. This is because history, exclusively on its own grounds, does not merely produce a one-sided weltanschauung. Actually, it produces no weltanschauung that deserves the name. If it is consistent, every historicism ends in relativism, even in nihilism. Or it conceals its futility and emptiness by arbitrarily singling out this or that specific configuration of historical life in order to draw from it the content for a weltanschauung whose horizon tends to be much narrower than that of a naturalistic weltanschauung. In light of its character, history must confine itself to the historical, and thus to what is temporally conditioned. Philosophy always has the task of proceeding beyond the historical to what is timeless or eternal. So if, for the foregoing reasons, we also advance the struggle against the one-sided quality of methodological naturalism, it is precisely the investigation into the character of historical science that should lead us to understand the following point: Philosophy will progress, on the one hand, only if it takes into consideration not *merely* the natural sciences but the historical sciences *as well* and, on the other hand, only if it also attempts to establish a standpoint beyond *both*. This should suffice as a defense against misunderstanding of our enterprise of exhibiting the limits of natural science.

In the foregoing, we spoke of a lacuna in the totality of the empirical sciences. In the interest of a comprehensive theory of weltanschauung, this lacuna should be exhibited. In order to advance toward this goal, we propose to undertake an investigation of scientific *methods*. Again, we will reach a point at which it will be perfectly clear that our ideas depend on the contemporary state of philosophy, even if in a different respect. Fundamentally, it is problems of how the world and life are to be conceived that are at stake – in the final analysis, the only kind of problem with which philosophy is concerned. In all of its essential aspects, however, ours is a *logical*, or a methodological and epistemological, investigation. It approaches more general questions of how the world and life are to be conceived only where the perspective of logic leads – as it were, by itself – to a more comprehensive perspective. Therefore this book does not propose to achieve scientific clarity concerning how the world and life are to be conceived. On the contrary, it aims only to exhibit the means with which a universal and comprehensive weltanschauung – subject to no limitations by natural scientific prejudices and narrow-mindedness – is to be established. This sort of inquiry can easily create the impression of an enfeebled, uncertain, and exhausted form of thought. Why all this inconsequential reflection concerning the path to philosophy instead of a bold attack?

In fact, the logical-epistemological bent that characterizes modern philosophy and is most clearly represented in many of its best achievements may have helped to alienate philosophy from the interests of a larger public. At this point, moreover, there is not much hope that philosophy as epistemology could again exercise a direct and material influence on such an audience. Not only is this mode of philosophizing difficult. On the basis of a cursory view, it must also seem extraordinarily unproductive for the solution of problems of weltanschauung. And from many sides, of course, we have been told that we have finally had enough in the way of epistemological investigations. Even someone who actually takes the view that a solution of philosophical problems is possible only on the basis of an inquiry into the logical character of science may occasionally be gripped by the feeling that, in comparison with the conceptual systems of the halcyon days of German philosophy, in which an image of the world was projected and an attempt was made to develop a conception of life on its basis, such an effort is remarkably insipid, colorless, and prosaic. What splendor and enchantment for the emotions and the imagination! Among all theories, on the other hand, it is epistemology that is especially "gray." We may be overcome by envy when we read how Hegel proclaimed the courage to pursue the truth as the first condition for philosophical study and admonished his audience that the closed nature of the universe has no intrinsic power to resist the bold spirit of knowledge. Perhaps we cannot blame those who, recalling these times, find that the extraordinary "prudence" of our philosophy seems to give them little cause for enthusiasm. Should we not finally give up being "analysts" and advance to "synthesis"? Is this not the surest way to avoid all natural scientific or psychological narrow-mindedness, as well as all historical narrow-mindedness?

No one familiar with the intellectual history of the nineteenth century can accept this position. Perhaps philosophy will again enjoy another age. For now, the epistemological method seems to be completely indispensable. We know in how short a time the proud intellectual systems of German idealism lost their spiritual dominance. This did not happen for purely extraneous reasons. The philosophical spirit radically underestimated the power of the universe. A period of philosophical pusillanimity set in, and we continue to suffer its aftereffects.

Especially in our own time, there is a particular reason to be cautious in philosophy and spend quite a long time at analysis before proceeding to synthesis. At least among the younger generation, that reactionary period finally seems to be behind us, and the interest in general problems is growing. Unless all the evidence is deceptive, the era of pure specialization – a form of scientific enterprise that rejects all more comprehensive considerations as "unscientific" in principle – has passed its peak. Although natural science and psychology are still very much in the foreground, we once again venture to pose the central philosophical questions. Today, in particular, the incapacity for more comprehensive thought *in the natural sciences* is allowed to occupy itself zealously with levers and screws – where formerly the human mind was called on to concentrate on energetic reflection concerning the problems of weltanschauung. But of course this fact has only extraneous significance. Consider the view that before one takes up philosophical problems, it is first necessary to give them an "exact" foundation in one of the most specialized of the special sciences: experimental psychology. The transition from this view to what is on the agenda – that is, to philosophy – can be swift. On the other hand, precisely because this "inexact" state of mind has reappeared – the only atmosphere in which it is at least possible for philosophy to flourish, namely, the antispecialist state of mind – every form of uncritical enthusiasm is all the more hazardous. We can make lasting progress only by proceeding cautiously and judiciously, considering every step of the investigation beforehand and justifying it. We give priority over every substantive assertion to an investigation into the extent to which science has a right to make any assertion here at all. Thus every problem of the general conception of the world and life is transformed into a problem of logic, of epistemology. Perhaps this can be described as a kind of concession we make to the zeitgeist, which in part remains a spirit of specialization. For of all the parts of philosophy, it is epistemology that most exhibits the character of a special science. Be that as it may, our courage to pursue knowledge, at least in the sense that Hegel possessed it, has been broken. For us, epistemology has become a matter of good conscience, and we will not be prepared to listen to anyone who fails to justify his ideas on this basis.

Perhaps this will appear to later – and happier – times as a sign of weakness. Today those who imagine themselves beyond this sort of "weakness" have not yet provided proof that philosophy as a *science* can make progress in any other way. The metaphysical constructions of the cosmos that we are obliged to witness in our own time either bear a suspicious similarity to older, and mostly much more dynamic and illuminating, intellectual schemes, or are products of the most execrable dilettantism. Nor should the circumstance that, now at least, some people are familiar with the grand *past* and thus rely on originals – for example, on this or that system of German idealism – rather than on insipid modernizations mislead us concerning our epistemological prudence. Whatever is not produced independently and from the ground up but, rather, is taken merely from the past cannot really be "vital" in our time. Dogmatic attempts at restoration are just as worthless philosophically as the restriction to the exact special science. At this point, those who are contemptuous of epistemological investigations must all be seen as fanatics who pose a greater threat to the establishment of a comprehensive theory of life and the world on a scientific basis than those all too modest and undemanding natures who want nothing more than specialization in science.

Thus the philosophy of our time also has its Scylla and its Charybdis. Either it must make its own way between dogmatic enthusiasm and skeptical or narrow-minded specialization or it will not progress at all. We do not require that courage of an earlier age, which occasionally was a form of arrogance. We do not require "audacious" metaphysical constructions of the cosmos that are based on some sort of "intuition" that cannot be substantiated. Attempts of this sort can only bring discredit on a philosophy that proposes to be a scientific theory of weltanschauung. What we need is the courage to persist on the difficult and thorny path of logic and epistemology, the path that Plato and Kant took. This is the locus of the most important tasks for a philosophy that – cognizant of its relationship to the great thinkers of the past and aloof from current fashions – continues to work on the traditional problems.

If this happens, there is also no danger of losing sight of those great *aims* the attainment of which has always been regarded as the real purpose of philosophical inquiry. Our path should also lead to clarity in questions concerning a comprehensive conception of life and the world. This is a task no age can neglect. In any philosophy that deserves the name, there can be differences of opinion only over which path to take, never over the goal. Because of the path we have taken, our ultimate aim may remain unclear for quite some time. At the outset, therefore, it will be useful to give some indication of this aim, and in a way that is independent of the special form in which we shall subsequently cast our problem and attempt to solve it. In other words, we should like to point out the philosophical problems to which our work is intimately related, the problems that have repeatedly occupied the reflections of the human spirit.

This process of reflection moves in grand oppositions. Our task is to identify these oppositions – insofar as they concern the significance of the historical for a philosophical weltanschauung – in the most familiar form, even the most trivial form, possible. Thus we will return to the philosophers already mentioned, those for whom their position on historical life is especially characteristic of their weltanschauung. In considering these philosophers, it could be said that Schopenhauer has no *positive* relationship to history at all. He rejects history as a science, and thus he has no place in our account. Hegel and Comte, on the other hand, can serve as types for the two directions in which the great Either/Or of weltanschauung is expressed precisely in the way they treat history.

For Hegel, what is world history? The primary history in which the author himself narrates what he has experienced – supplemented if need be by the reports of others – or in which a survey of the entire history of a people, a country, or even the world is provided, is not enough for Hegel. Nor can the various kinds of reflective history – pragmatic history, which relates the past to the present; the critical investigation of history with reference to its credibility; the developmental history of certain specific concepts in art and religion – satisfy the philosopher. For him it is a presupposition that history does not simply run its course. On the contrary, it has a *meaning*: *Reason* governs the world. The authentic philosophical task is to search out and describe the plan of history, to discern its "spirit." For Hegel, however, the essence of spirit, in contrast to matter, is freedom. But the spirit is free only insofar as it knows itself as free. Thus Hegel proposes to exhibit world history as the process in which the spirit attains self-consciousness, and thereby freedom. Every historical event is related to this process, and in this way the whole is amalgamated into a unity.

Today, the Hegelian philosophy of history is regarded by some as obsolete, and to a certain extent this is true. First, as Hegel himself knew perfectly well, it stands or falls with his own metaphysical system, which defines the content of the meaning of history. Aside from this issue, however, one will be inclined to pose another question: Who can guarantee that there actually is a "meaning," a "reason," and a "plan" in history, and that they are possible objects of human knowledge? As a result of these considerations, the possibility of any treatment of history that resembles Hegel's in principle becomes at least questionable. And as long as it lacks an epistemological basis, it must remain powerless against such objections.

Comte's position on history seems to be completely different. We are, of course, obliged to focus on one tendency of his work that exists alongside others, and not ask whether he always carried this tendency through consistently. That is permissible, since it is this tendency alone that has become influential in the subsequent development of the philosophy of history. In short, we can call it the naturalistic tendency. According to Comte, history should become "positive," just as the other sciences are. Positive research, however, recognizes only facts and their laws. For the most part, the natural sciences have already attained this insight. What is of importance now is that, at long last, inquiry into the historical life of mankind should also be limited to the search for facts and natural laws. Thus Comte's belief that he has knowledge of the "law" of all historical development is just as uncompromising as Hegel's belief that he has knowledge of the "meaning" of history.

Here too, it can be noted that Comte's sociology stands or falls with his famous law of the three stages: the theological, the metaphysical, and the positive. In addition, the following epistemological question cannot simply be dismissed without further consideration: Are there actually natural laws of history? Or at the very least, are such laws possible objects of human knowledge? Comte did not pose either question. Indeed, to a great extent he left the logical structure of his fundamental law unclear. Only someone who favors a one-sided natural scientific mode of thought can regard this lapse as less serious than Hegel's "uncritical" manner. Comte's philosophy of history is no less defenseless against epistemological criticism than that of the German idealist, regardless of how "modern" it may still seem to many.

At the outset, therefore, philosophy as theory of science is obliged to reject both the Hegelian and the Comtean way of treating history. But Hegel and Comte can still serve as typical representatives of the two directions in the philosophy of history, the tendencies between which our own investigation will have to reach a decision. Thus it is with reference to their doctrines that we propose to clarify the problem under consideration here.

We lack the proper epigrammatic terms for unambiguously characterizing the opposition between these two tendencies in its most general form. As regards the direction typified by Comte, the word "naturalism" can perhaps be used here. This conforms with Comte's endeavor to make history into sociology – in other words, into a science that proceeds according to the manner of natural science. The question of whether the logical character of Comte's "law" of the three stages is actually that of a natural law does not concern us here. But what should we call the other direction? Without further clarification, the term "idealism" is too imprecise and ambiguous to be useful. Here we will be content to define the opposition by means of a negation, which is sufficient for the purposes of this preliminary orientation. We can also employ the concepts of immanence and transcendence. One mode of thought proposes to restrict itself exclusively to the world, which it believes to be immediately and perceptually given as reality. The other tendency attempts to establish a relationship between the reality in which we live – the immanent, visible, and tangible world – and another world that is at least not given to us perceptually. Moreover, this latter view holds that the essence of life is to be sought by immersing oneself in the relations between the natural, perceptual world and that other supernatural or supersensible world.

It is obvious how these different views on history taken by Comte and Hegel must be expressed if they are to be developed consistently: Here the concept of a self-contained, self-sufficient being governed by purely immanent laws; there reality as a process structured in terms of the relationships between its component events and a transcendent principle. Here the world that – because it is subsumed under general laws – constitutes a *nature* that is fundamentally always the same; a *cyclical process* indifferent to the profusion of individual configurations that come to be and pass away and that, as transitory phenomena, have no real being; there reality, the particulars of which are meaningfully structured with reference to the transcendent principle, a unique *development* of different stages each of which has its own unique significance. If naturalism is valid, then in fact historical research remains possible only in the form of sociology: as a theory of the general natural laws that govern every process of historical reality in a uniform fashion. The result is different if it is permissible to establish a relation between empirical reality and a world that lies "beyond" it. Then the *unique* phenomenon in its individual *distinctiveness* also acquires an interest according to the position it occupies in relation to that other world. Under these conditions, it makes sense to interpret the plan or the reason of the totality of historical development.

Perhaps the distinction between these two views can be best clarified by reference to a specific problem. Is there *progress* in history? This is a question that has often been considered, and from the most diverse philosophical positions, a question that no philosophy of historical life can altogether avoid answering. Even Comte called his social dynamics a theory of progress. But we must understand the word "progress" in the following sense: When something is said to be progressive, a *value* distinction between different states is to be drawn. Thus progress also signifies an *enhancement of value*. Otherwise the question of progress in history would have no particular interest, since it is self-evident that everything in history changes. Can naturalism, assuming that it remains consistent, make these value distinctions among different levels of change in such a way that they have more than an arbitrary significance? Moreover, can Comte's law – assuming that it really is to have the status of a natural law – also be a law of progress? Must not every purely immanent valuation – beyond which naturalism, because of its character, cannot proceed – seem to be nothing more than a transitory phenomenon and a scientific nullity? And must we not at least limit ourselves to the claim that progress is what will take place according to necessary laws, and that, for this reason, the later of two events always represents progress over the earlier? But does this not imply that the word "progress" necessarily loses its established meaning as an enhancement of value?

This is not yet the time to decide these issues. It should be stressed only that there is a difficulty for naturalism that does not arise for the other perspective, because this latter perspective places reality in a relationship to a world that lies "outside" it. This is because the transcendental world provides a *criterion* for a valuation of different states that is more than arbitrary and transitory, and thus the possibility of actually understanding progress as an enhancement of value. The unique and distinctive phenomenon is assigned its place as a stage in the developmental progress toward a goal. This goal not only has an objective meaning of its own; it also transmits this meaning to the whole by means of which it is realized. Thus the question of progress in history cannot avoid the choice between an immanent and a transcendent weltanschauung.

As noted, this question does not form the real theme of our inquiry. In addition, we wanted only to sketch this problem in quite general terms and in a way that comprehended the most diverse features, a sketch that, for this reason, was somewhat imprecise. Ultimately, however, our investigation should lead us to a point where we will also be required to take a position on the question of whether we can get by with an immanent weltanschauung or whether a transcendent weltanschauung is indispensable. Then the meaning of this question will be defined more rigorously. The general philosophical justification of these logical investigations seems to lie precisely in the fact that we will necessarily reach such a point. Thus, at this juncture, we should at least provide some anticipatory indication of the direction our ultimate decision will have to take.

As the foregoing makes clear, a consideration of history from the purely naturalistic standpoint seems to be an error in principle. We will have to show in detail that historical research as natural science is intrinsically impossible, a logically contradictory task. This also implies that our standpoint exhibits an affinity with that other supranatural mode of thought for which Hegel served as the model. But only an *affinity*. Most of the attempts made thus far in this direction – and, above all, the system of Hegel – do not achieve what they should. If their logical consequences are developed, they inevitably lead to a result that reveals all the inconsistencies of naturalism. However, we take the view that if history is to be pursued as a science, transcendent assumptions are indispensable. We will even be able to show that an immanent naturalism is not logically feasible. The theory of science compels us to recognize that *every* science rests on transcendent presuppositions. The natural sciences may be able to deceive themselves on this point because the use of the transcendent in these sciences has become so self-evident that it is usually completely overlooked. The historical sciences will have to reflect explicitly on their transcendent factors. In demonstrating this necessity, logic leads into a general theory of weltanschauung.

These few remarks can suffice as a *general* orientation to the character and purpose of this inquiry and also as an indication of the philosophical framework within which it will move. At this point, we will turn to the formulation of our *specific problem*.

Even the transposition of a general question concerning the conception of life and the world into a logical problem seemed to be a restriction of our task. Now we must proceed a step further in this direction. We do not propose to define the limits of natural science in a comprehensive and exhaustively elaborated *systematic* theory of science, and then on this basis clarify the nature of history. In particular, we do not propose to solve the widely discussed problem of a "classification" of *all* sciences. On the contrary, we will single out only a special case. But we have selected this case in such a way that we can exhibit the general logical principle and treat the essential questions systematically. This holds for the limits of natural science as well as for the fundamental logical concepts of the historical disciplines.

In logic, it is conventional to distinguish scientific *investigation* and scientific *representation*. Suppose we do not take this second term in a superficial sense in which only the linguistic formulation of ideas is at stake. Suppose instead we understand by a representation the logical form that must necessarily be taken by the *results* of scientific work. In that case, we can say that our purpose is not to exhibit the logical structure of the process of scientific research and demonstration. On the contrary, we will essentially try only to provide a logical understanding of one of its *means of representation*. If the intention of our investigation is not to be misunderstood from the outset, this must be scrupulously kept in mind. In the natural sciences, we use the name *concept* for the form in which the results of scientific investigation are – as this might be put – set down. Concept formation in our sense always forms, at least relatively, the *conclusion* of an investigation. Thus the concept represents as complete what has been established by research. Insofar as concept formation is the *goal* of all research in natural science, it seems that an examination of concept formation is an excellent way to clarify the essential nature of the method of natural science in general, especially as regards its relations to the question of the scientific treatment of history. Following the intention indicated earlier, our task is to inquire into the areas where the formation of concepts according to the method of natural science has a meaning and the areas where it must necessarily lose this meaning. In other words, our task is to investigate *the limits of concept formation in natural science.* In the first instance, this inquiry should exhibit the *gap* that natural science (including psychology as the science of "natural," empirically real mental life) – no matter how perfect its state of completeness – must necessarily leave in our knowledge. It should lead to what cannot be achieved by means of concept formation in natural science, even where it is only the aims of the empirical sciences that are at stake.

Once this question is answered, we will try to show what kind of science can fill this space in the *empirical sciences*. We believe that this task falls to the historical sciences. In our positive exposition of history, we will especially have to stress what is calculated to elucidate the logical *opposition* between the two methods. In this way, the basic significance of the limits of concept formation in natural science will be exhibited even more clearly. In addition, however, this opposition must also illuminate the definitive characteristics of the historical procedure itself, and especially of historical representation or the "historical concept," if this expression may be allowed in opposition to the concept of natural science. Nevertheless, it should be noted that what we mean by the historical sciences here at the outset is still not history in the narrower sense. When we employ the words "historical" and "history" in the basic claims of this book, our focus can only be on logical – in other words, *formal* – concepts. Thus we cannot be concerned with the historical sciences as characterized by their distinctive subject matter. Those who fail to keep this in mind will no more understand the central point of our exposition than those who lose sight of the restriction of the investigation to the concept. For this reason, we should offer by way of introduction a few more remarks, both on the plan of a "logic of history" in general and on the meaning of the word "concept" in the historical disciplines in particular. From the outset, this should prevent misunderstandings concerning the purpose of our enterprise.

At one time, the concept of "history" with whose logic we have to *begin* was quite commonplace – for example, in the philosophy of Christian Wolff and in the German Enlightenment, even though there was no perception of the problem that concerns us. More recently, a terminology has become conventional that employs the word "history" only in a narrower sense. This is why some of what we say here may sound paradoxical. In the interest of a clearly executed analysis of logical problems, this cannot be avoided. And we have even less reason to fear apparent paradoxes of this sort, since we are only returning to an old, well-established usage. If we intend to achieve *logical* clarity concerning the relationship of history to natural science, the concept of the historical with which we begin can only be formal.

Actually, this should be taken as self-evident. And yet it seems that it is precisely the acknowledgment of this *governing principle of our entire investigation* that encounters the most powerful resistance. In the "logic of history," everything conceivable is discussed, with the exception of its logical structure. We propose to make a fundamental break with these habits; although they are widespread, they are still not justified. Indeed, we see this as the main value of our enterprise. We would like to conquer a territory for logic that it has almost completely neglected. We will do this by asking what the concept of history as a *science* consists in. It is only the answer to this question that has an independent logical interest, and the concept of science can be logically defined only in a *formal* fashion. At the beginning of our work, this is why we especially cannot understand history in the sense of "human science" [*Geisteswissenschaft*] as one usually can. At the *outset*, we will even have to eschew what we will later see as the substantively most appropriate expression, "cultural science" [*Kulturwissenschaft*]. This is because these terms and others as well all refer to the *material* that history investigates and not the *logical* structure of a historical representation, which is our interest here. I do not see how the legitimacy of such a *problematic* can be contested on scientific grounds.

Contrary to what people seem to believe, the logic of history need not *conflict* with investigations concerning the nature of history that have a different orientation. At least it has its own theoretical value *alongside* them. It is, of course, possible to begin with differences in the *material* that the sciences investigate in order to show how, for example, the acquisition of knowledge of *mental* life in history poses other difficulties – and thus requires other methods of investigation – than the acquisition of knowledge of corporeal nature. In that case, we might quite rightly place concepts like that of historical "understanding" – in contrast to the concept of "explanation" in natural science – in the foreground. Insofar as we undertake a *logical* investigation of history, there is no sense in which we contest the justification of such distinctions. Indeed, in the long run we will also consider in detail the problems that arise here. For this reason alone, it represents a misunderstanding of our efforts to claim that they contain *only* a formal philosophy of history. The *content* of history is just as important to us as its *form. Subsequently*, therefore, I will present a full discussion of the distinctive substantive characteristics of the historical material. We cannot take up these questions at the *outset*, precisely because our concern is with a *logic* of history. The fact that, thus far, people have not been in the habit of treating the problem of historical science in a logical or formal fashion – and, in consequence, pose logically secondary questions – is, of course, no objection to our attempt.

A purely "historical" survey; or a classification of the different individual disciplines according to differences in their *material*, as is usually done in some systems of "logic"; or the attempt to link as closely as possible those sciences whose representatives depend on one another in their work to a particularly high degree – this can least of all constitute the ultimate goal of a *philosophy* of the sciences. The problem here is just not that simple, because in this way we would never reach clarity concerning the extent to which history qualifies as scientific *knowledge*. Naturally some of what passes for "history" today is either not science at all or is *more* than science, and of course its basis is also a problem for the theory of science. But it holds true for *all* sciences that they cannot be exhaustively incorporated into *any* logical schema just as they exist, as historical facts. More or less atheoretical motives also come into play in all scientific research. The respects in which history can go beyond scientific knowlege or the respects in which it can fall short can be understood only if the concept of history as a *science* has first been identified logically.

Nor does it matter at all – to mention this one further point – if logic should bring into formal opposition matters that are always most intimately connected with one another in the enterprise of science as it in fact exists. The reproach that such a way of thinking "mutilates" the sciences in an "unnatural" fashion would have no more justification than the reproach that the anatomist dissects a body in order to comprehend it scientifically. An articulation of the sciences according to their raw material or their nonlogical components in general may also have its significance, but it does not lie on the path to a *logic* of history. Indeed, it can even be useful as preliminary work for a logic of history only if we are equipped with logical concepts and know how to use such an articulation. Moreover, even the difference between natural science and history with reference to their distinctive substantive characteristics will be philosophically understood only in a logical fashion. In other words, only in this way will we comprehend what historical science means for an epistemologically grounded philosophy. The circumstance that the sciences can be classified differently on the basis of perspectives that differ from ours has no import at all for our enterprise.

It is obvious that only the following investigation can define the logical concept of history in the sense that it will be employed in the ensuing, the most comprehensive formal sense imaginable. Here we should note that in conformity with the limitations we placed on our investigation of natural science, the issue does not concern the process of historical research so much as the form of representation – in other words, the logical structure of the *results* of the historical sciences. These results alone can fill the gaps in the comprehension of reality by natural science. That is why they are the genuine object of philosophical interest. For this reason, we will also not take it as an objection to our theory if someone contests the view that scientific demonstration in the so-called human sciences is conducted according to a different method, or that the identification of its *initial premises* takes place differently, than in the area of the natural sciences.[5] These problems simply do not come under discussion here. They would be treated in other parts of a systematic theory of science. From such a theory, it would certainly follow that the processes of research and demonstration in all the empirical sciences exhibit far-reaching common features. For our purpose, however, this is of secondary importance.

As we have already noted, here we will establish only the nature of the *historical concept*. It is always necessary to keep this in mind if the intention of the book is not to be misinterpreted from the outset. The circumstance that such an expression – in opposition to the concept of the natural sciences – is not in common use, need cause no difficulties. As we have already mentioned, it is connected with the illogical or nonlogical character of virtually all the work in the "logic of history" that has been done thus far. Those who propose to understand history with reference to the *material* it represents have no reason to speak of "historical concepts." We choose this word to convey the logical character of the investigation in its terminology as well, and also so that we can treat the different problems posed by natural science and history in a parallel fashion.

In what we designate as a historical concept, it is especially the *scientific* character of history that must be expressed. Finally, suppose the total process of scientific work is determined by its goal here as well. In that case, what is essential to the logical distinctiveness of the historical sciences, at least in its basic outlines and especially in distinction to the definitive quality of concept formation in natural science, can result from an investigation into representation in the historical sciences. It is in this sense and this sense alone that in the following we will try to provide a *logical introduction to the historical sciences*.

Although the distinction between the concepts of natural science and history is not a familiar one, it is all the more important to keep

[5]See A. Riehl, "Logik und Erkenntnistheorie," *Die Kultur der Gegenwart*. I, 6. 1907, p. 101.

it in mind because in the parts of logic devoted to the theory of the concept *in general*, we almost exclusively find *that* sort of concept formation considered that we believe must be designated as natural scientific. As a result, the theory of the concept thus far is quite one-sided. And even in the case of the concept of natural science, we cannot simply appeal to uncontested theorems of general logic. Especially since Sigwart[6] removed the theory of the concept from its place at the pinnacle of the system it occupied in traditional logic, no one has as yet succeeded in giving this theory a generally acknowledged position and configuration. There is a considerable difference of opinion concerning what a "concept" really is, or what this expression should most properly be used for. The word "concept" is employed for both the simplest logical components or elements as well as for the most complicated logical entities. It allegedly designates not only the most primitive meanings of words that cannot be reduced by further analysis but also the ultimate consolidations of scientific theories. Indeed, the ambiguity of the word "concept" is so great that recently people have actually avoided the term altogether. We are delighted to be able to discuss, "without any help even from the mere word 'concept,' "[7] problems that were formerly regarded as the main problems of the theory of the concept.

Obviously what is at stake here is not the *word* "concept." Because of the lack of clarity produced by its ambiguity, it would be preferable to replace it with several precise terms. But it will surely be extremely difficult to decide to dispense altogether with the expressions "concept," "conceive," and "conceptual" in logic. Perhaps we will succeed in bringing somewhat more unity and clarity to the discussion of these questions if, in a specialized logical investigation, we explicitly do the same thing that the general part of logic has almost always done implicitly, namely, completely restrict ourselves in the first instance to the concept of the *natural sciences*. In other words, we will disregard altogether the question of the extent to which what we deal with pertains to the nature of the scientific concept in general. Only then will we fix the limits of concept formation in natural science. From this point, we will be able to penetrate the nature of the historical concept. . . .

---

[6]In his *Logik*, 1873–78, 4th ed., 1911, a work that still has a powerful influence on the more recent developments in logic.

[7]Benno Erdmann, *Logik*, I, 1892; 2nd ed., 1907, p. 255.

3

Nature and History

The sciences, since they are systems of concepts,
always speak of types. History, on the other hand,
always speaks of individuals. Thus it is a putative
science of individuals.

Arthur Schopenhauer

INTRODUCTION

If logic provides no justification in principle for a distinction between
natural science and the human sciences, why do we still search for a
method of concept formation that differs from that of natural science,
and what can this method be? Consider those who hold that natural
science is the only science, that there are no limits to natural science
that would make another kind of concept formation necessary. Does
not the rejection of a logical opposition between natural science and
the human sciences indicate that they are correct? Will not the
ensuing inquiry at best show the limits of *concept formation in science as
such*?

In turning to the answer to these questions, we finally reach the
main ideas of this work. All the earlier discussions had the purpose of
leading up to them,[1] so that the first decisive step of the inquiry must
now appear as a basically self-evident consequence of the foregoing –
to some readers, perhaps all too self-evident. The remarks that
immediately follow are self-evident [*selbstverständlich*] because they are
purely logical and because all that is purely logical, once it is
understood at all, is "understood by itself" [*sich von selbst versteht*].

There is no doubt about the path we have to take to make further
progress. We know that the limits of concept formation in natural
science cannot be fixed by reflection on the substantive properties of
the material, properties exhibited only by this or that *part* of empirical
reality. Thus we need to consider *in what relationship concept formation*

[1][On the theses of Chapters 1 and 2 and their role in laying the groundwork for the
development of Rickert's main ideas, see the translator's Introduction.]

in natural science, or generalizing concept formation, stands to empirical reality itself.

Once we are clear on this point, we will attempt to show the following: What for purely logical reasons can never be subsumed under a concept of natural science – namely, the "individuality" of empirical reality – can be represented only in sciences we are obliged to call *historical*, if it is to be the object of scientific treatment at all. This is because the concept of what sets a limit to natural science, the concept of the unique and the individual, coincides with *the concept of the historical* in the most comprehensive sense of this term conceivable – in other words, the purely logical and formal sense. The result is a *logical* opposition between nature and history. In the Introduction, we stressed as energetically as we could that this opposition, in its most comprehensive form, is not to be identified with that usually drawn between nature and history. But there is no reason why this circumstance should create difficulties for a logical investigation: Our opposition is *intended* to be more comprehensive than the usual one. Only by starting from this comprehensive opposition and proceeding *step by step* can we define the concept of "history" in the currently accepted narrower sense.

For this reason, the *subsequent* respects in which this most general concept of history requires qualification should not be conceived as "concessions" or accommodations to received views. On the contrary, the nature of our logical investigation requires that we *begin* by forming a concept of history that is *too* general from the perspective of the "historical sciences" as they happen to be conceived at present. Only by means of the ensuing analyses will this concept be structured and defined so that it is applicable to the historical disciplines that actually exist. *At the outset*, therefore, we do not establish much for the concept of historical science in the narrower sense. Nevertheless, our purely logical concept of history is indispensable for a logically grounded methodology. This is because we can clarify the fundamental significance of the logical differences between the sciences only with its help.

Once our analysis has produced the most general logical opposition between nature and history, which as such can*not* yet provide the basis for an articulation of the sciences, we can turn to the problem of establishing the principle for a logical articulation of the empirical sciences that actually *exist*. In the first instance, this will show that the concepts of nature and history are, in a certain respect, relative if we employ them in the quite comprehensive and formal sense that is at stake at this preliminary stage of our investigation. In consequence, *historical components also* play a role *in the natural sciences*. They even condition the logical articulation of the natural sciences. Thus the purely logical structure of the natural sciences in all their *diversity* can be made fully clear only with the help of the logical concept of the historical.

The considerations of the foregoing paragraph cannot be regarded as an objection to our theory, however. On the contrary, they only confirm the view that progress can be made in the theory of science only with the logical concepts of nature and history, not with the substantive differences between nature and spirit. In that case, we shall find historical elements – in the most general, logical sense of the term – both in the sciences of bodies and in the psychological disciplines. This should provide no occasion for surprise. In the same way that our concept of nature includes both physical and psychic phenomena, so the concept of history formed in opposition to it must be understood in its most comprehensive sense as independent of the difference between body and spirit or mind. Thus we will find elements that are more or less historical in *all* the sciences that conceive reality as nature, in the sense that is relevant to this work. In other words, we do not want to dispute the *interpenetration* and *concomitance* of the two logical factors, although, astonishingly enough, that is how we have been interpreted. On the contrary, we propose to draw explicit attention to it.

In the final analysis, however, it can be shown that the relativity of the concepts of nature and history and their concurrence in the most diverse disciplines of the natural sciences have no bearing on the significance of these concepts for the *logical* articulation of the empirical sciences. Regardless of how the concept of the historical sciences is more narrowly defined in order to approximate more closely what is usually understood by this term, there are no conditions under which a natural scientific or generalizing representation of *history* is possible. Thus concept formation in *natural science* and concept formation in *history* must always remain in radical logical opposition. With this insight, we first reach the idea of a scientific *goal* that can never be attained by the kind of concept formation characteristic of natural science. In this chapter, it will suffice to show that there is such a goal.

At the outset, therefore, the concept of historical science will be identified *only* as the concept of a *task* that is thus far unresolved. We will not proceed to the *positive* determination of the nature of concept formation in history until the fourth chapter. There we will try to develop, in opposition to the definitive features of representation in natural science, the fundamental logical concepts and presuppositions of a historical representation. At that point, it will finally be possible to define *the* concept of history that we invariably have in mind today when we speak of historical science; for by that point, we will also be able to say something about the *material* with which historical science is concerned. We will see that this material qualifies as *culture*, in opposition to nature. Here we arrive at a *substantive* distinction. Just as it stands, it obviously need not coincide with the logical opposition between history and nature. But the analyses in this chapter must remain purely *formal*. This is because the aim of our investigation is always to distinguish the purely logical from the material as rigorously as possible. We can return to the problem of the *integration* of the formal and the material only when this distinction has been carried through consistently. That is, only under this condition can we consider the relationships between formal and material differences in the sciences, relationships that obviously no one will attempt to deny.

1. NATURAL SCIENTIFIC CONCEPT FORMATION AND EMPIRICAL REALITY

What is it that fixes the limits of concept formation in natural science, limits that, for logical or *formal* reasons, the natural sciences can never traverse? This is our *first* question, even though it need not remain our only question.

To answer it, suppose we focus our attention on what is necessarily eliminated by the transformation and simplification that take place in the representations and systems of the natural sciences, or the generalizing disciplines. At this point, therefore, we will examine what might be called the opposite side of concept formation in natural science. For this purpose, we will proceed from the relationship in which concept formation in natural science stands to the *concrete actuality* of the empirical world. Only after that will we turn to what can be called the *individuality* of empirical reality, whose relationship to the concepts of representation in natural science is our primary concern.

Even a description employing words with a general reference abstracts from the perceptual manifold every single entity presents to us. In many cases, however, the content of the concept is still represented by perceptions. Yet, as we know, this sort of representation can actually be a source of trouble in the context of scientific research. This is due to its indeterminate manifold. Thus, as we were able to show, its elimination is a further task that concept formation is obliged to confront. Once this task is resolved by means of the definition of the concept, perception can no longer render its content adequately. Should certain vestiges of perception remain, they will tend to disappear as the process of concept formation advances. And finally, if the logical ideal of a theory in natural science is attained, we will find that the content of its concepts contains nothing more of *that* sort of perception that experience directly presents. Therefore we can flatly claim that the complete logical articulation of a concept in natural science depends on the extent to which empirical perception or sense perception is eliminated from its content. . . .

. . . The meaning and purpose of natural science are to establish an opposition between the content of *concepts* and the *reality* of sense perception that is as rigorous as possible. The creation of this sort of fissure is the necessary result of every perspective that conceives reality as "nature," that is, with reference to what is general. Regardless of the content of concepts, the opposition of this content to the empirical world of sense perception becomes all the more uncompromising the further advanced, in a logical sense, natural scientific concept formation becomes.

This is directly related to another point that is essential to the complete clarification of the significance of this opposition for our problem. If what we call the "individuality" of reality is intended to designate the real itself, it is linked not with perception in the homogeneous, mathematical sense but, rather, with the heterogeneous, empirical sense perception that natural scientific concept formation eliminates from its descriptions. For this reason, the elimination of empirical perception as carried out by natural scientific concept formation invariably implies the removal of the individual character of the given reality from the content of concepts as well. In other words, natural scientific concepts contain progressively less of the individual as well as of empirical perception the more complete they become in a logical sense. The individual in the strict sense is absent from even the most primitive form of natural scientific concepts. In the final analysis, natural science entails that everything real is fundamentally one and the same, and thus no longer contains anything that is individual.

It is not necessary to demonstrate this point in more detail for the different sciences. As we have seen, regardless of which part of the invariably perceptual and individual real world in which we live is under consideration, the natural sciences always represent bodies as the motion of atoms; and for mental life, an analogous conception is at least attempted. If something is the object of a natural scientific concept, then, together with the manifold of empirical perception, everything is eliminated that constitutes it as a *real individual*.

To assess the significance of this result, suppose we define more precisely exactly what "individual" and "individuality" mean in this context. In the case of these words, we are primarily inclined to think of personalities. At this point, that sense of these expressions is irrelevant. In accordance with the general logical intention of our analyses, the concept of the individual under consideration here is much more inclusive. The human individual forms only one of its types. We need to keep in mind that *every* corporeal or mental process, just as we directly observe or experience it, is an "individual." In other words, it is an entity that really occurs only once at this particular juncture in space and time, it is different from all other corporeal or mental processes, and it never recurs. Thus when it is destroyed or lapses into the past, it disappears from the real world forever. Even if we disregard personalities, there is still, of course, a second concept of the individual that does not coincide with the unique and distinctive reality we have in mind here. In the ensuing, this concept will occupy us fully. In any case, we also use the word "individuality" to designate the distinctiveness, singularity, and uniqueness of every reality. In this context, we only want to underscore the nonrecurrent distinctiveness, singularity, and uniqueness of every real entity *as such*. We do this to mark off what cannot be subsumed under a natural scientific concept because it disappears with empirical sense perception.

Although these claims are basically self-evident, it is easy to over-look them. We are inclined to link individuality as the unique and the distinctive with only one *part* of reality. Natural science itself is responsible for this disposition. When we abstract from the individual configuration of things in natural science, this does not bother us in most cases; especially when a body is under consideration, we hardly notice it. We have no interest in the fact that every leaf on a tree appears different from the leaves next to it, or that no fragment of a chemical substance in a retort is exactly like any other fragment of the "same" substance and will ever reappear. The common name satisfies us for the purpose of denotation, and this is why we are only concerned with what must be present in order to apply the name. In other words, we unwittingly translate the content of perceptual reality into the content of general concepts. Then we suppose that because we always find something that corresponds to the content of these concepts, it is the real entity itself that either reappears or is the same as another real entity.

But this is actually never the case; and as soon as we consider this, we must realize the significance of the fact that all natural scientific or generalizing concept formation ignores the concrete reality and individuality of unique empirical reality. If the individual and the perceptual are not included in the content of concepts, it follows that nothing of the *real* as such remains in them either – where by the "real" we obviously mean only the immediately experienced or given reality in which we live our sentient existence. Thus the fissure between concepts and individuals produced by natural science is a fissure between concepts and empirical reality as such in its uniqueness and distinctiveness. A natural scientific representation that proceeds by generalizing no longer refers to this or that distinctive real thing. On the contrary, it abstracts from all properties that constitute objects as these distinctive realities, the very properties that are essential to their status as real entities.

Thus we arrive at the following result. The content of reality can be an object of immediate "experience" or "acquaintance." But as soon as we attempt to conceive it by means of natural science, precisely those properties that constitute it as reality always escape us. We have access to the full content of reality only through the immediacy of life, never by means of the concepts of natural science. The circumstance that the word "reality" can also be the name for the *form* that we ascribe to the immediately experienced, perceptual, and individual content is of no significance in this context. We designate as real the *content* that is both individual and also an object of sense perception. Thus it is clear that all the claims that could be made about the relations of natural scientific concept formation to concrete actuality and individuality must also hold true for its relationship to empirical reality itself. The more completely we develop our natural scientific theories and representations, the further we depart from reality as unique, perceptual, and individual – in other words, from the real as such. And so it becomes all the more certain that in the process of research, both the concrete actuality and the individuality of reality slip from our grasp.

This thesis can easily be established for the different stages of the natural scientific concept. In our use of words with elementary meanings, the content of reality that is retained remains relatively significant. The perceptual representations of concepts that provide a picture of the perceptual manifold of reality continue to impose themselves on us, but we have no interest in them. On the contrary, they even disturb us. And if we conceive the theories of the natural sciences as complete, we are talking about things or processes concerning which we negate everything of reality that immediate experience presents to us at every point, everything that is exclusively entitled to be called empirically real. This distance from the real holds true for the content of concepts that arise from the analysis of single processes as well as for concepts that occur through an empirical comparison of several objects. Concerning this point, therefore, we can say in all brevity: The substance of perceptual and individual reality that is still contained in the concepts of natural science has not yet been comprehended by natural science. If, on the other hand, a logically complete natural scientific concept has been developed, all of the individual content of reality and all of its content determined by sense perception – in the respect just discussed – have vanished from it.

As a result, we have a general answer to the question that lies at the focal point of this chapter. *What fixes the limits of natural scientific concept formation, and which the natural sciences can never surmount, is nothing but unique empirical reality itself*, just as we directly experience it in sense perception, in its *concrete actuality* and *individuality*.

Initially, the conclusion of this investigation may sound paradoxical. Do the concepts of natural science, we will be asked, become more complete the less they contain of reality, for the knowledge of which we form them? That cannot be so, for on this assumption, natural science would fail to realize its goal. It should lead us to reality, not away from it. Thus it cannot result in a system of concepts whose content stands in opposition to the content of empirical reality. There is another reason why this conclusion seems to be mistaken. Not only do theoretical considerations speak against it, but also the fact that we orient ourselves in reality with the help of natural science; we are even able to calculate its properties in advance by this means. These and similar objections will immediately be raised against our exposition. For this reason, we are obliged to make it somewhat more complete, both with reference to the concept of natural science and with reference to that of reality.

As regards the concept of natural science, we can limit ourselves to the point that everyone is obviously free to conceive whatever he likes under the term "natural science." In that case, he can reject our definition, which holds that in order to establish knowledge of the totality of an unlimited reality, natural science has to conceive it with reference to the general and, wherever possible, has to discover its laws. At the same time, however, we may take note of the fact that the sciences that attempt to establish natural laws are usually called natural sciences. We know that these nomological sciences cannot have the purpose of encompassing the concrete actuality and individuality of reality within its theories. Like the content of every concept of natural science, the content of a nomological concept is general. The content of all empirical reality, on the other hand, is individual. This gap can never be bridged, for the meaning of knowledge of the real as nature rests directly on it. Thus the conclusion of our exposition must be acknowledged as valid for all scientific research that proposes to represent any aspect of reality systematically by means of general concepts. There are purely logical reasons why the attempt to develop a system is inextricably linked with a disregard for the real, individual, and perceptual configuration. It remains equally certain that all reality with which we are acquainted consists solely of perceptually and individually formed constructs.

Therefore, it is incontestable that empirical reality – just as it exists, individual and perceptual – cannot be incorporated into any system of concepts in natural science, and thus also that it defines the limits of all knowledge in natural science. That is the only point at issue in this context. It lies in the *concept* of the law of nature that it has nothing to say about what really occurs here or there, now or then, with a uniqueness and an individuality that cannot be repeated. This can be made clear by the consideration that any natural law can be formulated in a completely adequate fashion in a so-called hypothetical judgment: *If* one thing occurs, then so will another. The names of the two things in question are always names of general concepts. Concerning the objects subsumed under these general concepts – their actual perceptual and individual configuration, the number of such objects that really exist, and their real location in space and time – the law of nature can and will have nothing to say. Indeed, it would immediately cease to be a law of nature if it undertook to represent individual objects of this sort. Since only unique, perceptual, and distinctive objects in a certain number, in specific places, and at a specific time are real, the natural law also can and will have nothing to say about the real itself just as it exists, perceptually and individually. As soon as the "if . . . , then . . . " relationship in the law of nature is at issue, *whether* the antecedent holds true is no longer explicitly in question. On the contrary, it is only implicitly presupposed that there is a real entity that falls under the general concepts linked in the nomological concept. But the individuality and concrete actuality of this real entity are necessarily bracketed. If we do not use the name "natural science" for the kind of representation of reality in which reality as unique, perceptual, and individual, and thus as reality itself, disappears, we cannot demand knowledge of the corporeal world or of mental life *in general* from natural science and its natural laws.

Nor can the fact that we are able to orient ourselves practically in reality with the help of knowledge in natural science, and that reality can even be calculated in advance in this way, be regarded as an objection to the view that the content of individual and perceptual reality is eliminated from the concepts of natural science. We are, rather, obliged to take the contrary position: If the concepts of natural science comprised the perceptual and individual configuration of reality, then neither a practical orientation to reality nor a prediction of its properties would be possible with the help of these concepts. As we have already stressed in our critique of pragmatism,[2] we can orient ourselves to reality only by means of the *simplification* of reality that is undertaken in concepts. We must abstract from its unique distinctiveness and particularity in order to find our way in the real. Otherwise the infinite manifold of its content eliminates any possibility of orientation. If we did not have general concepts by means of which we could simplify reality and thereby divest it of its bewildering individuality and concrete actuality, in our practical conduct we would stand helpless before reality.

In addition, the fact that we calculate the real in advance does not imply that the concepts of natural science comprehend its total contents. We only need to be clear about what calculation means. It is not a question of grasping individual and perceptual realities in their individuality and concrete actuality. We are able to say only that in the future, an object will appear that can be subsumed as a case under this or that genereal concept. But this does not give us knowledge of the individuality and concrete actuality of future objects. Should we be interested in this sort of knowledge, we are always obliged to wait until the objects are really at hand. Then we can substantiate their individuality and concrete actuality, that is, their complete reality, which lies beyond the general content of concepts. If we ignore this point and assume that natural science predicts what really happens, that is because, in these cases, we are simply not *interested* in knowledge of how the future entity is formed in its concrete actuality and individuality. On the contrary, if we know the general concept under which these future realities can be subsumed, we are satisfied.

Thus the usefulness of natural science in practical life is not an objection to our position. On the contrary, when this point is correctly understood, it provides a new proof for the thesis that reality in its concrete actuality and individuality – that is, reality as such – can never be subsumed under the concepts of natural science. . . .

The view that a theory in natural science fails to reach its goal when it does not succeed in representing reality itself as it actually exists is possible only on the basis of a quite specific *concept of knowledge*, namely, on the assumption that the task of knowledge is to provide a *complete reproduction* of empirical reality. A reproduction is obviously all the more perfect the more closely it approximates the original as it really *exists*. So if the picture theory were correct, natural science

[2][The reference is to discussions in chapter 1 (*Die Grenzen*, pp. 40, 84) that are not included in the translation. Here Rickert stresses that his thesis concerning the logical basis of concept formation in natural science is independent of any genetic or evolutionary claim concerning its origins.]

would even have the task of reproducing the concrete actuality and individuality of empirical reality. But can scientific knowlege be regarded as equivalent to a reproduction? The unequivocal answer to this question is no. Our earlier exposition was directed just as much against this conception of knowledge as against the idea that the individual object of sense perception can be incorporated into the theories of natural science.

It can be shown on the basis of general logical considerations that no knowledge can possibly provide a reproduction. This is because every knowledge claim must take the form of a *judgment*. In other words, it is impossible, as this is usually expressed, for the truth of knowledge to consist in the "agreement of the *idea* with its object." The relationship between an original and its copy will never obtain between reality and the content of the judgments made about it. There is, of course, a certain kind of description that also makes it possible to represent reality with judgments in such a way that a kind of perceptual *picture* of reality is produced. As we have shown in detail, however, this sort of description is never natural scientific. So it seems that the theory of the concept developed in the foregoing can provide a definitive refutation of the picture theory. Knowledge of nature can only undertake an analysis and transformation of empirical reality. That is because the totality of this reality simply cannot be pictured: The attempt to provide an exact reproduction of what has no limits is an absurd enterprise. In fact, natural science would never have accomplished anything if knowledge of nature had comprised an exact reproduction of reality. If we reject the picture theory, however, it does not follow that knowledge is worthless because it is unable to incorporate the content of reality itself into its concepts. Consider the following two claims: on the one hand, the proposition that reality invariably confronts us as an infinite manifold; on the other hand, the proposition that a theory in natural science is more advanced the more it has surmounted this infinity and thereby reduced the irrational to the rational. From these it follows with complete self-evidence that a natural scientific theory is more complete the *less* its concepts contain of the immediately given and infinite reality of sense perception. As soon as this point becomes clear, for the most part the result of our investigation must already have lost its appearance of paradox.

This impression of paradox will disappear completely if we underscore one further idea. Although the concepts of natural science encompass only a bit of the content of the immediately given and infinitely diverse empirical reality, it is obvious that these concepts stand in a most intimate *relationship* to this reality. They cannot in the least be represented as products of caprice. We have repeatedly stressed that the *mere* conceptual simplification of reality is not equivalent to scientific concept formation. Just as we emphatically reject the view that a conception of reality with reference to the general could provide the reproductive representation of this reality itself as it actually exists, so we insist just as emphatically that a cognitive content can be ascribed to the generalizing concept formation of natural science only if the general it represents holds *validly for* individual reality.

As regards this relationship between real being and nonreal validity, in almost all cases recent epistemology still finds itself in a kind of transitional stage. Quite frequently there is an attempt to provide a conclusive refutation of conceptual realism, which regards valid concepts as reproductions of reality. This is not always undertaken with the requisite consistency, however. And even where it succeeds, a frame of mind usually develops that is necessarily inclined to make skeptical assaults on the significance of all science, especially natural science. It is easy to identify the basis for this. It is not enough simply to dismiss Platonic "conceptual realism" and reject the view of concepts as pictures of real entities. The attempt to put something new in its place is also necessary, something that can fulfill the function that realism formerly served; namely, to ground the "objectivity" of natural science. In the absence of such an attempt, it seems from an epistemological standpoint that every systematic science based on general concepts is suspended in midair without any foundation. In this context, nevertheless, we cannot undertake the epistemological reconstruction that vindicates the objectivity of generalizing concept formation.[3] It must suffice to point out that another "object" must take the place of the real entity whose perceptual content cannot be comprehended by concepts. The concepts of the natural sciences are true, not because they reproduce reality as it actually exists but because they represent what holds *validly* for reality. If this condition is satisfied, there is no longer any reason to require that natural science encompass reality itself. Moreover, a reproduction of the content of reality by the content of concepts would *not* be able to achieve precisely what we require from knowledge of reality. As a *mere* duplication, it would be worthless; and most important, it would have no *theoretical* significance. Thus the rejection of the false concept of truth, according to which knowledge is a pictorial "image" of a reality, must finally eliminate every appearance of paradox created by our conclusion.

[3]The attempt to provide such a foundation may be found in my book *Der Gegenstand der Erkenntnis*. See especially the sixth edition, chapter five, section five, pp. 401 seq. The fifth chapter of the present book is also concerned with these problems.

Basically what comes to the fore here is an ancient idea. It is so far from being paradoxical that it could even be called trivial. Since Socrates, logic has revolved around the opposition of the general to the particular or the individual. When we say that every object of sense perception, everything individual and distinctive, is incomprehensible in its individuality and distinctiveness for generalizing natural science, this is really nothing more than the claim that the general is not the distinctive and the individual. This claim takes on a new significance as a result of the consideration that we no longer acknowledge "general realities" as objects of knowledge. On the contrary, for us, every real object of knowledge is perceptual and individual or distinctive. We could show that up to now, logic has been almost exclusively concerned with the sciences that are oriented to a representation of the general. In this way, it has overlooked what is necessarily lost in such a representation. By "nature" we understand reality with reference to the general. Because logic, with only a few exceptions, has been solely concerned with scientific representations that subsume the particular under the general, it inevitably constituted itself as a one-sided logic of natural science. In the ensuing, we propose to identify the direction in which the completion of this one-sidedness is to be sought.

2. THE LOGICAL CONCEPT OF THE HISTORICAL

If we consider what the foregoing exposition has already established as regards a method of representation that differs from that of the natural sciences, we can see at once that insight into the logical *character* of concept formation in natural science has, in a certain sense, opened up the field for this other method of representation.

As long as it is regarded as the task of knowledge to provide a reproduction of reality by means of ideas, or to incorporate the given content of reality into concepts, the claim that two logically juxtaposed scientific representations of reality are both possible will appear unacceptable. Suppose the objective of science is reproduction. In that case, because only *one* reproduction can be correct, every scientific representation must pursue one and the same objective; and insofar as the logical structure of concept formation in a science is determined by its objective, it follows that there can be only *one* method of representation. As a result, methodological differences are always a consequence of the substantive properties of the *material*, which will pose one task for research in one context and another task in a different context. But if the copy theory – in the sense that it has been understood here – is rejected, the situation is different. In that event, we have a concept of knowledge that admits logical *differentia-tions* in the mode of concept formation, but without necessarily jeopardizing the import of knowledge in any way. What we mean by conceptual knowledge could then branch off in several directions without losing its value. Concepts comprise what is abstracted from the material of knowledge as "essential." Their significance for knowledge lies exclusively in the consideration that their content is united to form a necessary – in other words, a valid – unity. We no longer discern the nature of concepts in their capacity to provide a reproduction, but rather exclusively in their validity. Thus the perspectives that govern the selection of what is essential and its union in valid concepts – that is to say, the analysis and transformation of empirical reality – are the exclusive determinants of cognitive value. At this point, moreover, it is not at all clear why an analysis and transformation of reality, or a valid selection of what is essential, and the scientific synthesis of interrelated elements in a conceptual representation of the real should proceed only on the basis of *one* perspective and in only *one* direction.

The first result of the proof that natural science does not reproduce reality or incorporate the content of reality as it exists into its concepts, but rather *transforms* this content in a generally valid fashion and on the basis of specific perspectives, is the *possibility* of a science that proceeds in a completely different way and undertakes a trans-formation of reality on the basis of different *perspectives*, even though this need not make it less valid than the natural scientific representation.

This possibility is translated into a logical *necessity* as soon as we identify not only the nature but also the *limits* of concept formation in natural science. Then we will be in a position to pose questions that natural science can never answer.

By this point, it is obvious which questions are at stake here or which gaps natural science, even if we take this term in the most comprehensive sense imaginable, must always leave in our represen-tation of reality. There is a profusion of things and events that interest us not only because of their relationship to a general law or a system of general concepts but also because their distinctiveness, uniqueness, and individuality are significant to us. Wherever this *interest* in reality is present, we can do nothing with natural scientific concept forma-tion. But – and it is always necessary to emphasize this point – this does not mean that a representation of unique and distinctive objects by means of natural science is impossible, nor does it diminish the significance of representation in natural science. On the contrary, it only clarifies its *definitive character* and, of course, its *one-sidedness* as well. This point should make the following explicit: Regardless of its significance for knowledge of nature, a science concerned with whatever has no spatiotemporal reference but is generally – and therefore universally and invariably – valid can have nothing to say about what exists at a specific point in space and time, and what really and uniquely holds true here or there, now or then.

Thus we come to the *central problem* of this book. Suppose we want to know something about the uniqueness, distinctiveness, and individuality of the real. Then we cannot turn to a science for whose concepts the unique and individual configuration of the real event, as well as its perceptual configuration, sets a limit. On the contrary, if there is to be a representation of reality with reference to its uniqueness and individuality, a science is required that diverges logically from natural science in essential points concerning the form of its concept formation. From this point on, our task is to identify the logical structure of this science, to distinguish its mode of concept formation from that of every natural science, and thus to establish the principle for a logical articulation of the empirical sciences, a task directly linked with the demonstration of the limits of concept formation in natural science.

If we consider what *name* a science concerned with the unique and the individual should bear, only one simple consideration remains necessary. Recall that all empirical reality is situated in time and space. Insofar as things are instances of general concepts, the particular place where they are located and the specific time in which they exist are irrelevant. It belongs to the character of the natural scientific concept that it is valid for objects that exist in different places and different times. The unique and the individual, on the other hand, always exist in a specific place and at a specific time. In this context, spatial determination is of no further importance. But the temporality of everything that is real results in a distinctive quality of unique and individual realities that should be taken into account.

If we understand the word "present" in the strict sense, then in the scientific investigation of the uniqueness and individuality of real objects, they are never conceived as present. They are always situated in the *past*, and their existence in the past always occupies a certain period of time. Thus the questions germane to unique and individual reality must always assume the following form: What *was formerly* the case in the world, and how did what now exists come to be? In short, the science of the unique and the individual is necessarily the science of the *event* that has occurred in the past. As a name for the representation of this event, however, language has only one word. Every account of reality itself, every account that on the basis of the foregoing reasons, concerns the unique, individual event that takes place at a specific point in space and time, we call *history*. Therefore, should there be a science of the unique and individual event, it must be called historical science.

Thus we always turn to history when our interest is not satisfied by natural science, in the most comprehensive sense of this term. History alone can fill the gap that natural science inevitably leaves in our knowledge insofar as it excludes from its concepts everything individual as such. History views reality from a completely different logical perspective. For this reason, it is also necessary that it employ a completely different method of representation and concept formation. Only in the ensuing will we be able to show exactly what this method consists in, how it discriminates the essential aspects of reality in such a way that the individuality of the unique event is retained, and how these essential aspects are also unified into coherent and valid concepts. At this juncture, however, we can already establish that the most general governing perspective of historical science diverges from that of natural science, that it is logically opposed to natural science. Even as a science, history can never attempt to represent reality with reference to the *general*, but only with reference to the *specific* and the *individual*. Only the individual and the unique *really happened*, and only a science concerned with the unique, real event itself can be called historical science.

On the basis of the foregoing considerations, however, it seems that much remains to be established concerning the logical foundation of history as a distinctive *science*. The advocates of natural science as a universal method will perhaps make the following reply: Although there is nothing objectionable about this definition of the concept, it is precisely what deprives history of the character of a science, from the outset and for all time. It may be true that the conception of reality as nature – that is, with reference to the general – is one-sided. But the essence of science itself consists in just this one-sided character. The mere determination of unique and individual facts in their uniqueness and distinctiveness could, at best, qualify as *preliminary work* for science. Ultimately science depends on applying the generalizing method, which goes beyond this preliminary level of analysis, to *those* objects that heretofore have been treated *only* "historically," in other words, ascertained as mere facts in their uniqueness and individuality. In the modern era, Schopenhauer was one of the first for whom the *logical* difference between natural science and history was completely clear. As we have already noted, he employs this clarity to deny history the character of a science. This has been done repeatedly. As Schopenhauer quite correctly remarks, precisely because history would have the status of a "science of individuals," it cannot, in his view, qualify as a science at all, for this concept is contradictory.

We are obliged to show that this sort of objection is essentially of no significance. At this juncture, we can make the following point. If the view of the science of the general as the *only* genuine science is regarded as sound, then, as Schopenhauer consistently held, there is *no* sense in which history could qualify as a science. At present, however, we will not consider *this* question. We note that the term "history" can be applied only to a science that provides an account of what, as a unique and individual event, really happened. All history has taken up this task, and this remains true today without exception. Even those who maintain that history must achieve the rank of a science by imitating the procedure of natural science do *not*, in fact, proceed according to the method of natural science. On the contrary, they too provide an account of what took place once upon a time and what will never be repeated in its individuality. Now that we have established the limits of concept formation in natural science, we know that natural science *cannot resolve* the task of history. This is sufficient. To designate as "history" some part or other of the generalizing sciences, which obviously can be extended to every part of reality, seems a capricious terminology. Here we presuppose that history should be pursued as a science of the unique and individual real event. That is because not only the general but also the individual or the distinctive is an object of scientific *interest*.

It seems thoroughly dogmatic and unjustified to abjure such an interest as unscientific from the outset. We live in the individual and the distinctive, and we really exist only as individuals. The proof that the scientific interest in the individual is unjustified should first be produced. Without such proof, claims such as the statement that only the general can be the object of a scientific representation have no methodological significance. They contain a *petitio principii* of the most objectionable sort. And yet we encounter this form of reasoning frequently in the theories of "natural scientific historians," even though it could never be translated into the praxis of scientific research. Every historian represents his subject matter in its uniqueness and individuality. This is a fact that cannot be seriously doubted. We are obliged to begin with this *fact* and to ask what constitutes the logical character of history as a science.

There are more significant objections, however. Suppose history as a representation of the real event in its uniqueness and individuality qualifies as a science. In light of our earlier exposition, do we not arrive at the concept of a task that is logically contradictory? As we have shown in detail, the perceptual and individual configuration of reality is not encompassed by *any* science. On the basis of this claim, we were able to deduce the necessity and the distinctiveness of the natural scientific, generalizing method. Thus there are no circumstances under which we can now set history the task of *reproducing* in its concepts the individual and perceptual content of reality. Such an attempt would in fact be a logical absurdity. Moreover, the extensive infinity of reality is exclusively accessible to natural science, which forms concepts of unconditionally general validity for all of its parts. A science that does not try to discover laws simply cannot surmount *this* sort of infinity. So whenever the task is to discern the *totality* of empirical reality, *only* a natural scientific method can be employed. It follows that an empirical science that does not qualify as a natural science will have only a *part* of reality as its subject matter.

Even if we bracket the extensively infinite manifold of reality and restrict history to an intensively infinite part, it still seems that the concept of a method different from that of natural science is not logically unobjectionable. We know that the intensive infinity of every single process also poses insuperable obstacles to a form of knowledge that proposes to represent reality just as it really is. It follows that the historical disciplines, those that do not fall within the natural sciences, are also obliged to undertake a transformation and an analysis of the reality that is given to them. Here too, however, the aim of this analysis can only be simplification by means of a selection of what is essential and a synthesis of correlated elements into valid concepts. Does the concept of history, therefore, not remain thoroughly problematic, at least *the* history to which we set the task of incorporating the unique, real event, in its uniqueness and individuality, into concepts?

Thus far, of course, we have identified nothing more than a *problem*, and to avoid misunderstandings, we must stress this as forcefully as possible. But the principal point here is the following. If we restrict historical science to a *part* of reality, its task is no longer contradictory in the sense that would hold true for a historical representation of reality in its totality. Only where both extensive and intensive infinity had to be overcome did the law of nature appear as the exclusive, logically complete means required for the resolution of this task. Only in this case could the objective of all science consist solely in the formation of unconditionally general concepts. But if extensive infinity is not at issue, the following sort of scientific analysis at least seems possible: Although it cannot represent exactly the content of reality itself, just as it is, in concepts, its relationship to empirical reality is quite different from and – as this might be put – more proximate than that of natural science. Such an analysis can never comprehend the *complete* intensive manifold of its perceptual material. Like every science, it must translate perception into concepts. However, its object need not be to progressively depart in the content of its concepts from the individuality of empirical reality.

On the contrary, this analysis and transformation of perceptual reality may be able to accomplish something that seems to have the following significance: It is as if the unique, individual, real event itself were represented by this means. To indicate the direction in which this might be possible, we need only recall the kind of *description* discussed earlier, which reproduces a real entity from the perspective of its distinctiveness and uniqueness. For exactly this reason, such a description cannot be the objective of a natural scientific representation. It is, of course, true that such a description still lacks the governing perspectives that make it possible to distinguish the essential from the inessential in a necessary fashion, and thus to arrive at valid scientific concepts, but it is sufficient to dispose of the idea that historical science is an a priori logical absurdity. For the rest, we can regard the concept of a historical science as the concept of a necessary *problem* in the theory of science. There are, in fact, sciences that represent reality in its uniqueness and individuality. Thus we are obliged to ask what their logical structure consists in.

We do not propose to answer this question until Chapter 4. In this context, our aim has been to obtain a logical opposition to the tasks of natural science, first by identifying an *interest* that can never be satisfied by concepts formed on the basis of generalization. Without exploring its logical structure further, we can at least show that there is a representation of reality that proceeds not by generalizing but by *individualizing*, a representation that is therefore able to satisfy the interest in the unique, individual event itself.

In direct connection with the identification of the character and limits of concept formation in the natural sciences, we reach the concept of history, at least in the most comprehensive, formal, and purely logical sense of the term, the only sense relevant at this point. Even if we have arrived only at a methodological *problem* – in other words, even if we still do not know how a scientific representation of history is "possible" – its opposition to the representation of natural science is already established. In the light of its task, history can never attempt to subsume its subject matter under a system of general concepts that becomes more complete the less it contains of the individuality of reality. On the contrary, history at least attempts to approximate a representation of unique and individual reality itself, insofar as this can be claimed for any science. If history, like every other science, must abandon the domain of sense perception, conceived as complete and immediately given, it must still remain dependent on the unique and individual process of the event itself.

In comparison with natural science, therefore, which always moves from the specific to the general and thus to the unreal, we can designate history as a *science of reality*, here following Simmel.[4] But this expression can be understood only in the following way. The historian attempts to represent the distinctiveness and individuality of reality. Even if he cannot reproduce the content of reality itself, his concepts still stand in a relationship to unique and individual reality that is in principle different from and actually *more proximate* than what holds true for the concepts of generalizing natural science.

But perhaps even this position will be contested, and on the grounds of a consideration we also cannot pass over at this point. Suppose the content of reality as such cannot be incorporated into *any* concept, but must first always be recast. In that case, we also have no right to claim that the individual is more intimately related to the real than holds true for the general, assuming that we have in mind the sort of individual that can be incorporated into a scientific representation. On the contrary, if we follow the idea of the unintelligibility of the real to its ultimate consequences, we reach the conclusion that reality as such is neither individual nor general. The former property can no more be ascribed to it than the latter. This is because the concept of the individual acquires an import only in opposition to that of the general. If we designate reality as individual, then we already undertake a conceptual transformation, in the same way that this takes place when we subsume something under a general concept.

Reality itself, the infinite manifold of which scorns *every* conception, can at best be called "irrational," and even this designation could be applied to it only on the grounds that it *resists* every conception. Therefore such a designation would make no positive assertion about reality, but merely a negative claim. Moreover, it would actually make no claim about reality itself – only about our inability to conceive reality. As regards the intrinsic and essential nature of reality itself, there is *nothing* at all we can say about it. Thus, even with the preceding restriction, the concept of history as the science of reality remains a self-contradiction in every respect. Individuality seems to be no less unreal than generality. So it seems we are obliged to conclude that there can be no scientific interest of any sort in the real itself.

Truth and falsity are compounded in such a consideration. On the one hand, it is true that the content of reality itself, just as it is and

---

[4]*Probleme der Geschichtsphilosophie*, 1892, p. 34. [*The Problems of the Philosophy of History*, trans. Guy Oakes (New York: Free Press, 1977), where the distinction appears at pp. 128–34.]

independent of *all* conceptualization, can be called neither general nor individual. On the other hand, it is false that the individual is no more closely related to the real than holds true for the general and that the concept of a science that represents the reality of the unique, individual event is self-contradictory. It is, of course, true that the concept of the individual has a specific content only in opposition to the concept of the general. But we would not understand the meaning of the word "individual" unless we could become explicitly aware of it in the irrational content of immediately given reality itself. From the fact that the concept of individuality can be clearly defined only in opposition to the meaning of the word "general," it does not follow that we cannot call the real itself individual. The individuality of the real is most intimately connected with its "irrationality," in opposition to the *general* concept. This consideration alone establishes why the individual is in principle more closely related to the real than the general is.

In another respect, it must be admitted that this connection between the individual and the irrational renders the concept of a *science* of individuals quite problematic. The proposition that the individual is ineffable seems to quash every attempt to bring the individual itself under *concepts*. But *for the time being*, as we have already noted, we *propose* to identify no more than a problem. In order to make this problem explicit, we point out that historical science must attempt to approximate reality *more closely* than is ever possible for the general concepts of natural science. How can "irrational" reality be conceptualized in *this* way? Put another way, how can it be "rationalized" in such a way that, in spite of this, its "individuality" does not disappear? This is the subsequent question the theory of historical concept formation has to answer. We will see that two types of the *individual* are to be distinguished from one another. Only one of these coincides with reality itself. Nevertheless, they retain something *in common*, and it is precisely this common feature that justifies our regarding history as the science that represents the real event itself. History too, insofar as it is a science, can produce only a *conception* of reality based on a specific logical *perspective*. As a result, the immediacy of reality is necessarily destroyed, but that consideration does not alter the legitimacy of this *point of departure* for a logical investigation.

In order to avoid misunderstandings, however, it is useful at the outset to note once more that *every* science – and thus history as well – has *to recast* and conceptualize its perceptual material. Therefore we propose to formulate the opposition between natural science and history at stake here in the following way: Empirical reality can also be brought under a logical perspective that differs from that of nature. *Empirical reality becomes nature when we conceive it with reference to the general. It becomes history when we conceive it with reference to the distinctive and the individual.* Every empirical science proceeds from immediately experienced reality in its concrete actuality and individuality, and every empirical science must single out what is essential from reality. In other words, it must destroy the immediacy of reality. The ultimate difference in methods is to be sought exclusively in what different concepts make of reality. For logic, the question is whether they attempt to discover the general or the individual in the real. Natural science has the former task, historical science the latter.

As we have repeatedly stressed, *provisionally* we take the concept of "history"["*Geschichte*"] in the most comprehensive sense conceivable, a sense that is purely *logical*. Corresponding to this intention, the initial and most general concept of *the historical* [*des Historischen*] will be employed the same way. This can be our name for the subject matter of history [*den Gegenstand der Geschichte*] wherever the ambiguity of the term "history" ["*Geschichte*"] leaves a doubt as to whether we mean the science or the object it represents.[5] It is obvious that this concept of the historical [*des Historischen*] comprehends not only the part of reality that is the material of the historical sciences [*Geschichts-wissenschaften*] in the usual and more narrow sense. On the contrary, in its purely logical aspect, it must be applicable to *every* part of the totality of empirical reality whatsoever, insofar as reality is conceived as invariably consisting of individual constructs. From this perspective, the totality of reality itself in its individuality becomes a "historical" ["*historischer*"] process, even if there can be no total history [*Gesamtgeschichte*] as a representation of this process.

With what *part* of the historical in this sense [*dieses Historischen*] is the historical representation [*die Geschichtsdarstellung*] concerned; and thus what qualifies as the historical [*das Historische*] in the narrow sense? These questions can be answered only on the basis of a more precise analysis of the concept of the historical sciences [*der historischen Wissenschaften*]. Throughout we will not attempt to identify the science

[5][The German nouns *Geschichte* and *Historie* both translate as "history," and their adjectival forms *geschichtlich* and *historisch* are rendered as "historical." Although the two pairs of German terms are generally used synonymously, they permit a distinction that is not marked by the English terms "history" and "historical," which refer to a science and also to its subject matter. When the context does not indicate whether the science or its subject matter is under consideration, Rickert proposes to reserve *Geschichte* for the inquiry or science of history. Its object or subject matter is *das Historische*: the historical. After introducing this distinction, Rickert immediately proceeds to muddle it somewhat by referring to both the *Geschichts-wissenschaften* and the *historische Wissenschaften*.]

by reference to the concept of its object. On the contrary, we will attempt to identify the concept of the object on the basis of the concept of the science that investigates it. Regardless of the concerns of history as a science and how its concept may be more precisely defined, we can already see that the concept of the historical in its most general logical significance is independent of substantive differences, such as the distinction between nature and "spirit." The corporeal can be conceived with reference to its distinctiveness and individuality in quite the same way as the psychic. In defining logical concepts, it is not legitimate to begin with properties that are possessed only by a part of empirical reality. We can understand the distinctive methodological properties of the empirical sciences only by means of a *purely* logical concept of the historical.

For a complete elucidation of the logical concept of the historical, it is necessary for us to be clear on the following point: The considerations presented in the foregoing are the only truly decisive grounds that prevent science from conceptualizing historical material according to the method of natural science. It is not infrequently claimed that for one reason or another, "historical life" – the reality with which historical science in the narrow sense is concerned – is not *uniform* in the same way as nature, and for this reason cannot be subsumed under concepts of natural laws. This is the view of Sigwart, for example, who claims that with regard to the objects of historical research, we "cannot presume a regularity similar to that which obtains in the domain of nature."[6] This is probably true to the extent that it may be more difficult to discover laws for *the* reality with which history is *usually* concerned than for the reality with which the natural sciences, and especially the sciences of bodies, are concerned. On the basis of this consideration, however, it will never be possible either to ground a fundamental logical opposition between nature and history or to determine the logical significance of the historical. On the contrary, in opposition to such arguments, the view that real historical life is just as much a part of empirical reality as the real being of "nature" must always remain correct. Although it may be more difficult to discover historical laws, there is not the slightest reason to regard the resolution of this task as impossible for all time. The more difficult the task turns out to be, the more powerful will be the inducement to attempt its solution.

In order to make clear how thoroughly weak such arguments are, we stress the point that discussions concerning whether a nomological science is more or less *difficult* are irrelevant to what we will establish

[6]*Logik*, II, 4th ed., p. 636.

here. Of course, "historical life" is an aspect of empirical reality like every other. In the present context, however, this point is irrelevant. That is because *all* reality is "historical" in the most comprehensive, purely logical sense of the word; namely, unique and individual. Naturally we can attempt to discover laws for all reality; and in any case, it is also possible to subsume *that* reality with which history in the narrower sense is concerned under general concepts. Thus it is hardly our intention to contest the view that the fate of man as a cultural being *can* be subjected to a natural scientific or generalizing representation. At this point, however, we can see why the results of this concept formation could never be called "history": Such a representation could no longer have any reference to the unique, individual, real event in its uniqueness and individuality.

Where reality is to be comprehended in its individuality and distinctiveness, the intention of bringing it under general concepts or establishing laws of the historical – laws that, as we know, are necessarily general concepts – is simply a *logical absurdity*. Like all the concepts of natural science, nomological concepts of this sort would only result in what is no longer unique and individual. Thus the historical sciences would fail to realize their purpose – knowledge of reality in its individuality – all the more certainly the more successful they became in discovering the laws of the real material whose "history" we want to know. It is not more or less difficult to discover the laws of history. On the contrary, assuming that we understand the concept of the historical in the purely logical sense under consideration in this work, the *concept* of the "historical law" is self-contradictory. That is, historical science and nomological science are mutually exclusive concepts insofar as the former proposes to represent the individual and the latter, the general. The representation of the general can never be the representation of the individual.

At this point, we will apply this general principle to a specific case in which it has a special significance. Not infrequently we hear that the individual *personalities* of history, at least, cannot be conceived by natural science because they are too complicated to be fully comprehended. On the other hand, because of their simplicity corporeal processes do not present such a difficulty. This view should be categorically rejected as well. Independent of the grounds that have already been presented, the extent to which this position is erroneous should immediately become clear if we reflect on what we have established concerning the concept of the *individual*.

Each leaf on a tree, every lump of sulfur a chemist puts in his retort, is an individual. As such, it can no more be subsumed under a natural scientific concept than any great personality of history. As regards leaves or sulfur, however, we *automatically* conceive the single individuals as nothing more than instances of general concepts. In other words, we pay no attention to what constitutes them as individuals. This is necessary, for only under this condition do we obtain "leaves" or "sulfur" in the sense of natural science. Here we are *interested* only in individuals as generic cases. Thus we forget what we have done and, in consequence, make no distinction between "a leaf" in the sense of natural science and "this particular leaf" as a distinctive, individual historical fact. As regards other individuals, however – and this holds true especially for personalities – it is difficult, even impossible, to overlook the difference between the individual and the generic case. If we transpose an individual such as Goethe into a generic case, it is inevitable that we notice the difference immediately; for what remains is only a poet, a minister, and a person, but no longer Goethe. This difference, however, should not deceive us concerning the following point: Logically, the process by which we transpose this leaf and this piece of sulfur into "a leaf" or "sulfur" in the sense of natural science – that is, into a generic case – is precisely the same as the process by means of which we transform Goethe into "a poet."

How is it that we so easily overlook this point, which is basically quite obvious? In most cases, the answer lies in an extraneous circumstance. There are individuals that bear only generic *names*. Once we have formed a concept for one of them, then the name for the concept remains the same as the name of the real individual. Concerning individuals that bear proper names, on the other hand, the name changes as soon as the individual becomes a generic case. This circumstance immediately makes us aware of what we have done. As regards the point at issue here, however, the change of name is *incidental*. It makes no purely logical or *formal* difference whether, instead of referring to Goethe, we refer to a person or a poet in general. So it is misleading to claim that whereas a historical personality is too complicated to be incorporated into the concepts of natural science, a corporeal process is not. That would not rule out the possibility of a subsequent comprehension of the personality as well. It would also include the claim that there is a difference between the individuals of history in the narrower sense and other things that are also historical individuals in the most general, logical sense of the word.

This is exactly the view we contest. As a *complete* empirical reality, Goethe is no "more complex" than any given fragment of sulfur in its *complete* empirical reality. That is because the manifold of *both* realities is infinite. As long as only empirical reality as such is in question, to speak of one as being more or less complex than the other is senseless.

A "man of history" is incomprehensible for natural science, not as a complicated personality but rather as a unique individual, a distinctive construct that will never recur. In other words, he shares this incomprehensibility with everything real insofar as its individuality is at issue. There can hardly be anything "simpler" than a lump of sulfur. And yet every piece of sulfur we consider with reference to its individual peculiarities – instead of with reference to the general "nature" of sulfur – is an infinite manifold. As such, therefore, it is exactly as incomprehensible as Goethe or Kant; in other words, it is incomprehensible for a generalizing natural science. It follows that specific things such as historical personalities are never more incomprehensible in this sense than any other real objects. On the contrary, as regards *all* reality, it is invariably true that a natural scientific account can render only what no longer interests the historian, whose intention is to represent the individual and the unique.

Nietzsche once said; "The course of history can be divined only if individuals are eliminated, for then the single irrational factor is eliminated."[7] This claim is an admirable rendition of the received view. It is false, however, for in referring to individuals, Nietzsche has only important personalities in mind. They do not constitute *the sole* irrational factor. *Everything* real – and in consequence, everything historical in the logical or formal sense established here – is just as "irrational" in relation to the general, natural scientific concept as the great individual personalities. In principle, therefore, everything real is removed from a generalizing representation.

Finally, our determination of the concept of the historical is not only to be distinguished from all views that propose to understand the nature of the historical sciences on the basis of the distinctive character of a special subject matter – man as a cultural being, for example, or "spiritual life." We are also obliged to take a position on a widely held view that, like our own, attempts to establish a *logical* or *formal* concept of the historical. But because it does not touch the logically *primordial* opposition between nature and history, the view in question cannot qualify as logically unobjectionable. This position appeared quite early and in several independent forms. We will now have a look at them.

In, 1792, Condorcet's *Esquisse d'un tableau historique*[8] appeared, a text that, as is well known, contains many of the ideas that have frequently reappeared whenever the attempt is made "to elevate history to the rank of a science." In the same year, Friedrich Schlegel

---

[7]*Werke*, vol. X, p. 290.
[8][*Sketch for a Historical Picture of the Progress of the Human Mind*, trans. June Barraclough (New York: Noonday Press, 1955).]

published his critique in *Niethammers Philosophisches Journal*. Here he points out the basic error of the endeavors we are also exposing. He clearly sees that Condorcet completely misconceives the concept of history, and he claims, "The constant properties of man are the object of pure science. The variable properties of man, on the other hand, both in the individual as well as in the mass, are the object of a scientific history of mankind." By "pure" science, we should understand the same thing that we are calling natural science. In that case, the opposition between nature and history is equivalent to the opposition between the constant and the variable. Material differences are no longer at stake here. On the contrary, the distinction is articulated in a purely formal – and, in this sense, logical – fashion. But we can find no trace of the influence of Schlegel's ideas on this point, and his critique of Condorcet has remained as good as unknown.

Subsequently, Droysen[9] is one of the few who has also attempted to develop a logical concept of history, and Bernheim has followed him.[10] "If," Bernheim claims, "we survey the different sciences, we notice that there are three different ways that a science conceives its objects, corresponding to what it wants to know about them: (1) how the objects are in themselves and how they act – their being; (2) how they become or became what they are – their development; (3) what they signify in relation to one another and to the world. The natural scientific, historical, and philosophical conceptions are thereby distinguished from one another." If we disregard the concept of philosophy introduced here, from a logical point of view this distinction between natural science and history is essentially the same as Schlegel's. In any case, its opposition between being and becoming also focuses on method, not on subject matter.

Finally, the most fully developed theory of the historical sciences constructed on the basis of a logical opposition is found in a work by Xénopol.[11] He distinguishes two different kinds of facts. One he calls *phénomènes coexistants*, or later *faits de répétition*; the other *phénomènes successifs*. He holds that although the former constitute the object of natural science, history is concerned only with the latter. Accordingly, natural science is the science of recurrences, and history the science of succession. Natural science seeks laws; the historical sciences have to represent "sequences." It requires no proof to show how closely this distinction corresponds to that just discussed and how it too is purely

[9]*Grundriss der Historik*, 1867; 3rd ed., 1882.
[10]*Lehrbuch der historischen Methode*, 1889; 2nd ed., 1894, p. 1.
[11]*Les principes fondamenteaux de l'histoire*, 1889; the second edition appeared in 1908 as *La théorie de l'histoire*.

formal, and therefore logical. As Xénopol explains, there are recurrent phenomena everywhere, in the corporeal as well as in the mental. And on the other hand, the phenomena of succession are not limited to historical life in the strict sense. On the contrary, the entire corporeal world can be regarded as a sequence of successive phenomena.

What can be said in response to such views? From a logical point of view, there is no doubt that the distinctions between natural science and history just considered are the best we have encountered thus far. That is because they are concerned with method, not subject matter. In the strict sense, however, we cannot accept the view that the oppositions between constancy and change, being and becoming, recurrence and succession hold for the objects of empirical reality, just as they exist independent of every scientific conception. It is, of course, quite true that history is concerned with change, becoming, and succession, insofar as *all* unique and individual reality – and thus everything historical in the most comprehensive logical sense conceivable – is in a process of change, becoming, and succession. The work of Xénopol in particular shows that on the basis of his opposition of recurrence and succession, valuable conclusions can be reached. From a philosophical standpoint, however, the identification of the foregoing conceptual dichotomies with that between nature and history is inadmissible because they fail to articulate the genuinely decisive *logical* difference with sufficient *clarity*. The use of these dichotomies creates the impression – in fact, it is explicitly claimed – that empirical *reality itself* falls under constancy and change, being and becoming, recurrence and succession, as if the investigator were presented with two fundamentally different kinds of *fact* that he could accept just as they really are. Thus *here* we would have nature as a brute fact and *there* history, likewise as a brute fact; in both cases science would be only a "mirror of reality." But it is precisely this view that is untenable, and as long as it is held, we will never arrive at a *logical* understanding of the sciences. . . .

Thus the most general logical distinction between natural science and history cannot be based on the opposition between recurrent being and variable becoming. Since no real being recurs exactly as it was, this opposition is misleading without further explanation. On the contrary, we have to hold fast to the opposition between the *general* – that which is valid for different places and times, or that which is universally and invariably valid – and the only real, *individual* world of the event and change, in which nothing ever repeats itself exactly. This may suffice to clarify the concepts of nature and history in their most general *logical* significance. . . .

4

Concept Formation in History

The title "Hellenes" is applied to those who share our culture rather than to those who share a common blood.[1]

Isocrates

INTRODUCTION

Up to now, we have come to know the concept of historical science negatively, as that of a task that cannot be resolved by concept formation in natural science. In order to define this concept positively, we will again link the different logical problems it contains to *one* main problem. It must correspond, however, to the problem we placed in the foreground in our elucidation of the character of natural science. In other words, as already noted in the Introduction, here as well what matters is not the path that research takes, and especially not the *search* for the historical material, but rather the form of its *representation*. The entity in which the preliminary or final results of natural science are expressed is called a "concept." Accordingly our task now is to fix the principles of *concept formation in history*. The extension of linguistic usage that lies in this designation is justified by the consideration that the new problem is logically the same as the one that was placed in the foreground in the attempt to develop a logical understanding of natural science. Above all, our task is to understand how the elements of a historical concept are consolidated into a *unity*, or what the scientific validity of historical concepts is based on.

In that case, the solution to the problem may be articulated in the following way. Again, in order to exhibit its logical content as clearly as possible, here too we will begin by bracketing all the substantive particulars of the material of the historical sciences. Thus we will proceed from the limit of all concept formation in natural science, namely, the *individual*, in the most comprehensive sense of the word, in which it designates every unique and individual reality whatsoever.

[1] [In Rickert's text, the epigraph from Isocrates is quoted in Greek.]

First, not all individual realities are the object of history. Therefore we have to show how a special variety of objects – which we can designate as "historical individuals" in the strict sense, the only objects that are important for a representation of their individuality – are differentiated for historical representation from the infinitely extensive manifold of objects. Second, these historical realities cannot be represented in their complete intensive manifold either. Thus we also have to understand what is differentiated from the content of the manifold of the single historical individual and is consolidated as the individual content of a historical concept. In this way, we will grasp the most general principle of an *individualizing concept formation*, which stands in logical opposition to the generalizing concept formation of natural science. Finally, we will see how mistaken the view is that holds that in the representation of history, it is a question of the mere application of the general conclusions of natural science to the specific case.

As a result of the new mode of distinguishing essential from inessential aspects, the representation of the individual – and thus of the historical, in the logical sense of this term – is shown to be possible. Moreover, it will be shown that the formation of concepts with an individual content – or individualizing concept formation, as we will call it – takes place only through a theoretical "relationship" [*"Beziehung"*] of historical objects to *values*, a relationship whose nature we will have to define precisely. To that extent, this sort of concept formation could also be characterized as "teleological." However, this historical-teleological moment has nothing to do with the teleological concept of history that appears from time to time and often has been quite justifiably criticized as unscientific. In particular, here it is only a purely *theoretical* principle that can be in question. It is true that, in general, no notice is taken of this principle. However, it is necessarily employed by every historian, regardless of how much he may struggle against every kind of "teleology." Individualizing concept formation, therefore, also proves to be *value relevant* [*wertbeziehende*], and in this way too, it is opposed to the value-free concept formation of natural science. The concept of *theoretical value relevance* [*Wertbeziehung*] as the genuine logical principle of an individualizing or historical representation requires an exhaustive discussion.

This discussion will be advanced by the consideration that in historical reality, individuals are never *isolated*. All objects of history are rather parts of a larger whole with which they stand in a real nexus. As we have seen, the abstractions of natural science destroy this nexus and isolate instances. History cannot proceed in this way. It becomes the science of the unique, real event only by means of a representation of the *historical nexus*. Concerning this point, it is especially important to note that every individual object is *causally* linked with other individual objects. The causal connections of history, however, should be scrupulously distinguished from the causal *laws* of natural science. Contrary to what is frequently supposed, the representation of causal connections simply does not coincide with a generalizing representation of reality as "nature."

Finally, the fundamental logical principles of concept formation in history are united in the concept of historical *development*. It also holds true, however, that there is no sense in which this consideration implies that the methods of history and natural science approximate each other. First, *historical* development consists of unique and individual processes. And second, these processes fall under historical concepts only by means of the theoretical relationship to *values*. *This* concept of development remains foreign to those representations that, in a logical sense, belong to natural science. Even if this concept plays a role in some parts of the corporeal sciences, that is only because physical reality can also be brought under historical perspectives and represented in an individualizing fashion. This circumstance again proves how inadequate the opposition between nature and spirit is for clarifying the logical problems of history, as long as "spirit" refers to the psychic.

If the concept of developmental history [*Entwicklungsgeschichte*] defines the most general logical character of every historical representation, we can turn to the qualifications that must also be made here if our concept is to be applied to historical science as it really exists. We will extend this concept from the absolutely historical – at the outset, the exclusive object of our concern – to the *relatively historical*. In this way, we will become familiar with the *natural scientific aspects of the historical sciences*, which are just as important as the historical aspects of the natural sciences. Here again, we attempt to understand the *interpenetration* and *concomitance* of general and individual factors that are characteristic of *every* empirical science. And yet in spite of all the transitions and intermediate forms with which we will become acquainted, a fundamental logical distinction between natural science and historical science remains. Even though many, perhaps even most, historical concepts have a *general* content in the sense that they comprehend what is common to a plurality of individual realities, in the historical nexus of a unique developmental sequence this generality is always considered as something relatively specific and individual. Just like the absolutely historical, therefore, it must also form a limit for natural science. We will understand how even the general – in other words, what is common to several objects – can be represented in a value-relevant and individualizing fashion. The paradox in this idea is only apparent.

With this demonstration, the *purely* logical work of this chapter is concluded. However, if we want to understand not only the logical nature but also the scientific significance and indispensability of concept formation in history with regard to its substance, ultimately we must also know which specific part of individual reality *requires* a historical representation. This necessity can rest only on specific *material* determinations of certain objects, which then become "historical objects" in the strict sense. Thus we have to inquire into the extent to which there is a connection between the *content* and *form*, or between the *material* and *method* of historical representations. In this way we will also obtain the *substantive* concept of history, which is primarily what we have in mind today when we speak of "history."

At the outset, there is the consideration that the existing historical sciences are not *actually* indifferent to the difference between body and "mind" [*Geist*] that was intentionally disregarded at the beginning of our account. On the contrary, they are essentially concerned with mental processes, and *to this extent* they could also be called human sciences [*Geisteswissenschaften*]. We must ascertain why that is so and whether the historical *method* can also be crucially determined by this circumstance. But it will once again be shown that there is no sense in which the difference between natural science and human science [*Geisteswissenschaft*] – assuming that "mind" [*Geist*] refers only to noncorporeal, real being, or to psychic reality – can be regarded as a determining factor for method, as long as the issue concerns the classification of the empirical sciences into two *materially* different groups.

In opposition to the objects of natural science, it is rather the case that the objects with which the historical sciences in the strict sense are concerned fall under the concept of *culture*. This is because the *values* that govern value-relevant concept formation in history and determine what the object of history is, are always drawn from cultural life, or are *cultural values*. Of course, culture as well, like every reality, can be brought under the concepts of natural science. In other words, it can be represented in a generalizing fashion. But this mode of representation alone is never sufficient for culture. Therefore, it is the *historical sciences of culture* that must be opposed to the natural sciences, with reference to both method and content. They fall under the concept of history that is more than formal, the *material* concept. And yet this concept also remains formal to the following extent: In methodology, we can set up only a formal concept of culture.

Logic can never determine which substantively defined values govern historical representations or what the substantively defined concept of culture consists of. Only historical science itself and a comprehensive philosophy or a theory of weltanschauung oriented to historical science can do that. At best, methodology can make the attempt to fathom the nature of the much discussed process of *historical understanding* by starting from the concept of the cultural sciences. This concept of historical understanding is regarded by some as the true central locus of a theory of the so-called human sciences. But we can begin to solve the problem this concept contains only if we already know *what* is understood by the historian and only if we have grasped the extent to which *historical* understanding must bear an *individualizing* character. In a theory of history, this is also why we cannot *begin with* a distinction such as that between "explanation" and "understanding." Historical understanding cannot only signify the understanding of the real mental or psychic existence of the past. That is because, as a mere real event, it may remain just as unintelligible as corporeal existence. The task of history rather lies in the understanding of culture, which is *more* than a real psychic phenomenon. Thus it makes sense to include history in the human sciences and to employ this latter concept in a "classification" of the sciences that provides more than a superficial schema for the arrangement of the *material* of science only if "mind" refers to something fundamentally different from the real mental life that psychology investigates.

Finally, one further new problem is posed for the logic of history. In every historical representation as well as in every representation in natural science, we employ a series of *presuppositions* that can be designated as the "a priori" of scientific concept formation. Insofar as they are relevant here, these presuppositions primarily lie in the concept of the *law of nature* as that of an unconditionally general judgment, on the one hand; and in the concept of the *cultural value* to which every historical object must be theoretically related in order to become a possible object of historical representation, on the other. It is not only possible to pose the question of the *validity* of these presuppositions; because of the special character they have in historical science, the scientific *objectivity* of historical representation – in comparison with natural science – will seem problematic.

In this way, there is another aspect in which history as scientific *knowledge* is again placed in question. Here we finally arrive at the task of comprehending the relationship between natural science and history with reference to their presuppositions as well. This task no longer has any connection with *methodology*, however. In consequence, only the final chapter will deal with the *epistemological* or transcendental-philosophical problems of the *philosophy of nature* and the *philosophy of history* – the problems to which we are led by the question concerning the objectivity of concept formation in history – detached from methodological problems. This will bring our inquiry to its conclusion.

1. THE PROBLEM OF CONCEPT FORMATION IN HISTORY

In order to formulate our new methodological problem precisely, it is necessary that we also look at the *totality* of the questions historical science poses for logic, and then distinguish what we mean by concept formation in history from other forms of thought in historical science.

According to Droysen, the methodology of historical research has four parts: heuristics, criticism, interpretation, and representation.[2] Bernstein also adopts this arrangement. He summarizes the individual principles and operations that constitute applied methodology into four different groups: "*knowledge of sources* or heuristics, which comprehends the collection and apprehension of the material; *criticism*, which is concerned with the sifting of the material and the determination of the facts; the *conception*, which is concerned with knowledge of the significance and the connection of facts; *representation*, which reproduces the facts as known in their connection in a cognitively adequate expression."[3] For the purpose of a synopsis, we can accept this arrangement. We only have to define the meaning of some of the terms a bit more precisely.

As regards its most general meaning, the opposition between material and conception coincides in this context with that between matter and methodological form. We always regard empirical reality as the material of science. In the case of the corporeal world, for example, it consists of a "plurality" of "things." As we have already noted, there is an epistemological standpoint from which this reality – which qualifies only as material for the specific sciences – can already be regarded as formed material. In that case, plurality and substantiality, even reality itself, would be forms that are imposed on the material. This *epistemological* opposition of matter and form must be distinguished from the *methodological* opposition.[4] For an investigation that proposes to represent the forms of historical science in opposition to those of natural science, it can be important to know

[2]See *Grundriss der Historik*, 2nd ed., 1895.
[3]See *Lehrbuch der historischen Methode*, 5th and 6th eds., 1908, pp. 250 seq.
[4]On this point, see my book *Der Gegenstand der Erkenntnis*, 6th edition, 1928, fifth chapter: "Das Problem der objektiven Wirklichkeit" and "Konstitutive Wirklichkeitsformen und methodologische Erkenntnisformen."

which forms belong to *every* scientific conception of reality. This is because these latter forms – for example, the form of "reality" – are necessarily *common* to both natural science and history.

Here it is obvious that the boundary is not to be drawn in such a way that we inquire into the *system* of these epistemological forms. On the contrary, we can only undertake the distinction for the specific cases to which the investigation leads us. At the outset, however, it is necessary to note the following: In the ensuing, when we speak without further qualification of forms of scientific conception, general, epistemological, or "constitutive" forms are never intended, but only methodological forms; in other words, the forms that are distinctive to the historical or the natural sciences. Therefore, in a methodological investigation, empirical reality – which, from an epistemological standpoint, is already constituted as the formed material of the empirical sciences – can simply be characterized as material. This will be especially important to the question of the significance of the principle of causality in history.

Even so, the term "material" of historical science is still not unambiguous. This term can refer to *that* material that is directly given to the historian and from which he obtains his knowledge of the things and processes he wants to represent; and it can also refer to these things and processes themselves, which constitute material for methodology only as long as they have not assumed the methodological forms distinctive to historical science. Thus we will call the immediately given material that is not itself an object of historical representation *source material*. The things and processes of empirical reality, on the other hand, that history proposes to represent scientifically we will call its objects; or, to indicate the opposition to the methodological form of history, we will designate them as the *factual material* of history, which falls only under general epistemological forms. In consequence, when we refer to historical material in opposition to historical form, this should never be understood as a reference to the mere source, or to the object that has already been comprehended or analyzed by history, but only to individual historical reality as such.

Finally, with regard to terminology it should be recalled that we do not use the word "representation" merely for the external form of a statement, but for the "conception" as well. In other words, it should be understood as referring to what is meant by knowledge of the "significance" and "connection" of facts. Thus we can formulate our problem with reference to the four groups indicated in the following way: It is concerned not with the first two, heuristics and criticism, but with the last two, conception and representation. We can leave aside

the question of how knowledge of the historical facts or knowledge of
the reality to be represented is obtained from the sources. Regardless
of how interesting it may be to follow in detail the technique of the
collection and criticism of the historical material, the differences
between the methods of natural science and history that occur here
cannot be of such fundamental significance for us as those that
appear in the conception and representation of the material that has
been ascertained. In the discovery and confirmation of facts, *every*
path and detour is equally acceptable and justifiable as long as it leads
to the goal. The fundamental methodological differences arise only
when *one* group of sciences "conceives" its material as nature and the
other group "conceives" it as history.

What is to be understood by a "conception," and especially what is
meant by the ambiguous expressions "significance" and "connection,"
will be demonstrated more precisely only in the ensuing. Here it is
sufficient to note that our problem begins with the question of how
history becomes a science on the basis of established and historically
confirmed facts. Or, since we call the scientifically – and, to this
extent, conceptually – formed material a "concept" in history as well,
how does the historian form his historical *concepts* from his *factual
material* (not from his *source material*)? It is only in this way that our
problem conforms to that considered in the investigation of concept
formation in natural science.

It can also be asked, however, whether in general it makes any sense
in history to distinguish, even conceptually, the determination of facts
from concept formation. If we examine historical works from the
perspective of this issue, then it seems that the historian often
represents *everything* that he has taken from the real objects of
experience. Quite frequently, moreover, he does not know as much
about them as he would like. In that case, the idea that he still had to
"simplify" his factual material by a process of selection would never
occur to him. Has he not done his work when the facts have been
discovered in the sources and criticized? And is it not true that
representation is only a form of reportage that, although it may
require talent and taste, cannot be regarded as the real *scientific* task?
Will not the most faithful and genuine historical representation be the
one that explicitly limits itself to the reproduction of the critically
confirmed factual material and only "idiographically" narrates "what
really happened"? In natural science, it is legitimate to ask what it
selects as essential from the infinite profusion of the immediately
given real material, and thus to see the focal point of its task in the
correct formation of its concepts. But the historical facts obtained
from the sources are not infinitely diverse. Therefore, the problems

posed for the logic of natural science do not exist for the logic of the historical sciences. As a result, the discrepancy between source material and factual material seems to acquire an essential logical significance.

In fact, a simple reference to the infinite manifold of every empirical reality is not sufficient to exhibit the new problem as clearly as the problem of concept formation in natural science. Of course, we could claim that even if the facts are not given to the historian as an intensively infinite manifold, this still holds true for the *sources*. Thus he always requires a principle of selection to distinguish the essential from the inessential in the sources. On the basis of this consideration alone, however, we would not yet be able to define a problem that can be taken as parallel to the question posed for concept formation in natural science. From the standpoint of logic, that would be a defect. There is no doubt that history is also distinguished from natural science by the manner in which the facts are given to it. Therefore we have to try to understand this difference, insofar as it is germane to the most general logical opposition of nature and history.

In this context, the decisive point is the following. That which the "nature" of reality consists in and what natural science must take cognizance of in order to form its general concepts, is almost always present in a plurality of objects. In particular, the material for the discovery of timelessly valid laws of nature is present at many points. On the other hand, the specific and the individual in which history is interested have existed only on a single occasion – at least this holds true for absolute historical concepts. Thus the knowledge of such a phenomenon frequently is acquired only with difficulty. It follows that the material for the representation of an object in natural science can exist in its entirety. For a historical representation of *the same* object, however, it can be obtained only in an extremely incomplete fashion. . . .

Suppose we return to our problem of concept formation in history. Now we can understand how it is that history, unlike natural science, usually cannot directly experience its facts but must almost always infer them from the traces that are left, and thus why history does not confront its factual material, but rather only its source material, as an infinite manifold. In a few exceptional cases, the object *for* which history forms its concepts is the same as the object *from* which it can form them. Usually the object of direct observation and the object of historical representation – in other words, source and fact – differ. As a result, the view can arise that the historian has to represent *all* the properties of his objects that experience makes available in any way at all. In that case, there seems to be no basis for the claim that concept formation in history can even be conceptually distinguished from the determination of facts.

In spite of this consideration, such a basis can be demonstrated. Initially, of course, the incompleteness of the material of history results in a new difficulty that seems to place the point of our entire enterprise in question. Given the dissociation of sources and facts, it is not clear why the sources should always be available, even for the incomplete determination of precisely *that* factual material that interests the historian. From a logical standpoint, therefore, which processes he is able to represent seems *fortuitous*. This fortuitousness inevitably invests history with characteristics that cannot be derived from its purely theoretical or scientific objectives, and this simply cannot be conceived as logically conditioned. They lend history the appearance of an unstructured material. In understanding the relationship of the logical ideal of a historical representation to the historical sciences that actually exist, this point should be considered most scrupulously. This is because it is much more difficult to bring ideal and reality in conformity here than was the case for concept formation in natural science.

It does not yet follow from this consideration that setting up a logical ideal of historical representation or concept formation is impossible as such. In general, the fragmentary character of the material can be understood as a consequence of the logical concept of history as the science of unique and individual reality. In specific cases, however, this fragmentary character is random. For precisely this reason, we can ignore it in specific cases and employ the fiction that in any given case, the historian can obtain any piece of factual material from the sources. This is because it could randomly happen that all the sources necessary for this have been preserved. Thus we first set up a logical ideal for a conceivable case of this sort, and when the ideal is to be compared with reality, we add the reservations that are typically necessary in view of the usual deficiency in the material available.

But if this fiction can be employed, the *particular* difficulty that arose for our problematic and from which we proceeded is eliminated. To be sure, it is only the source material, and not the factual material of history, that possesses the quality of infinite multiplicity. However, if this signifies nothing more than an *incompleteness* in the factual material, then we need not concede to it any influence on the logical development of a theory of historical representation. This is precisely because the fragmentary character of the material resists logical comprehension in every specific instance. Rather, we can again pose the same question we posed in the elucidation of concept formation in natural science: Why does historical science always attempt to represent only a part of reality in its individual configuration, and which part is this? Assuming that this issue is not governed by caprice, there must be a scientific principle according to which the selection is made. As a result, the logical structure of historical representation and concept formation necessarily depends on this principle.

Although the aforementioned fiction is justified in the interest of logic, it is useful to add that we need it *only* to pose our problem in a perfectly *general* fashion. In actuality as well, there are almost always more facts for the historian to extract from the sources than he represents or incorporates into his concepts. For this reason as well, a principle of selection and simplification is indispensable for him. Concerning this point, we must, of course, distinguish several different cases from one another.

When the sources and the facts coincide, the necessity of a simplification by means of separating the essential from the inessential is self-evident. If the historian can interrogate the persons that form his object, or if he is concerned with geographic arenas of historical events that have been preserved unchanged, or with cultural artifacts such as buildings, works of art, tools, and so on – not only as sources but also as historical facts or objects – then he confronts them, exactly as the natural scientist does, as an infinite manifold. In the same way, he always knows much more than he can and will represent about all the historical events he has witnessed. For example, anyone who has actually seen Bismarck himself knows an inordinate number of facts about him that do not belong in any history, not even in the most exhaustive biography.

The case is not very different for some historical events that lie quite close to us temporally, even though we never experienced them at first hand. Here too on the basis of reliable sources, we could discover a wealth of details that do not have the slightest historical interest. In that case, we will always insist that the historian know how to distinguish the essential from the inessential. That Friedrich Wilhelm IV declined the German imperial crown is a "historical" event, but the question of which tailors made his uniforms remains a matter of complete indifference for political history, even though we could probably acquire precise knowledge of this too. Suppose it is objected against this point[5] that although this fact will indeed always remain inessential for political history, in a history of fashion or haberdashery or prices, it could become historically essential. This is,

[5] As Eduard Meyer has done in *Zur Theorie und Methodik der Geschichte*, 1902. See also my book *Kulturwissenschaft und Naturwissenschaft*, 6th and 7th eds., pp. 89 *seq.*

of course, true, but it proves nothing about the general principle at issue here. It is rather the case that the objection even admits the necessity of a principle of selection for political history. Moreover, facts can easily be cited that are inessential to *every* conceivable historical representation. Of course, the illustrations chosen for this purpose will always seem somewhat "farfetched" because the sources for completely inessential historical facts have usually been lost, and no one has an interest in remembering them. There is no doubt, however, that we could ascertain a multitude of facts about a personality such as Friedrich Wilhelm IV that are historically inessential under all conditions. Simply suppose that a historian possessed a substantial number of letters written in the king's own hand. If he concerned himself with the way the king distributed ink on the page, he could fill volumes with the description of absolutely indubitable facts from the past, but not even the most specialized specialist would maintain that this qualifies as historical science. Thus the "historical concept" of the king certainly cannot consist of *everything* that might be reliably established about him.

The situation seems different when the sources are meager. In such a case, there are in fact circumstances under which we will perhaps omit no individual characteristic that can possibly be discovered. Because of the lack of material, even the most trifling phenomenon acquires a significance here that it perhaps would not have if an ample body of information were available. But can we really say that in these cases the historian represents *everything* that he knows or could know? Here too the mere fact does not yet have any meaning. We can even discover much more about completely "unknown" things than can be incorporated into history. Concerning every person, all that natural science teaches us about bodies and all that general psychology teaches us about mental life can be claimed with confidence. Precisely because he is engaged in a science of individuals, however, the historian is not concerned with this knowledge. Thus even when history knows *too little* about its objects, it still knows *too much* about them. For this reason, it can never confine itself to narrating "what really happened" or to proceeding "idiographically." On the contrary, it always has the task of *separating* the essential from the inessential. For this purpose, however, there must be governing *perspectives*. As principles of historical representation, they should be made explicit. As a result, the problem of concept formation in history clearly emerges, irrespective of the fiction that is justified in the interest of logic.

But does this give us the right to speak of historical representation as a formation of historical *concepts*? Precisely on the basis of our earlier exposition, the following objection could be raised against this claim.

Even if history does not have to report *all* the facts it can ascertain, it remains true that whereas history *substantiates* this or that individual fact as *real*, natural science forms concepts that *hold validly*. Insofar as its concepts are intended to hold validly for reality and only for reality, it is true that *every* empirical science is concerned with real things and processes. If someone proposed to incorporate the products of the imagination into a system of concepts, no one would call that natural science, or a science of any sort. Nevertheless, generalizing natural science, in contrast to history, remains a science of concepts [*Begriffswissenschaft*] not only in the sense that the more comprehensive or general these concepts become, the less the content of its general concepts resembles the content of individual, empirical reality, but also in the sense that the existence of its objects need not be *explicitly* set out in judgments. Propositions such as "a corporeal world really exists," "water exists," or "there really are living human beings" do not comprise the content, but rather the implicit presuppositions of the natural sciences, which are concerned with the corporeal world in general, water, or human beings. In other words, precisely because such judgments are self-evident, they no longer belong in these sciences. In natural science the crucial point is always the question of the validity of concepts, not the question of the real existence of objects. In historical science, on the other hand, purely existential judgments have a fundamentally different significance. The historian is continually claiming that this was really the case, and that was really otherwise. His main concern lies precisely in the assertion and confirmation of the purely factual truth of such judgments. Contrary to natural science, therefore, the crucial issue is the real existence of objects, not the nonreal validity of concepts. This is why it seems that we cannot posit a historical *concept* formation parallel to that of natural science. In history, the word "concept" must receive a meaning completely different from the meaning it has in natural science. What can be said in response to this objection?

There is, of course, a fundamental difference. Indeed, the purpose of our entire account was to establish this difference. But consider the process in history by which a selection of the essential from the inessential is made, and which determines that a historical representation consists precisely of these and not those existential judgments. The fundamental difference in question cannot prevent us from characterizing this process as concept formation as well. Up to now, of course, we always used the word "concept" in such a way that it designated a nonreal construct with a *general* content. This is because when logic speaks of scientific concepts, it tends to focus almost exclusively on what the distinctive character of the concept of the *natural* sciences consists in. Here we see precisely that one-sidedness that we want to overcome. Unlike the generalizing disciplines, therefore, history does not form general concepts. On the other hand, history can no more incorporate its real objects themselves – for example, Caesar, the Thirty Years' War, the rise of the manors, or Dutch painting – into its representation than natural science can. On the contrary, it is obliged to form "ideas" *of* Caesar or "ideas" *of* the rise of the manors that hold validly and therefore are nonreal. Because the content of these ideas never coincides exactly with the infinitely diverse real processes, they are still "concepts" – even though they have no *general* content – in the sense that in them, what is essential for history is singled out from reality and comprehended, in quite the same way that natural science forms concepts by singling out what is essential to reality and comprehending it.

In addition, it is obvious that the content of historical concepts can be made explicit only if they are reduced to existential judgments that recount the things and processes they represent. As we have shown, however, the transposition into judgments is also necessary to the conception of the content of concepts in natural science. So in this respect, there is no basic difference either. In the one case, it is a matter of judgments that are formed in order to grasp the general, in accordance with the purpose of natural science. In the other case, it is a matter of judgments that give an account of specific and individual reality. But this exhibits only the general difference between representation in natural science and in history. In its most comprehensive meaning, we propose to maintain the term "concept" independent of just this difference. We will use it to refer to every logical construct whose content comprises valid knowledge of objects. Only in this way will we arrive at a truly comprehensive and universal theory of concept formation. In the interest of logic, therefore, it remains just as justified to designate as concepts those constructs in which the historical nature of reality is grasped in an individualizing fashion, as those constructs in which the general nature of things is expressed. In this sense, *all* scientific thought must take place in "concepts," individualizing history no less than generalizing science.

Apart from the use of this unconventional *terminology*, nothing is further from our intention than to invent a *new* method of historical representation that has never been employed and to set it up as the only justified method in opposition to that now in use. As in our investigation of natural science, we are rather guided by the purpose of understanding the scientific activity of the historian as it is really practiced. In other words, our purpose is to become acquainted with the logical structure that *every* historical representation must exhibit. Logic should never have any other relationship to empirical research. Reflection on the distinctive logical features of an investigation can do no more than proceed hand in hand with the investigation itself, and thereby structure it in a more systematic fashion. In the vast majority of cases, however, the sciences are developed to a considerable degree before reflection on their logical structure begins. Even if epistemology questions the basis of certain ultimate "presuppositions" of science and attempts to make their validity problematic in the philosophically justified interest of maximum unconditionality, there is no sense in which it brings into question the distinctive significance of the sciences as specialized forms of empirical research. Thus epistemology does not claim to direct science onto the paths it should take. On the contrary, it proposes only to follow science with a view to understanding it.

This can seem to be so self-evident that it does not need to be said. But it is precisely the logic of the historical sciences that has reason to stress the self-evident. Proposals to finally "elevate history to the rank of a science" by recommending a method it has never employed are still everyday occurrences. These attempts follow a period in which the historical sciences have been developed to an exceptional level. Taken on their own terms, they seem somewhat strange, even reactionary. This is because they invariably have recourse to the ideas of a – happily superseded – distinctively unhistorical or antihistorical philosophy of earlier times. Thus it is even more astonishing that the "modern" methodological constructions are produced not by speculative metaphysicians contemptuous of experience but by philosophers who take pride in their close contact with the empirical sciences, or even by historians themselves who cannot do enough to profess their antipathy to philosophical constructions. In view of these considerations, we can understand why other historians have become suspicious of *all* methodological investigations. Because even the modest philosophy of experience produces such exotic blossoms as the "new historical method," perhaps worse still will be expected from a logic that explicitly stresses that it will begin by proceeding in a "purely formal" way and even places itself in the service of an idealist weltanschauung. At the outset, therefore, we note that it is the naturalists and the alleged empiricists who are sufficiently remote from an understanding of the existing historical sciences that they demand a "new" historical method. The logic in which we are engaged here, however, can have nothing in view that proposes to inaugurate a new era of historical research. It proposes to understand the logical nature of *that* historical science that actually exists, for only in this way can it assess the significance of history for the theory of weltanschauung.

This obviously does not mean that the logic of history will declare the procedure of an individual hisorian, such as Ranke, or the special method of a so-called old tendency to be validly fixed for all time and pronounce the introduction of new "points of view" into historical science as unjustified. As an attempt to control the sciences, this would be just as futile as the proclamation of a universal scientific method, or the effort to banish Ranke's work from science. On the contrary, our concept of history must be just as general and comprehensive as our concept of natural science. It cannot exclude the most "modern" endeavors such as economic history, "cultural history," and the geographic and "materialist" conceptions of history, but rather has to understand them logically as well. Precisely for this reason, however, it remains a priori impossible for us to reach conclusions that are inconsistent with history as it was written by Ranke or other representatives of the "older" tendency. On the contrary, we believe we can show that the genuinely new perspectives in historical science, such as, for example, the more thorough consideration of economic life – to which logic cannot raise the slightest objection, since it has no judgment at all to offer in a case of this sort – signify the introduction of a new *material* and not the introduction of a new *method*. We also believe we can show that, as long as they write history at all, even the theoretically most radical proponents of the "new method" will always work in practice – even though they may not be aware of this – by employing the method that always has been used in history and always will be used as long as there is a historical science.

A different point, of course, should also be stressed, which will perhaps be regarded as a qualification of the foregoing remarks. Even though the *result* our investigation attempts to establish is "only" an agreement of logical theory with the method of the historical sciences that actually exist, for this reason the *path* on which we will arrive at concepts useful for the logical understanding of historical science cannot consist in a mere *analysis* of existing scientific activity. We even believe that an investigation that proposed to *begin* with such an analysis would never reach logically significant conclusions. We already indicated the basis for this claim in the Introduction. If no science amounts to description – in the sense of a mere reproduction of its material – for this reason, logic cannot qualify as mere "description" either. The sciences themselves are a part of historical reality, which, as we know, cannot be described at all without a principle of selection. The concept of "pure induction" – the name of this slogan, which still has not disappeared – is actually the ideal of a radically "empiricist" form of speculation that proceeds in a purely deductive fashion and has lost all contact with real scientific thought. The attempt to make progress in logic in a purely inductive way will necessarily remain completely fruitless.

The reason for this is obvious. How are we simply to read off the structure of the sciences if the issue concerns the clarification of two methods that are logically, and thus formally, juxtaposed? The division of scientific labor is in the first instance connected not with logical differences but with substantive differences in the material. These differences must inevitably come to the fore as soon as the attempt is made to describe the different sciences "inductively." To gain any sort of perception of the logical oppositions, therefore, we can *begin* only formally, construing them in their most elementary form and without regard to the existing individual sciences. We also find formal constructions of this sort in the work of scientific specialists who have attempted to clarify the method of their own work. Boeckh,[6] for example, in connection with his famous definition of philology as the "knowledge of the known," says the following: "First, it was necessary to formulate an unconditional concept of philology, with a view to eliminating all arbitrary definitions and identifying the real essence of the science." That is what we too will try to do here. Moreover, this is justified if we only keep in mind – again employing the words of Boeckh – the following point: "The more unconditional a concept, the more the conditions must be given in the development."

In the *general* parts of logic, this way of proceeding is regarded as a matter of course. When methodology turns to more specialized forms of science, however, we often find that from the very beginning, the content of the science in question plays the chief role. As a result, investigations of this sort offer more of an encyclopedic survey of the different disciplines than a development of logical concepts. In the ensuing, just as in our account of concept formation in natural science, we will make a scrupulous effort to avoid this encyclopedic tendency – as exhibited, for example, in substantial parts of Wundt's *Logik* – in order really to produce a *logical* methodology of concept formation in history. The empirical material can always occur only as an example for the clarification of a previously established logical principle. Moreover, no one should be troubled if logical principles that at first are developed in a purely formal way must subsequently be restricted when they are applied to the actual praxis of scientific

[6]*Enzyklopädie und Methodologie der philologischen Wissenschaften*, 1877, p. 20.

research. As historical facts, the existing sciences cannot be exhaustively reduced to any schema. This provides all the more reason why we need general logical schemata, both to understand the logical structure of the sciences and to distinguish conceptually the different logical components of the sciences that in fact are interconnected.

There is another reason why we are obliged to begin in a formal or "deductive" fashion. Where the theory of science set about its work with previously established concepts, it was usually not aware of this. On the contrary, it conceived the relationship between the general and the particular – as if this were self-evident – in such a way that it considered only the subordination of the particular case under the general concept. As a result, only concept formation in natural science conformed to its schema. Either it was as good as blind to any other possibility, or it attempted to compress everything into its schema. From the outset, our self-consciously deductive procedure considers not only *one* but *all* the conceivable possibilities of the representation of reality. We thereby propose to overcome this one-sidedness and do justice to the sciences that actually exist. Thus we begin by constructing the purely logical concept of a historical method, and we then apply it to empirical science. In other words, our strategy is exactly the opposite of the logical naturalists, who begin by proclaiming a pure empiricism in order to arrive at the purely speculative demand for a "historical science." Assuming that this science is expected to resolve the tasks that fall to history, it can never be realized. . . .

2. THE HISTORICAL INDIVIDUAL

As we have seen, the historical in its most comprehensive sense – in which it coincides with the unique, invariably individual, and empirically real event itself – forms the limit of concept formation in natural science. This is due to its perceptual reality as well as to its individuality. The empirical *perception* of reality cannot be represented by any science, because it remains infinitely diverse under all conditions. Thus it cannot be reduced to any concept. But this does not hold true for *individuality*. Although it is given to us perceptually, it does not follow that individuality must remain *identical* with perception. *The problem of concept formation in history, therefore, is whether a scientific analysis and reduction of perceptual reality is possible that does not at the same time – as in the concepts of natural science – forfeit individuality*, and yet also does not produce a mere "description" of facts that cannot yet be regarded as a scientific representation. In other words, we must now ask, From the infinite manifold of the perceptual content of reality, can certain aspects be accentuated and consolidated into scientific concepts in such a way that they represent not what is common to a plurality of things and processes but, rather, only what is present in *one* individual? This is the only way that concepts with individual content will occur that can claim to be historical concepts. It must follow from the foregoing that mere descriptions of individual facts, which obviously are always *possible*, do not yet warrant this name. We propose to reserve the name "concept" for *that* in which a scientific representation finds its conclusion. Therefore we ask, Are individual concepts logically impossible, in the same way that perceptual concepts would be logically impossible?

Obviously we do not contest the indispensability of a *generality* for all scientific concept formation. Even a fleeting glance at a historical representation shows that it too almost always consists of words that have *general meanings*. It could not be otherwise, for these are the only words intelligible to everyone. It is true that historical representations also include proper names, and they seem to constitute an exception. Without further specification of their sense, however, they mean something only to someone who is acquainted on the basis of perception with the individual designated or can reproduce this individual in his memory. The historian should never presuppose knowledge of such individual *perceptions*. If he happens to possess this knowledge himself – which is possible only if factual material and source material coincide – he can communicate it only by specifying its content by means of words that have general meanings. Thus proper names can appear in a historical representation only as proxies for a complex of words with a general meaning; for only then is the representation intelligible to everyone who hears or reads it.

Indeed, we are obliged to claim even more than this. It is not merely this external circumstance that forces the historian to represent everything he wants to express scientifically by using *general* concepts. Earlier we found that every judgment requires a generality and that, for this reason, even the elements with which we form a general concept in natural science are themselves always general. But if this "first generality" – as we propose to call it – is indispensable to all logical thought as such, then it is just as essential to a historical representation as to concept formation in natural science. In the sense that the *elements* of concepts and judgments are general, *all* scientific thought must be articulated in general concepts. So if the task of rendering nothing but individual contents is ascribed to history, then the concept of a historical *science* would in fact be a contradiction in terms.

But does it follow that the *use* of words with general meanings as elements of concepts is possible only in the *one* direction that we find in natural science? Put another way, by using words with general meanings, can unique and individual processes be described only in such a way that the contents of these descriptions can be nothing more than *material* for further conceptual analysis?

Each of the elements of a scientific concept must be intrinsically general. Earlier, however, we saw that considered on their own terms, they still do not qualify as scientific "concepts." On the contrary, only their *combination* is scientifically significant, and this combination certainly does not always have to be undertaken in such a way that another concept with a general content is formed by its means. Rather, it can also follow that the resulting complex of general elements as a *whole* has a content that occurs only in one unique and specific object. Thus it represents precisely that by means of which this object is distinguished from all others. To maintain that the fundamental opposition between natural science and history holds for concept formation too, we do not need more than such a possibility.

As regards the point that all thought requires the general, we can formulate this opposition in the following way. In natural science, the general – which is already present in the most elementary meanings of words – is also what the science endeavors to develop further. In other words, a general concept to which the profusion of specific phenomena can be subordinated is its *purpose*. Even the most restricted law of nature must always hold for an indefinite number of things and processes if it is to deserve the name of a "law." Although history also *uses* the general so that it can think and judge scientifically, the general is nothing more than a *means* for history. In other words, it forms the indirect path on which history attempts to return to the individual as its real object. History employs the general in the same way a description uses it to represent a purely factual individual reality that signifies nothing more than the material of science. The only important point here is to understand the scientific *objective* served by a historical representation of the individual. We propose to characterize the sciences, not with reference to their means but with reference to their objectives. Therefore, assertions such as the claim that all scientific thought employs general concepts are, of course, incontestable. But on this level of imprecision, they are meaningless for the question of whether historical science pursues the same *objectives* as natural science. It must be possible to resolve all concepts into judgments whose ultimate components are indeed general. In their totality, however, these judgments can represent something that is unique and individual as well as something that is general. This is the only issue of importance here. . . .

Therefore our problem does not begin until we pose the question of which principle governs the historical *combination* of conceptual elements? History as a science can never consist in the mere "description" of individual facts. Such descriptions – which we have, for example, in representations of the moon and which can be given for any individual reality at all – are "historical" only in that first quite general meaning of the word, in which it designates the unique and the individual as such. But they cannot serve as examples that clarify the concept of a historical *science*. In history as well, the elements of the concept must form a unity – in the sense of a *coherent* entity[7] – if science is to arise as a self-contained or closed system of ideas. For us, therefore, the tie that binds these elements into one concept with an individual content is the only important matter. This is the only perspective from which we can speak of a *validity* of historical concepts. If such a principle of unity specific to history cannot be discovered, we would have to accept the claim that the representation of everything individual should be regarded as nothing more than a preliminary analysis or a collection of material for a more advanced form of generalizing concept formation. Thus what does the "unity" of historical concepts consist in if the coherence of conceptual elements – unlike the case of a concept in natural science – is not based on the fact that the concept holds generally for all the cases subsumed under it?

To answer this question in principle, suppose we again consider the most comprehensive concept of the historical, in other words, the concept of the real *individual* as such. At this point, we stress that this word does not have only the meaning to which we limited our account in the foregoing, namely, that of the unique, the specific, and the singular. On the contrary, it also includes the *indivisible*. The concept of indivisibility indicates a *unity* that arouses our logical interest. We know that to qualify as singular, every reality must also be composite, for the simple, like the atom, lacks individuality. Thus the following question arises: Is it perhaps more than an accident that combined in the word "individual" are *two* meanings that are interconnected for our problem of the historical concept – that of the unity of a manifold in the sense of a coherence, on the one hand; and that of uniqueness, on the other? It at least seems noteworthy that we also designate as an individual – as that which is indivisible – something that is necessarily manifold. Has the expression "individual" lost its meaning when it is used to designate unique manifolds, and is only the simple atom indivisible? Or are there perhaps individuals also in the sense that

7[*Zusammengehörig* literally means "belonging together." *Zusammengehörigkeit* is a state in which things belong together, for example, a state of contiguity, unity, solidarity, or coherence.]

their manifold forms a unity – in the sense of a *coherence* – *because of* their uniqueness? If this is the case, here the uniqueness and unity of a manifold are connected with one another in the way that they must be connected in a historical concept if we are to speak of its *validity*. Does the concept of the individual perhaps contain the principle that links the coherent aspects in the historical material and thereby distinguishes them from aspects that are merely contingently related?

We will begin by attempting to establish quite generally whether the concept of indivisibility can be linked with that of uniqueness in such a way that uniqueness forms the basis or presupposition of indivisibility. In this way, we will at least take the *first step* along the path that should gradually lead us to the concept of the historical individual. . . .

Initially, the principle that is the basis of the unity of the indivisibility that arises from uniqueness can be clarified by the comparison of two *bodies*. In this way, of course, we will not yet reach the *final* concept of the historical individual, for there is no doubt that history is primarily concerned with real mental life. Indeed, we must remain with a preliminary concept in this context because we will completely ignore the consideration that all historical reality is an *event* that changes, and because we will consider only the individual as such, insofar as it is autonomous and self-contained, which is never really the case. But if we want to understand logically the method of concept formation in history, we again have to begin by representing the logical principles abstractly to determine them more precisely in the ensuing in a step-by-step fashion.

Consider the principle that alone is at stake at this point and that only concerns the distinction between two kinds of individuals as such. As the bodies with which we will clarify this principle in a logically abstract fashion, let us employ a particular lump of coal and a particular large diamond, such as the famous Koh-i-noor. The point that there is only one particular chunk of coal lying here holds true for it no less than for the diamond, which has a proper name. Like the diamond, its individual properties distinguish it not only from everything else that is differently constituted, but also from every other lump of coal. As regards *uniqueness*, therefore, both bodies are individuals in exactly the same sense. As regards their *indivisibility*, on the other hand, they are quite different. It is true that both *can be* split apart. A blow of the hammer would shatter one individual as well as the other. But while the splitting of a lump of coal is the most indifferent matter imaginable, the diamond will be scrupulously protected from this. Moreover, we do not want to see the diamond split, *because* it is unique. In the case of the diamond, therefore, the unity of its individual manifold is really connected with its uniqueness in such a way that its unity is based on its uniqueness. In the case of the lump of coal, it is true that uniqueness is also present, but it is simply not related as a unity to a possible splitting. The reason is as follows: Although another lump of coal can always be substituted for this one, another Koh-i-noor can never be produced. As a result, the difference between the two kinds of individuals must be clear. The unique is always necessarily indivisible as well – or an in-dividual [*In-dividuum*] in the strict sense of the word – when its uniqueness acquires an irreplaceable *significance*. In this sense, it is incontestable that not only minds, but also bodies, form individual unities.

There is no doubt that it is only this difference between two kinds of individuals that is applicable to *all* bodies in such a way that, from this perspective, the entire physical world falls into two groups of realities. From the extensively infinite manifold of things, a specific number is differentiated. The vast majority of bodies come into consideration only insofar as they are instances of general concepts. As regards those bodies that are not merely unique but, rather, are also unified in the sense of being indivisible because of their uniqueness, we do not want *just* to subsume them under general concepts. Indeed, we can even claim more than this. If we examine an individual in the strict sense – again, for example, the specific diamond – somewhat more closely, we find that the significance of its individuality does not lie in the *totality* of that which constitutes the content of its manifold. Like the manifold of everything else, this manifold consists of an infinity of determinations. Its irreplaceability can depend on only a *part* of them. It is this part alone that we consider when we "describe" the diamond. The multiplicity of its other properties could be different without thereby modifying or even nullifying its significance. But if the unity the diamond possesses by virtue of its individuality comprehends no more than a part of it, the principle we seek makes it possible not only to regard its individuality as a unity; at the same time, it allows a limited and precisely defined number of its attributes to be consolidated into an individual unity. In addition, this difference between merely coexisting and coherently related "characteristics" must also be found in every body that qualifies as an individual in the strict sense. Thus we see how a certain number of unique *and* – in the sense of indivisible – unified corporeal manifolds, each of which has a specific and determinable content, are discriminated from the totality of the known corporeal world.

Let us attempt to formulate explicitly the general *principle* on which this distinction is based, insofar as this is possible with reference to the example we used. In that case we can say the following: The meaning possessed by the diamond rests on the *value* attached to its irreplace-able uniqueness. The diamond *should* not be split because it is valuable. This must also hold true for all bodies that are in-dividuals. The mode of unity in indivisibility just characterized can arise only if its uniqueness is *related to a value*.

This is not to deny that there are other grounds on which a body is constituted as an indivisible unity. Organisms, for example, cannot be split without ceasing to be organisms, and the same holds true for tools and machines. But *this* sort of unity is not relevant to our discussion, because it does not concern the uniqueness of a specific, singular, individual thing. Our question is only how uniqueness can form the *basis* of unity, and here the answer must be that in-dividuals are always individuals that are related to a value. This and this *alone* is the only point we want to establish for the present. Thus we should again note that this is *not* yet sufficient to define completely the concept of the historical individual and especially that in the Koh-i-noor diamond, we do not yet have a "historical individual" of the *specific* kind that historical science in the strict sense deals with. As a *finished* stone, the diamond has no "history" at all, if for no other reason than because its development is unknown to us. Only if it is brought into connection with persons who value can the diamond acquire a historical significance *in* this connection. We will subse-quently become acquainted with the reasons for this. We have made use of the Koh-i-noor diamond and compared it with an arbitrary lump of coal only to clarify *the* difference between two kinds of individuality on the basis of which we shall define the concept of the historical individual more precisely in the ensuing. Thus all objections that amount to the claim that the diamond is not "historical" are unfounded. By means of this example, we want to take *only* the *first* step toward the definition of historical individuality. It is impossible to say everything at once.

At first, we have to ask whether the distinction just made can be carried out for all conceivable empirical reality, and especially whether it can be transposed onto psychic existence. If this is not immediately obvious, the reason is as follows: Among the animate beings with which we are familiar and of which we take note, there are presumably none in whose individual character one part of the determinations is not differentiated from the others and consolidated to form a distinctive individual unity. In particular, we know of no *person* whose individuality does not comprise an essential "core" as the real personality, in opposition to inessential and peripheral processes. Because we find this unity of indivisibility in all human mental life, we are easily led to believe that it is tied to the nature of the psychic itself.

But that is a mistake. If we disregard both the epistemological unity of consciousness as such as well as any metaphysical unity of a transcendental mind, the distinction between center and periphery in the empirical manifold of a human mind is based on no other principle than that with which we become acquainted in the comparison of the diamond with the lump of coal. In other words, individual unity as the indivisibility of a personality is grounded on no other consideration but the following: We associate a *value* with this unity, and as a result, the aspects that are irreplaceable or essential with reference to this value form a whole that *should* not be divided. In short, the individual unity or indivisibility of the unique personality is no different from the unity of the individual as such that is related to a value.

On the basis of this consideration, the concept of the "psychic structural nexus" [*des psychischen Strukturzusammenhanges*] also becomes intelligible. The *historical* unity of a personality is not constituted by an "experienced" unity. On the contrary, as long as we have not grasped its nature, the indivisible unity of the personality that is related to a *value* leads us to the mistaken conclusion that an *individual* unity may already be discovered in the experienced unity of the real psychic structural nexus as such. This becomes especially clear when the structural nexus is also characterized as a *purposive* nexus [*Zweckzusammenhang*]. That is because a *value* is implicit in the concept of a purpose, and the unity of individuality rests on this value alone. The difference between the corporeal and the mental individual lies *exclusively* in the fact that there is no person whose individuality is so indifferent to us as that of a lump of coal. It follows from this, however, that the indivisible unity of uniqueness is still not tied to the psychic as such. Independent of value, we not only can easily *conceive* a unique mental life that possesses no individual unity – even though it always has to have the unity of the psychic structural nexus; when we consider animals, for example, quite often there is really no "bond" that constitutes uniqueness as the unity of indivisibility – although the unity of the experienced structural nexus cannot be wanting here either, assuming that this unity pertains to the mental as such.

At this point, it is irrelevant why *all* persons are linked with values or are related to values and thus qualify as individuals in the strict sense of indivisibility. It is important to show only that our principle is truly *general*, and therefore that by its means any reality at all – regardless of whether it is physical or psychic – can be analyzed as individuals in the strict sense and the more comprehensive sense. In that case, we also understand why we so easily forget that with reference to uniqueness, *all* realities exist in the same way as individuals in the more comprehensive sense. In the overwhelming number of cases, they are *only* unique. We *take note* of uniqueness and have occasion to become explicitly aware of it only when they are related to a value and thereby become indivisibly unified in their uniqueness, which almost always holds true for psychic individualities. This is why it sounds paradoxical to call leaves or nuts individuals, even though – in the most general sense of this expression – they are exactly as individual as the personalities of history.

Consider, however, the clarification of the principle on which the distinction into two different kinds of individuals rests. What it initially makes explicit is nothing more than the perspective that guides every feeling, willing, and acting person – in short, everyone who takes a position on values, and thus every genuinely "vital" person – in his conception of the world, the perspective on the basis of which the essential and inessential aspects of real existence are distinguished for him. On the one hand, anyone who *lives* – in other words, anyone who sets goals for himself and wants to realize them – can never regard the world *exclusively* with reference to the specific. This is because he can orient himself and act practically in the domain of reality, which is always individual, only by generalizing. Thus he is concerned with some objects only insofar as they are instances of general concepts. On the other hand, many objects will be important for the person who values precisely because of their uniqueness. For him, therefore, they are necessarily indivisible or unified individuals. This distinction is made with such consummate self-evidence that we only rarely take note of its basis and simply do not consider that in such a case, *value perspectives* govern a *selection*. In fact, this is the primordial conception of reality, which is prior to every science. For the real person, therefore – who is always a person who wills, values, and takes positions – reality conceived in the manner just described, as in part generalizing and in part individualizing, actually becomes reality simpliciter. This is why we must explicitly stress that the world of unified individuals – quite like reality as an object of aesthetic perception or as an object of general concepts – is *only* a specific *conception*. As a third conception, we differentiate it in principle from the natural scientific and aesthetic conception. Initially, it can be designated as the world of practical life.

What is the relationship between the prescientific, individualizing conception of reality and the problem of concept formation in historical science?

We have repeatedly stressed that the concept of the *historical* individual in the *strict* sense still cannot be clarified by the concept of the diamond. Our analysis will proceed from the concept of the limits of natural science to the progressive determination of the concept of historical science. At this point, we can say the following: If individual reality as such was identified with the most general concept of the historical *object*, the individualizing conception of reality characteristic of practical life must be designated as the primordial and most comprehensive *historical conception*. Here, however, the "historical" still means nothing more than reality with reference to the unique, the specific, and the individual per se. We have identified the historical interest in this most comprehensive sense with the interest in the individual. Thus those individuals that qualify as in-dividuals for the person who wills and values can be called *historical individuals*, as long as the concept of the historical is regarded exclusively as the concept of the unique and the individual.

Initially even this more narrow concept of the individual still has no significance for the concept of a *scientific* history. Nevertheless it is still important in our methodological context. This is because we can define the most comprehensive logical concept of the historical, which heretofore only comprised a problem, with reference to this concept. In this way, we can at least come *closer* to a solution to the problem. In the foregoing, we designated nature as reality with reference to the general and history as reality with reference to the individual. Although it is true that this formulation comprises the most general concept of natural science, it still has *nothing* to say about the concept of a historical science. Suupose we now claim, in opposition to this formulation, that reality becomes history with reference to the meaning the individual possesses by virtue of its uniqueness for the being that wills and acts. In that case, the *possibility* of a historical *representation* in the logical sense is immediately opened up for us. Because the historical conception or the formation of in-dividuals as just described surmounts both the extensively and the intensively infinite manifold of empirical reality, the perspective that is definitive in this context must also be suited to be the principle for the formation of concepts with an individual content. At the same time, this more precise definition does not alter in the slightest the fundamental logical opposition between nature and history. This is because empirical reality, as the volitional person of practical life would represent it with reference to its uniqueness and singularity, would have to set a limit to concept formation in natural science, just as this holds true for reality itself as an infinite manifold that lies beyond any representation.

But how can the prescientific conception of *volitional* or *practical* life bring us closer to the concept of history as a *science*? At this point that is the crucial question. Does not the prescientific conception remain necessarily opposed to the scientific conception precisely *because* it is the conception of the volitional person? The historical conception, of course, cannot be identical with that of the practical or volitional person. It is true that both share the distinction between individuals in the strict sense and the more comprehensive sense, and both consolidate individual manifolds of this sort into unities – in the sense of entities that have an indivisible coherence. But they also differ in two fundamental respects. We will arrive at the *scientific* formation of in-dividuals only by taking note of these differences.

First, in opposition to the volitional person, the historian as a scientist is not practical but theoretical. Thus his mode of activity is always *representational*, and not *judgmental*. In other words, he shares the perspectives of considering something with the practical person, but not the activity of willing and valuing itself. This can also be expressed in the following way: History is *not* a *valuing* science but a *value-relevant* science. We will establish precisely what counts as "considering" something under value perspectives or the purely theoretical "relation to values," in opposition to volition and practical valuation. Here we only note that this is another reason why we cannot yet regard the Koh-i-noor diamond as a historical individual: We distinguished it from the lump of coal precisely on the ground that, for the person who makes practical valuations, a greater value is ascribed to it than to any lump of coal, which we do not value. The diamond would be intelligible as an individual that is merely theoretically value relevant – and thus as a historical individual in the scientific sense – only in a larger context, which for the time being we cannot yet examine.

At this point, suppose we establish the second difference. In practical life, it always holds true that the volitional person also esteems certain values that qualify as such for him alone. This is why there are many individuals that become in-dividuals for him, even though others have no reason to acknowledge these individual manifolds as necessary unities, in the sense of being indivisible. History, on the other hand, assuming that we want to grasp the concept of the science as well, must always strive for a representation that is valid for *everyone*. That is why only the content of its concepts, but never the principles governing its representation, can be "individual": in other words, valid for only this or that individual person. Thus we are not only obliged to distinguish practical "valuation" from a theoretical "value relationship." We also have to define the value perspectives that are decisive for the theoretically value-relevant formation of historical in-dividuals more precisely than was possible in the comparison of the diamond and the lump of coal.

We will begin with the second point, deferring for the time being the difference between practical valuation and theoretical value relevance. Then the inadequacy of the concept of the historical individual obtained thus far is demonstrated by the fact that in practical life, we regard *all* persons as individuals. There is *no* person whose individuality is as insignificant to us as that of a lump of coal. History, however, never represents the individuality of all persons. What is the basis for limiting it to a part of them?

Obviously it is based on the consideration that history is interested only in what – as we usually put it – has a *general* significance. This must mean that for history, the value with reference to which objects become historical individuals must be a general value: in other words, a value that is *valid for everyone*. All persons become individuals in the strict sense by virtue of the fact that we relate every human individual to some sort of value. On the other hand, suppose we consider which individual life is consolidated as a unity by virtue of its uniqueness and with reference to *general* values. Then we will see that from the totality of persons – just as from the totality of all other objects – a certain number is *set in relief*. In comparing two bodies, we chose the diamond because, with reference to a general value, it becomes an individual that is valued by everyone. If we compare a personality such as Goethe with any average person, and if we ignore the consideration that even the individuality of this average person means something with reference to some value or other, it follows that Goethe is related to such a person in the same way the Koh-i-noor diamond is related to a lump of coal. In other words, with reference to the *general* value, the individuality of the average person can be replaced by any object that falls under the concept of a person. The significance of Goethe, on the other hand, lies precisely in what distinguishes him from all other instances of the concept of a person. There is no general concept under which he can be subsumed. Thus the individual Goethe is an in-dividual in the same sense as the individual Koh-i-noor: His distinctive status as an individual is valued by *everyone* for its individuality. As a result, we see how the relation to a general value makes it possible not only to distinguish two kinds of individuals in every reality whatsoever but also to draw this distinction in such a way that we can expect everyone to acknowledge its validity.

History, therefore, represents objects that become individuals from this perspective by replacing practical valuation with the purely theoretical value relationship. In this way, history as a science distinguishes the essential from the inessential in a *generally valid fashion* and consolidates the essential as a *necessary* unity.

But does this not invalidate the concept of the historical established in the foregoing, and especially the opposition to natural science? Are we still justified in speaking of a science of the distinctive and the individual if the value that constitutes objects as historical individuals is a *general* value?

In addition to the general *elements* of concepts already discussed – which we called the "first generality" – there is a *second generality* in history as well. This circumstance also explains why the difference between natural science and history could be overlooked in discussions about the method of the historical sciences, and why a natural scientific or generalizing method could be proclaimed as universal. It seemed quite self-evident: Science is always concerned with the "*general.*" And yet if we make clear what this "second generality of history" signifies, it will be seen that the general value that makes the general validity of a historical conception possible has even less to do with the generality found in natural science than do the general elements of historical concepts. At least as regards their content, historical concepts are general in the same sense as a concept of natural science. In contrast, the general value to which individuals must be related in order to become historical in-dividuals is not supposed to comprehend several individual values as its instances, but rather to be a value that everyone acknowledges, or a value that is *valid for everyone.* And second, if something has a general significance – insofar as it is related to a general value – that does not mean that this thing itself is general. On the contrary, the general significance of an object can even be augmented to the same extent that the differences between it and other objects increase.

Thus, precisely *because* it gives an account of what is related to a *general* value, history has to give an account of the individual and the distinctive. So the historical individual is significant for *everyone* by virtue of that in which it is *different from everything else.* Those who hold that it is never the individual but rather only the general that has a general significance fail to see that it is precisely the most general values that can attach to what is absolutely individual and unique.

Thus it is true that historical representation requires something general as a principle of selection, but this second generality of history is not the *goal* for which its formations of concepts strive, no more than is the case for the elements of concepts. It is rather the *presupposition* on the sole basis of which a generally valid representation of what is unique and individual can be undertaken. . . .

. . . At this point, we will show only that if reality is analyzed into essential and inessential aspects with reference to a *general* value – in other words, a value that is universally acknowledged as such – and if the essential aspects are consolidated as individual unities, the resulting conception of reality is not arbitrary and thus not a priori unscientific: On the contrary, it must be acknowledged as necessary by everyone who presupposes the governing values as generally acknowledged; in consequence, it satisfies a necessary condition of the scientific conception.

We have, however, repeatedly identified a second difference between the scientific conception of history and that of the volitional person in practical life. The concept of the historical individual can be conclusively defined only by a thorough clarification of this difference as well. The foregoing exposition is to be regarded as a preliminary account. Whoever proposes to take a position on our concept of the historical individual should rely not on these preliminary definitions but only on the *final* definition, which will now be undertaken.

If the illustrations we used for the concept of the historical individual are considered, the Koh-i-noor diamond and Goethe, it might be supposed that *those* parts of reality become historical individuals when they themselves embody values, or when they are *goods* to which values are attached; moreover, values of a kind that are positively valued by everyone. The concept of a "good," however, is much too narrow to identify the historical individual; nor does it suffice to extend this concept in such a way that negatively valued realities or *bad* things – which is how we draw the opposition to goods – are also reckoned among the historical individuals. On the contrary, it is simply not the business of historical science to offer positive or negative *valuations*: in other words, to assert that the individual realities they represent are either good or bad, valuable or antagonistic to value. For in that case, how is history to arrive at *generally* valid value judgments? It is rather the case that we have to scrupulously distinguish what we mean by the "relation" of an individual to a value from the direct positive or negative *valuation* of this individual. Indeed, if our view were conceived as if we held that rendering positive or negative *value judgments* is a task of historical *science*, and thus that history is a *valuing* science, this would be the *most reprehensible of all misunderstandings*. On the contrary, we must regard the dissociation of every "practical" positive or negative value judgment from the *purely theoretical relation* of objects to values as an essential criterion of the *scientific* historical conception. Indeed, insofar as the value perspective is decisive for history, this concept of the "value relation" – in opposition to "valuation" – is actually *the* essential criterion for history as a pure science.

But what does it mean to relate an object to a value theoretically, without valuating it as good or bad, as valuable or antagonistic to values? In order to understand this, let us return once more to the conception of practical life, which always values objects as well, and consider two persons who have pronounced disagreements in what they love and hate – in other words, in what they value. In spite of this, may it not be that with reference to specific values – such as, for example, political values – they both *agree* that reality falls into objects of the following sort: those that if they think about them at all, are regarded as instances of a generic concept, and those they regard as significant because of their individuality?

One of the two may be a radical democrat and a free trader, the other an extreme aristocrat and a protectionist. In that event, there will certainly be few cases in which they agree in their valuations or value judgments about political events of their own time or the past, in their own country or in other nations. In other words, they will regard very different things as good or bad. But does this mean that one of them will be interested only in those individual political events that are indifferent to the other? Of course not. Even among politicians who take the most diverse positions imaginable, *the same* individual events form the object of *interest*. In other words, differences in evaluation must be based on a *common conception of reality*. If such a *common* conception of reality did not obtain, in a case in which two persons are of a different opinion concerning the value of a condition, the antagonists would not even be talking about the same thing. Therefore a controversy over the value of the object in question would be utterly impossible.

Even this example must make it clear that goods and acts of valuation can be regarded not only in such a way that we inquire into the validity of the values that are linked with them and then attempt to establish the justification with which positive or negative valuations are made – in other words, the justification with which things are regarded as good or bad; there is another view of values as well, which is not concerned with the value of things or their lack of value and does not inquire into their quality as being good or bad. This view singles out from the infinite manifold only that which stands in some sort of *relation* to values, so that it somehow *makes a difference* with respect to values. Here we are concerned solely with this sort of value relationship. History as a pure science is not concerned with the justification of valuing objects as good or bad, positive or negative. Thus whoever is opposed to such valuations in a purely scientific historical context certainly cannot be refuted. A theoretical *relation* of objects to values, however, – by virtue of which they fall into those that are indifferent to values and those that have some sort of meaning with respect to values – cannot be dissociated from the purely scientific perspective of history.

The theoretical value relationship is of such crucial significance for historical science that without it, we would not be able to distinguish historically relevant material from the phenomena of reality that remain historically indifferent. For example, we can regard the personality of Luther as either a good thing or a bad thing. In other words, we can believe that it was a stroke of luck for the cultural development of Germany or that it brought misfortune. On this point, the opinions of historians will probably always be in disagreement. But no one who knows the facts will doubt that Luther had some sort of *significance* with reference to generally acknowledged values, and it can never occur to a historian to claim that Luther's personality is historically *unimportant*. So it cannot be doubted that positive or negative valuation is in principle different from the theoretical relation of objects to values. Valuation is always positive or negative, and the value judgment declares that its object is either good or bad. The purely theoretical relation to values, on the other hand, stands aloof from such an alternative. If an object is essential to this relation, that does not mean we have to consider the character of the object good or bad.

If, in spite of this indubitable difference, the concepts of positive and negative valuation are not distinguished from the concept of the theoretical value relation, the reason perhaps lies in the following consideration. If one event is explicitly judged to be important and another event is explicitly judged to be unimportant, *that* is certainly an act of valuation or a commitment. Such a commitment, however, does not simply coincide with the theoretical relation of objects to values, as a result of which *historical* individuals are formed. It is rather the case that in *all* scientific concept formation, the explicit distinction into essential and inessential features implies a *valuation*. To this extent, natural science is not free of valuations either. Distinguishing the essential from the inessential always presupposes the value of *science*, with reference to which certain components are essential and others are inessential. Where science is not valued as a *good*, a distinction between the essential and the inessential aspects of reality simply cannot be made.

In consequence, the difference between the natural scientific and the historical conception can also be expressed in the following way. If someone regards natural science as a theoretical good and is guided in his thought by the aim of forming general concepts of nature, different factors of empirical reality must become essential and inessential for him than for someone who regards historical science as a theoretical good and distinguishes essential and inessential aspects in empirical reality from one another with reference to the objective of developing a historical science. In methodological investigations, however, we intentionally leave these *logical* values to which the investigator is committed, and which are implicitly presupposed in *all* scientific concept formation, in the background. We are concerned only with the relationship in which the *material* of conceptual representation stands to values, and in this regard we can state the following. It is characteristic of concept formation in natural science that the objects it represents are dissociated and must be dissociated from all relations to values if they are to be regarded as nothing more than generic instances of general concepts. Although it is true that historical science also has to maintain its autonomy from the practical valuation of objects and their evaluation as good or bad, it can never lose sight of the relations of objects to values as such. Otherwise it would be utterly impossible for historical science to distinguish the historically essential from the historically inessential events in empirical reality. The circumstance that *all* concept formation in science presupposes the value of *scientific* objectives should not mislead us concerning the points that the relation of objects to values is distinctive to concept formation in history and that the theoretical value relation must be distinguished from practical valuation.

In any case, we should not confuse diverging positive or negative valuations with the *common* conception of reality by virtue of which only certain objects and not others become historical individuals. For history, the distinction between essential and inessential elements is made in a way that is *independent* of the difference in practical value judgments. On the other hand, the conception that is common to the differing parties also remains "tied" to the "relation" to values. Suppose that by virtue of its individuality, an object acquires political, aesthetic, or religious significance. And suppose it becomes the object of a controversy and appears as historically important or unimportant. In other words, it is set in relief as an in-dividual from the infinite profusion of objects. In that case, we cannot regard political, artistic, or religious life as indifferent or neutral to values, but must rather explicitly *acknowledge some* sort of political, aesthetic, or religious values *as values*. For persons who do not do this, there would be no occasion to ascribe a different *interest* to one individual configuration of specific objects rather than to any other arbitrary configuration. Suppose we designate as the mere relation of reality to values that by virtue of which a conception of reality arises that is *common* to the most divergent value judgments and that, as reality, is neither positively nor negatively valued. In that case, we can rigorously distinguish this relation as purely theoretical from practical valuation. Valuing is always either positive or negative. The relation to values is neither. This consideration alone makes the fundamental difference clear. By means of this mere relation, therefore, a world of individuals is formed for everyone in *the same* way. The value of these individuals, on the other hand, can be assessed quite *differently*. The purely theoretical relation to values has absolutely nothing to say about what is good or bad, valuable or antagonistic to value in such a value-relevant world of individuals.

Now we can understand the following point: Assuming that history proposes to be nothing but a *science*, the *logical ideal* of the historical conception is characterized by the fact that it stands aloof from all practical *volition* concerning objects, and thus it abstracts from all valuation as well; on the other hand, it preserves the mere *relation* to generally acknowledged values in the sense just indicated. For history as a science, therefore, reality is divided into in-dividuals and in-stances of generic concepts in such a way that even the most radically opposed partisans with their divergent valuations can agree to this conception as held in common.

When we speak in this context of an "ideal" of historical represen-tation, this concept should be guarded from misunderstandings. Like the ideal of the "last natural science," it must also be understood in a *purely logical* sense. In other words, there is no sense in which we claim to impose practical prescriptions on the historian concerning how he *should* proceed. What is at stake here is rather only the question of understanding theoretically what in a scientific representation is purely scientific and what may transcend this. In particular, with the statement of our "ideal," we do not propose to deny that many – or perhaps all – historians *actually* make atheoretical value judgments as well. Finally, it is not our idea to prohibit them from doing this. In that regard we would have little success. We want only to state the following: Although atheoretical valuations, which are always positive or negative, do not belong to the logically *necessary* nature of history as a science, the theoretical relation of objects to values remains *concep-tually* inseparable from every historical representation and does not compromise its scientific status in any way. Thus our distinction between practical valuations and the theoretical value relationship would have to be made in the interest of logic even if it could be shown that the historian actually can *never* manage without practical valuations, or even if a purely theoretical representation of history, which abstains from every atheoretical position, were regarded as unacceptable from the standpoint of the interests of the general, *extrascientific* culture. For the statement of a purely *logical* "ideal" of a value-free historical science, even this circumstance is unimportant.

There is another special reason for emphasizing this point. The dominant *state of mind* concerning questions of *value* changes from time to time. *Logic* must hold itself aloof from such a change of mood, which is not based on theoretical grounds. At times, a general mistrust of *every* sort of value factor in science prevails. Then it is most important to point out the minimum value content without which no historical representation of the individual is *possible*. At other times, however, extrascientific interests intrude so powerfully into the foreground that science is required not *only* to provide theoretical truth but also to "be of service to life." Then something else is important for logic. In other words, then a different disposition concerning value questions can easily gain a foothold. It is obvious that every "vital" person is also a *valuing* person, and that abandoning all extrascientific valuations cannot be of service to "life." Where such life interests predominate, the historian will not want to be denied the right to practical valuations.

With regard to this issue, the primary task of logic is to make clear that every practical valuation introduces a factor into history that is no longer purely scientific. It is obvious, however, that this statement itself should not include a valuation in the sense that it disparages *valuative* history in any way. It is rather the case that here as elsewhere, logic only attempts to achieve theoretical *clarity*, and for this purpose alone it requires the conceptual distinction between valuation and the value relation. On the one hand, logic can show in this way that there is no completely value-free science of history. On the other hand, it can stress just as emphatically that in spite of this, a historical representation free of practical valuations is logically quite *possible*, even though it may not be desirable from the standpoint of the interests of a "vital" culture.

Here the principal issue is the theoretical value relation, and we can also make its indispensability explicit in the following way. We may presuppose as given that history is primarily concerned with *persons*, and that within human life not everything has the same importance for history. That, it will be said, is "self-evident." Of course. But there must also be reasons for this. *Why* does history provide an account of one person and remain silent about another? Intrinsically the individual differences between them are no larger than those between all other things. Unless we differentially stress one thing as essential and ignore another as inessential, every thing of a specific type differs from every other in infinitely many respects. It is only value relations that determine the "magnitude" of individual differences. They alone are responsible for the fact that we take note of the one event and disregard the other. The more we are inclined to pass over this point perfunctorily as something that is self-evident, the more reason logic has to underscore its self-evidence and stress that without the relation to values, individual differences in the historical life of persons would be just as indifferent to us as are differences in the waves of the sea or leaves in the wind.

Any example we might choose shows what is at stake here. If a historian proposes to write a history of the Renaissance or the romantic school, he can certainly form an ideal of historical objectivity in the attainment of which no one would notice whether his political or aesthetic convictions and the valuations linked with them make him sympathetic or unsympathetic to the Renaissance or romanticism, or whether they appear to him as the ultimate flowering of the development of humanity or as stages of its deepest decline. And even if he does not actually reach this ideal, he can at least regard an abstention from a judgment concerning the value of the objects in question as his scientific obligation. The reason is that, as a historian, a scientifically grounded opinion is possible for him only concerning the empirical process, but never concerning its value. And yet values play a decisive role in his work, for he simply would not concern himself with the unique and individual processes called the Renaissance or the romantic school if they did not stand in a relation to political, aesthetic, or other generally acknowledged values by virtue of their individuality. Thus the belief that we could ever maintain an absolutely value-free standpoint in history – in other words, that we could not only avoid practical positive or negative value judgments, but also theoretical value relations – amounts to self-deception.

Everyone will freely admit that history has to represent only the "essential." When the historian does not follow this rule and incorporates inessential matters into his representations, we raise a serious objection against him. But the word "essential" – and the words "interesting," "characteristic," "important," and "significant" as well, which must always be applicable to the historical – loses all specifiable meaning if there is no relation between the objects designated in this way and some sort of value. Fundamentally, therefore, the claim that every object that falls within the domain of history must be related to a value only articulates in *logically useful* terms the quite trivial truth that everything history represents is interesting, characteristic, important, or significant. The interesting, the characteristic, and the important can be good as well as bad, but the question of whether it is good or bad does not have to be considered at all. To this extent, its *valuation* is unimportant. But everything immediately loses the quality of the interesting, the important, and the characteristic when every sort of *relation* to values is terminated. Thus for this reason as well, valuation and the value relationship should be rigorously distinguished.

At this point, let us have another look at the foregoing. The definition of the concept of the historical individual has proceeded in three stages. At first, the historical was the unique and distinctive reality simpliciter, which is always individual in the sense of being singular. This concept was sufficient to clarify the limits of concept formation in natural science. Second, the historical was whatever a volitional being associated with a value, at the same time being a real entity unified in its uniqueness, for example, the Koh-i-noor diamond. Here we became acquainted with the conception of reality characteristic of practical life. Finally, we were able to define the historical individual as the reality that is consolidated for everyone as a singular and unified manifold by means of a purely theoretical relation to a general value – a reality that insofar as it breaks down into essential and inessential aspects from the perspective of this theoretical conception, can also be represented scientifically by history. It is only here that we arrive at the concept that comprehends the historical as the object of the historical *sciences*.

Now, the first two stages of the definition of the concept have no further interest for us. In particular, we must eschew examples such as the Koh-i-noor diamond in order to avoid the misunderstanding that it qualifies as an example of a "historical" individual in the strict sense. The first two stages only form the path on which we gradually attempted to reach the concept of the true historical individual. In the ensuing, when we speak of historical individuals or in-dividuals without further qualification, it is always the concept of the third stage of the definition that is intended.

It is obvious that this concept also remains, for the present, formal; thus in comparison with the substantive concept of history, it is still much too *broad*. Logically, however, the concept of history can now be formulated as follows. It is a science of *reality* insofar as it is concerned with unique, individual realities as such, the only realities of which we have any knowledge at all. It is a *science* of reality insofar as it adopts a standpoint in which we merely consider something, a standpoint that is valid for everyone; thus it is solely by means of a relation to a general value that history constitutes significant or essential individual realities or historical in-dividuals as the object of its representation. It is only owing to this definition that the concept of a science of reality is no longer merely a problem, as it was at the outset, and no longer includes a contradiction, insofar as the real – *exactly* as it exists independent of every conception – does not enter into *any* science.

Perhaps it is not superfluous to point out that linguistic usage is also quite compatible with the three stages of our definition of the concept. *First*, we use the ambiguous word "historical" to designate mere facticity, as was conventional in the linguistic usage of earlier times, in the philosophy of the Enlightenment, for example. Thus when we say that Galileo's frequently cited remark "And yet it moves" is not historical, we mean only that Galileo did not really say this. Here, "historical" has exactly the same meaning as "*real*." Therefore we also understand why all rationalists take a negative view of merely factual truths as truths that are "merely historical." This first sense of the word "historical" was our first concept.

Second, we speak with emphasis of a "historical moment," meaning that an event possesses great significance by virtue of the fact that it is a good to which a value is attached. Indeed, we regard ourselves as important if we are allowed to experience such a historical moment. This significance can arise only by the association with a value that is then transferred to us. Thus the second meaning of the word "historical" coincides with the second stage of our concept.

Third and finally, we say that this or that has "become historical," or better – because this can easily be understood as the negative value judgment that it is antiquated – that it "belongs to history." By this claim, we again intend something different. We want to say that an event of the past no longer has any positive or negative value for contemporary life. Thus it is dissociated from what we want. Some philosophers, for example, wish that Kant would finally become "historical" in this sense. In other words, they want to eliminate him from the philosophical controversy of the present. On the other hand, regardless of how "historical" Kant had become, he would still remain in certain relations to scientific values, and only because of these relations would he belong to history. So we see how the third meaning of the word "historical" coincides with the last concept we were obliged to add to the concept of the individual in order to obtain a concept of the historical individual that is useful to the theory of science.

In short, as regards the three different meanings of the word "historical" – namely, real, significant, and what has been withdrawn from controversy – we can claim that we could take them all into account in the same way or "sublate" them in our concept. This may at least provide a small contribution to the justification of our exposition.

3. VALUE-RELEVANT CONCEPT FORMATION

Now that we know what a historical individual is, the *principle of concept formation in history* will no longer be in doubt, at least as regards the absolutely historical and single individuals that have not yet been drawn into the stream of events, which is all we are concerned with at this point.

What falls under historical concepts is what is set in relief from reality and consolidated as individual unities by means of the purely theoretical relation of an object to generally acknowledged values. No further discussion is needed to show how both the extensively and the intensively infinite manifold are overcome in this way in a manner that differs in principle from the mere description of an arbitrarily selected aspect of reality. Only a small part of the extensive manifold of different configurations falls under historical concepts. In the same way, only a small part of the intensive manifold of a single historical individual forms the essential content of the historical concept. As regards simplification, therefore, the product of this sort of concept formation is analogous to that of natural science. As regards the substantive result of concept formation, however, they are logically antithetical. The concept of natural science comprises what is common to several individual configurations. What belongs to single individuals alone is excluded from the content of the concept itself. When the concept is formed *on the basis* of a single individual reality, however, the historical concept includes precisely what distinguishes the different individuals from one another. Either it completely disregards what is common to them, or it retains this only insofar as that is indispensable to the definition of their individuality. Thus we meet a kind of conceptualization in which the content of science does not become increasingly remote from the individuality of reality, which was the case for the sort of simplification produced by concepts of nature. On the contrary, by its means the content of science is formed in such a way that it expresses the individuality – even if not the perceptuality – of empirical existence.

In order to clarify the sense in which this solves the most general logical problem of historical representation, we must again explicitly note that the principle of value relevance thus obtained serves to surmount both the extensively infinite as well as the intensively infinite manifold of reality. It might be supposed that value relevance comes into play only when specific objects are set off in relief from the *extensive* manifold of things as essential for history. The representation of the *intensive* manifold of the single historical individual, on the other hand, would be independent of the principle of value relevance. As a result, the significance of this principle for concept formation in history would be considerably restricted. We would be obliged to say the following: Although the question of which objects in general are essential does indeed depend on values, this means only that the historian has to discriminate some objects or other from the infinite manifold to represent them historically. His real scientific work would begin only after the selection was made. Under this condition, if the principle of value relevance extends no further than the selection of historically essential objects in general, then it could not be called a principle of historical *concept formation*.

This view is untenable, however. If the principle of value relevance has an important role in historical science, it must be decisive for surmounting both the extensive and the intensive manifold. It is only *because of* the individuality of an intensive manifold that the object in question comes to have importance for the general value. Thus it is only with reference to the individuality of its infinite manifold that the single individual can be differentiated as a historical individual from the infinite multiplicity of other individuals. Therefore the principle of value relevance is just as crucial for the representation of intensively infinite content as it is for the selection of the object in question from the extensive infinity of things and processes in general. . . .

Insofar as the unity of the historical individual is always based on a value relation, it can be called a *teleological* unity, and historical individuals can be called teleological individuals. This is connected with the consideration that the concept of purpose is conceived as the concept of a future *good* that is to be realized. In other words, it is linked with the concept of a value that is attached to it. In consequence, we generally call every way of thinking in which values play a decisive role "teleological." In that case, concept formation in history, which has to conform to this sort of teleological formation of in-dividuals, can also be seen as *teleological*. Accordingly, concept formations in history can be distinguished from those of natural science as teleological *concept formations*. If it were permitted to coin a philologically unjustified term, the historical individual could also be called "what is not to be divided" [*Individuendum*], and concept formation in history could be called the "formation of entities that are not to be divided" [*Individuendenbildung*]. But wherever it is indicated that an individual is understood as a teleological individuality – in other words, an individuality that *is not to be divided* – it will be better to employ the term "in-dividual" [*In-dividuum*], even though it does not express the teleological moment of what *should* not be divided.

Nevertheless, the expression "teleological" certainly arouses suspicions in the minds of many. In particular, whoever makes any reference to teleology in the historical sciences must guard himself against misunderstandings. It is precisely historical teleology that has such a bad reputation, and justifiably so since there is in fact an unscientific historical teleology. Thus we should define precisely the exclusive sense in which value-relevant concept formation can be called "teleological."

It often happens that the concepts "causal" and "teleological" are opposed to each other. In that case, all teleology is regarded as untenable because it seems to be incompatible with the conception of causality. Terminologically, of course, this antithesis is not a particularly happy one. Assuming that the teleological conception is meant to exclude the causal, the difference intended here can consist only in the following. In the causal conception, the effect is conceived as produced by causes that precede it temporally. In the teleological conception, on the other hand, the effect as purpose is supposed to have the capacity to act before it is realized. Thus *both* conceptions are really "causal," for the fact that the effect is regarded as a purpose and is linked with a value makes no difference to causal relations as such. So we should speak of an opposition not between causality and teleology in general but, rather, between two different *kinds* of causality, as this is expressed in the "efficient cause" and "final cause." If we disregard all value perspectives, the final cause remains an *efficient* cause. The difference intended, therefore, consists only in the following: In the teleological conception of causality, the temporal sequence of cause and effect is *reversed*. In other words, in the one case there is a sense in which the cause thrusts the effect forward; in the other case, however, the final objective with which the value is linked – that is, the purpose – has the capacity to draw to itself the means by which it is realized.

Regardless of these considerations, for an empirical conception of reality, it is in fact always the first kind of causal concept alone that is applicable. So in historical science as well, the struggle against *that* form of teleology that amounts to a temporal reversal of the causal relationship insofar as it assumes operative purposes is quite justified. Causes that function before they really exist can never be given to us as historical facts. Thus the question of whether reality is influenced by causes that have the capacity to draw to themselves the material for their own realization cannot arise for a history that qualifies as an empirical science. The problem of a teleological causality in the sense at issue here – assuming that it is a problem at all – belongs rather in metaphysics. We propose to call this kind of teleology – which must take into account causes that lie beyond all empirical reality – *metaphysical teleology*, to place it at a distance from historical science.

And yet a certain reversal of the temporal sequence of cause and effect also seems to obtain when a conscious being has an objective in view and reaches it by his volitionally governed actions. Indeed, perhaps the concept of metaphysical teleology would not have arisen if it could not have been formed in an analogy with processes of this sort. Nevertheless, it is clear that this teleological conception must be distinguished from the metaphysical teleology of causality. It does not require a reversal of the sequence of cause and effect that is inconsistent with an empirical science. The *idea* of the objective, not the objective itself, is operative, and the idea also temporally precedes the intended effect. A teleological process of this sort, therefore, conforms completely to the only concept of causality that is valid for empirical reality.

This sort of teleology is germane to historical science to the extent that it *can* in fact be used to understand historical processes. If things occur that obviously fulfill some purpose, and if this purpose cannot be identified as the motive of an agent, then to explain such events, an inference will be made to the activity of a being whose actions are guided by a conscious and purposive will. This mode of thought can be generalized to all human life; in other words, conscious intentions and purposes will be sought *everywhere*. There have been times when history has done this as well. In that case, it can comprehend the course of historical events only by showing what value historical constructs have for persons. On this basis, it infers that they were always intentionally produced by rational beings who had this value in view. In such a case, therefore, history also proceeds in a fundamentally "teleological" fashion. We propose to call this sort of teleology *rationalistic teleology* because, on this view, historical events are shown to be intended consequences produced by rational and purposive beings. The role this sort of teleology has played in history is well known. Human beings allegedly created language because they needed it for mutual understanding. They supposedly founded the state in order to regulate their lives, arrange matters auspiciously, and so forth. By means of presuppositions of this sort, the content of every historical representation must assume a rationalistic-teleological character.

Do we have this teleology in mind when we speak of a value relevant method of historical science? There is no doubt that the essential aspects of some historical events have been influenced by persons who acted rationally according to conscious purposes. The aim of making rationalistic teleology into the general *principle* of history is quite out of the question, however, because historical individuals in our sense certainly do not always have to be beings that set purposes for themselves and act on them; on the contrary, bodies as well can become historical individuals. Like metaphysical teleology, therefore, rationalistic teleology lies outside our province.

We also have another reason to stress this point. Namely, it can be claimed that the rationalistic teleology of history is "individualistic." Those who see the setting of a conscious purpose and the conduct that follows from it as the motive force of all historical movements, and in consequence regard purpose as the explanatory principle of history, must not only see individual personalities as the chief object of history – because the setting of conscious purposes can be confirmed in them alone; as a result of this, they must also take the view that single individuals *make* history, so that everything becomes a product of individual intention. But we are far from advocating an individualistic conception of history in this sense. If we see the individual as the object of historical representation, this does not mean that we regard individual *wills* as the determining factor in the historical process. On the contrary, it means only that history is concerned with the individual as the unique and the distinctive. As a purely logical claim, this idea remains compatible with the most varied views imaginable as to what the genuinely operative factors in the historical process are. The determination of these factors cannot be the task of logic, but only the task of history itself. At this point there is no sense in which we are concerned with the question of whether the setting of individual purposes ever occurs in the *factual material* of history. Consider the extent to which there are necessary relations of logical significance that obtain between the governing values with reference to which the essential aspects of a historical concept are linked to form a unity and the distinctive characteristics of history that follow from the fact that it is concerned, among other things, with personalities who set purposes. This is, of course, a question that eventually can be posed as well. But it is one of those problems that results from the distinctiveness of the historical *material*. In this context, therefore, we are obliged to disregard it completely.

Thus the "teleological" character of history is not determined by purposes that appear in the historical *material*, but rather by value perspectives with reference to which historical *concepts* are formed. This is why we should not be surprised if nothing of teleological import is to be found in the content of many historical representations and if, as a result, many historians believe that they remain detached from all value relations. In most cases, the elements of the historical concept that cohere with reference to the governing value are simply placed *next to one another*, as if something purely factual were stated. Thus their unity – which consists in the fact that for the historian, they *alone* form what is essential to a process – need not be linguistically expressed at all. Rather, their coherence, which obtains with reference to the value, is exhibited only by the fact that they appear in the representation at all. The mere fact that they are spoken about sets them off as essential. For this reason the logical structure of a historical representation must first be explicitly investigated. Indeed, we should not expect to be able to prove what we have in mind with regard to *every* statement in a historical work. There are historical representations in which the governing value perspectives of concept formation can be discovered only in the context of the whole. In that case, an exhaustive and detailed analysis would be required to identify the value-relevant principle. We only occasionally find passages in historical writings that clearly exhibit, even on superficial examination, what we have in mind here. This will hold true especially when the historian needs to explicitly justify the representation of an event that may perhaps seem inessential to many. In that case the presupposition that is usually taken as self-evident – that only the essential has a place in the representation – must become problematic and explicitly formulated. These cases are exceptional, however. In history, "what matters" is what in this sense is essential or teleologically necessary with reference to the leading value. That is why there is an account of it, but not of other matters. It is in this sense alone that we can say that there has never been a historian who would not proceed in a value-relevant or "teleological" fashion. . . .

In the natural sciences, the validity that is more than empirically general is most clearly exhibited in the possibility of discovering laws of nature. In historical concept formation, we also encounter an analogous problem; namely, the validity of the historical representation must depend on the validity of the values to which historical reality is related. Thus the claim that historical concepts have an unconditionally general validity presupposes the acknowledgment of unconditionally general values. We have shown in detail – and we cannot exaggerate the importance of this point – that this acknowledgment does not imply the possibility of a consensus concerning the *valuation* of historical objects. However, it remains necessary that values in general be acknowledged on which we all – even as scientists – take a position and to which reality must be related. This is the only condition under which its individual, unique course can never be completely indifferent to us, and thus a representation of its individuality can never seem purely arbitrary or superfluous to us.

Therefore it is not sufficient that we rule out purely individual values and designate as the governing principles of a historical representation those values that are common to all members of a certain community. On the contrary, if history is to compete with the kind of general validity that natural science claims in stating laws of nature, we must not only assume that certain values are in fact acknowledged by all the members of certain communities; we must also assume that the acknowledgment of values in general can be required as indispensable for every scientist, and thus that the relation of unique and individual reality to *some* values that have a general validity that is more than empirical is *necessary*. Scientific necessity can be ascribed to a historical representation only under this condition.

We will not consider the question of what is to be understood by the validity of unconditionally general values and how they are connected to the problem of value-relevant concept formation until Chapter 5. We can understand the sense in which the claim of the historical sciences to "objectivity" depends on the validity of unconditionally general values only when the logical structure of the historical sciences has been exhaustively clarified and we are better acquainted with the values that in fact govern concept formation in these sciences. Here our sole purpose was to point out the *problem* in historical science that corresponds to the problem of the supraempirical, unconditional validity of natural laws. In the foregoing, we did not answer the question about the validity of natural laws either. We presupposed without any further basis that it makes sense to make judgments of a generality that is more than empirical. Thus all we showed was the following: In the investigation of reality as nature, a formation of concepts that is more than arbitrary is possible only *if* there are unconditionally general and valid laws. Here too we will limit ourselves to the following claim: An investigation of reality as history that is more than arbitrary is possible if and only if the acknowledgment of the validity of values in general and the relation of individual reality to them cannot appear as arbitrary from any scientific standpoint. The issues of whether and with what justification we may speak of unconditionally general laws of nature, on the one hand, and a scientifically necessary relation of reality to unconditionally general values, on the other, are no longer purely methodological questions.

Of course, we do not deceive ourselves concerning the fact that although the use of unconditionally general values as a scientific presupposition of history encounters the greatest suspicion, the question of whether there is anything such as an unconditionally general law of nature can be regarded as a rather superfluous epistemological speculation. But prejudices of this sort are connected with the one-sided conception of the nature of "science," opposition to which is the goal of this entire investigation. At the outset, at least, an unbiased conception should treat the question of the unconditional validity of values as just as open as the question of the unconditional validity of natural laws. In *both* cases, a supraempirical factor is inescapable. For the present, we can let the matter rest with this statement.

4. THE HISTORICAL NEXUS

Nevertheless, even if we disregard all problems of value, what we have said thus far about the representation of individual realities by history is still not sufficient to define the logical concept of historical science. To articulate the concept of the historical individual in its simplest form, we must first conceive the objects of history as configurations that are not only individual but also – in a certain sense – self-contained and thus *isolated*. But we should not regard the individual or the singular as what is isolated. In the real events of the empirical world, nothing is ever isolated. Not even history as the science of the individual process of empirical reality can be "individualistic" in the sense that it analyzes its material into *isolated* individuals or "gestalts." From the perspective of our presuppositions, isolation would be unhistorical. It is only generalizing conceptualization that is tied to an isolating form of abstraction. In history, it is true that there are descriptions of states that ignore the connection between the objects described and other things and processes, but historical science will not regard its task as exhausted by isolating representations of this sort. On the contrary, its work is done only when it places every object that it considers in the *nexus* in which this object actually exists.

What follows from this for the logic of history? First, it seems that this further step again places in question the correctness of the concept of the historical developed earlier. In opposition to the single historical individuals, the nexus in which they belong must be called *general*. In light of the consideration of this nexus, therefore, does not history cease to be a science of individuals?

Here again, we in fact encounter a "generality," and in addition to the general *elements* of concepts and general values, it is the *third generality* that appears in every history. It can easily be shown, however, that the historical representation of an individual object in its general *historical* nexus and the subsumption of the same object under a general concept of *natural science* are two intellectual formations that have a fundamentally different, even a mutually exclusive, logical significance. The "general" historical nexus is a comprehensive *whole*, and the single individuals are its parts. Generality in the sense of natural science, on the other hand, is the general content of a *concept* under which single individuals are subsumed as *instances*. It should not be necessary to prove that the relationship of the parts to the whole differs from that between the instances and the general concept under which they are subsumed. Whenever the "individual- istic" conception of history is contested with the claim that each individual belongs to a "general" nexus and for this reason the historian must proceed – as the preferred expression has it – in a "collectivistic" fashion, and *thus* on the basis of natural science or generalization, these two relationships are confused with one another. It is not merely the generality of the natural scientific *concept* and the generality of the *value* that we have to distinguish; we must also scrupulously distinguish these two generalities from a third: the generality of the historical *nexus* as the comprehensive historical *whole*. Thus the historical individual considered in the foregoing is always articulated in a historical whole. But there is no sense in which such an articulation coincides with *subsumption* under a general concept or a natural law.

The distinction is so clear and self-evident that we are obliged to ask how confusion on this point was ever possible. It can arise only in the following way. The whole, whose part is the single historical individ- ual, forms a *group* whose parts can all be brought under *one* general concept. In consequence, this whole has the same *name* that is usually used to designate each of its parts. In that event, the whole is called a *class* [*Gattung*]. If a historical individual as a part of such a class is given the general class name, it looks as if it is thereby subsumed under the general class concept. Thus it seems to be comprehended in a natural scientific, generalizing fashion. However, we should not forget that the word "class" [*Gattung*] refers not only to the general concept of natural science, but also to a concrete *plurality of individuals*, and from the fact that something is a part of a concrete class, it does not follow that it can be seen only as an instance of the class concept. On the contrary, the concrete class, the nexus – or however we propose to describe a historical *whole* – is individual and distinctive, just like each of its parts. In other words, it is more comprehensive and extensive, but not conceptually more general, than the single individuals of which it consists. The Italian Renaissance, for example, is just as much a historical individual as Machiavelli, the romantic school just as much as Novalis.

Suppose we want to know whether a part of a whole is considered from the standpoint of what it has in common with other parts of this whole, in which case it becomes essential only as an instance of a general concept; or whether it should be grasped in its individuality, the basis on which it is distinguished from all the other parts of its class. In that event, we will always speak, in the first case, of the *instance* of a class concept and, in the second, of the individual *constituent* of the concrete class or collectivity. For history, therefore, Machiavelli and Novalis are not instances but constituents. Their inclusion in the "general" historical nexus of the Renaissance or romanticism signifies the inclusion of one individual in another more comprehensive individual. That this intellectual operation does not coincide with the subsumption of an object as an instance under a general concept can be doubted only by someone who has not learned to distinguish the general *content* of a concept from its general *extension*. That should pose difficulties only for beginning students in logic – even though their number is not inconsiderable among the "modern" theoreticians of history who propose to make history into a natural science.

They should take note of the following. The content of a concept is general because it comprises what is common to a plurality of individuals, or because it applies to an indefinite plurality of individuals. Its extension is general because it comprehends *all* members of a plurality of individuals in an individual nexus or whole. Thus if history is obliged to consider every historical object as a constituent of a "general" – in other words, a relatively comprehensive – nexus, this does not mean that the historian no longer proceeds in an individualizing fashion. He represents even the "general nexus" as an individual and unique construct. Insofar as the whole or the collectivity is relevant to history as a unique and individual reality, there is no *logical* opposition between the individualizing historical method, as we understand it, and the only kind of historical method that can be regarded as "collectivistic." . . .

In short, we see that the principles of historical conceptualization are not altered by the inclusion of the single individual in the general – that is, more comprehensive, but in other respects still individual – nexus. Since the relationship of the part to the whole remains relative, it cannot be otherwise. In other words, every extensive manifold of parts can also be conceived as an intensive manifold, and thus every individual must be conceived both as a constituent of a whole and also as a whole that has its own constituents.

Precisely for this reason, however, one point seems to pose difficulties. If we place every individual within a new whole, ultimately we must reach a whole that no longer belongs to a nexus that is even more comprehensive. This "ultimate whole," therefore, would necessarily have to be an isolated entity – in other words, something whose existence history does not admit. In fact, however, this poses no new problem for us. From a logical standpoint, the ultimate historical whole would be the actual universe. As long as there was a "universal

history" in the true sense of the word, as was the case during the
Middle Ages, its most comprehensive nexus, which lay between the
Creation and the Last Judgment, in fact had to be an isolated
individual. The world as a whole was bounded by nothingness or the
nonworld. But we no longer regard the real "cosmos" as an object of
possible experience. As we could show, there is not even a generalizing science of the cosmos as a whole. Thus this concept no longer has
any significance for a logic of history. Of course, it is always true that
the "ultimate" *historical* whole can be placed as a constituent in a more
extensive nexus, which actually is an individual as well. But in the final
analysis, this more comprehensive nexus can no longer have significance as a whole, but only through the uniqueness of one of its parts.
In consequence, it possesses historical individuality only in this
respect. Therefore, its other parts come into question only as instances of natural scientific concepts, in the way we have already
shown. If we consider the cosmos in the strict sense, natural science
has to form concepts of it, but only in the sense that these concepts are
valid for all of its aspects. History, on the other hand, underscores one
of its aspects, because of the significance the individuality of this
aspect has with reference to values. In this aspect, history sees the
ultimate whole with which, as history, it is still concerned. Therefore,
this aspect of the cosmos, conceived in an individualizing fashion by
means of value relevance, is the "ultimate" or the most comprehensive
historical nexus conceivable.

To make this quite clear, suppose we attempt to elucidate the concept of the ultimate historical whole and the relations between the
historical constituent and the historical nexus with some examples. We
begin with a historical personality. It is an individual whole and at the
same time an individual constituent, an extensive as well as an intensive
historical manifold. It forms a unified whole insofar as it comprehends
everything that is historically significant to it. Each of its acts and every
aspect of its fate are individual. Insofar as its acts and its fate are
historical individuals, the personality is constituted for history by its
acts and its fate as its parts. These parts unite in the personality to form
a unity with reference to the significance the personality as a whole
possesses for the governing value. At the same time, however, such a
personality is a constituent of a more extended whole – a family, a
generation, a people, an age – to which it is related in the same way
that each of its parts is related to it. This is because each of the more
comprehensive nexuses can also be seen as a unified individual whose
components are formed by personalities, families, or peoples that
belong to it as its essential constituents. This whole, then, is included
in a still more comprehensive individual whole, and so on, and so on.

In the final analysis, the ultimate historical whole can be the culture of humanity, or humanity itself. In that case, the culture of humanity would be a constituent of humanity. The latter, however, would also be a constituent of the organic world. Or does the organic world form a historical individual as well? In other words, among its parts, is it not merely humanity that is conceived as a historical individual? On the contrary, can its other parts also be regarded as historical individuals? Finally, can the limit perhaps be extended further still? Can our planet qualify as a historical individual, and is it the ultimate historical whole? Or must it be seen as a constituent of a more comprehensive nexus, the solar system, and is it only the latter in which we would have the most comprehensive, "ultimate" historical individual? In any case, we have to stop with the solar system. This is because we know too little of the other parts of the whole of which it is a constituent in order for them to become historically significant on the basis of their individuality as well. For the present, at any rate, they come into question only as instances of general concepts. This is logically fortuitous, however, for without knowledge of the content of the governing values of the selection, the concept of the ultimate historical whole cannot be substantively defined. Here it is essential to note only that at some point, the most comprehensive historical whole is included in a still more extensive nexus that is no longer a historical individual. On the contrary, its other parts are of interest only for a generalizing science.

For the rest, the chief purpose of our reflections was to show how historical science, even when it links its objects to the "most general" – that is, most comprehensive – cosmic nexuses, still does not cease to be a science of the individual, the unique, and the specific. . . .

5. HISTORICAL DEVELOPMENT

In another respect, the idea of the causal nexus is even more important.[8] We need only recall a famous saying of Schopenhauer's, that causality is not a taxi we can halt at will, for it to seem that the firm bond the theoretical relation to a value imposes on a process, thereby consolidating it into a necessary unity, is again broken. Every individual cause we ascertain is itself an individual effect that also has

---

[8][In the foregoing part of section 5 that is not translated here, Rickert distinguishes seven different concepts of development. His aim is to identify the concept of historical development required by his idea of historical individuals that are connected in a causal nexus.]

its own individual cause. If we consider that no historical object would be as it is without the individual character of another individual cause, then the relation to the value that constitutes a process as a historical development is transposed onto the individual configuration of events that is causally connected with this process, even though the content of this configuration need not be essential or significant for the value. Then it is first of all the case that every developmental sequence must be traced into the past. And second, it seems that if our requirement of causality is to be satisfied, every developmental sequence must be extended not only longitudinally but also laterally, for every stage of a historical process is causally determined both by past events and by events that are contemporaneous with it.

Thus we will have to introduce another new concept to completely understand the logical structure of the representation of historical developmental sequences. Indeed, it is necessary to distinguish two kinds of historical in-dividuals. The first has a direct relation to the governing value, the second an indirect relation *mediated* by the causal nexus. As a result, we can speak of *primary* and *secondary* historical individuals.

It will not always be easy to specify in detail which historical objects belong to one kind and which to the other. It can happen that an individual with a primary historical significance from one governing value perspective has only a secondary historical significance – or no historical significance at all – from another perspective. Friedrich Wilhelm I, for example, can have only a secondary interest for the history of *philosophy*, insofar as he influenced the destiny of Christian Wolff. For the *political* history of Prussia, on the other hand, he can be an eminently primary historical individual. There are only a few individuals who can be claimed to have a primary historical significance from every perspective, but there are many of whom it can be said that there is no perspective from which they have a primary historical significance. For example, Schiller's father is considered only in the history of German literature, and here he can be regarded only as a secondary historical individual, in other words, as a man who would have no interest for us had he not been Schiller's father. In any case, the division of primary and secondary historical individuals is conceptually clear as soon as we set down the following. For a given governing value perspective, one kind of object is consolidated as a historical in-dividual directly as a result of the peculiar character of the content of its manifold. In the case of the other kind of object, the historical interest in it arises only by means of the intermediate link of the causal connection that obtains between it and the directly essential or primary historical individual. . . .

6. THE NATURAL SCIENTIFIC COMPONENTS OF
THE HISTORICAL SCIENCES

The foregoing analyses were intended to work out the difference
between historical and natural scientific concept formation as rigorously as possible. Thus attention was focused on what we call the
absolutely historical. In consequence, it was necessary for us to exaggerate the logical opposition of natural science and history, in other
words, to set up a logical ideal to which science, in part, cannot even
aspire. We know, however, that such an "exaggeration" belongs to the
methodical principles of our investigation, and it is harmless as long
as the necessary restrictions are not absent. Thus the restrictions that
follow should not be regarded as "concessions" that would again
weaken the clearly articulated logical principle. Now the point is
rather to show how the logical principle takes shape when *applied* to
the actual *praxis* of science. Its application would not be possible had
we not previously overstated the principle in working it out in its pure
state.

The reason why the concepts developed earlier require further
determination in order to be employed for the understanding of
historical science as it actually exists should be clear from the
foregoing analyses. When we set up the most general form of the
opposition of natural science and history by means of the difference
between the general and the individual, we saw the extent to which
the different parts of natural science form more or less general
concepts and thus, in our terminology, also exhibit components that
are more or less historical. As a result, the concept of nature became
relative.[9] Because the purely logical concepts of nature and history
are interdefinable, it follows that just as there are historical components in natural science, so there are natural scientific components in
history. Thus the concept of the historical must become relative as
well. But as long as the concept of historical *representation* remained
purely problematic, we could only allude to this consequence without
saying exactly what should be understood by a *concept* that is relatively
historical. Now that we are acquainted with the principle of historical
concept formation in its most general form as individualizing value
relevance, we have to define it in such a way that it can be applied to

[9][This refers to the discussion in chapter 3, section 3 (*Die Grenzen*, pp. 237–258),
which is not included in the translation. Here Rickert argues that the extent to
which concept formation in natural science abstracts from the perceptual and
individual properties of reality is a matter of degree. This means that there are
historical components of the various natural sciences, for example, a historical
biology or a natural history of the organic world, as well as a natural science of
biology.]

the relatively historical. Only then will it be possible to understand the logical structure of the historical science that actually exists, for there is no historical representation that employs concepts that are only absolutely historical. . . .

We arrive at the problem that concerns us here only when a concept with a content that is general in the sense of natural science also produces an exhaustive historical representation, or when *generalization* is also capable of *individualization* in such a way that nothing which is historically essential with reference to value relevance is lost. This will always be the case where historical meaning attaches to a complex of characteristics that occur not only in a single real object but also in several individuals that otherwise are quite different from one another. Then these individuals not only comprise a group; a group concept can also suffice for their historical representation. As always, the group as a *whole* is unique and individual, consisting of nothing but individuals. But since none of these individuals exhibit historically essential characteristics that are not also shared by all the other individuals that belong to the group, history need not form an absolute historical concept of such a historical whole. In other words, it need not represent its individual parts for their own sake. On the contrary, in such a case, the historian too sees the individuals that make up the group as *equivalent*. By virtue of these same characteristics, every individual is both a member of a historical whole as well as an instance of a general concept. As a result, individualizing historical concepts are formed by means of value relevance. And yet they have a general content: In other words, they comprehend what is common to *all* the individuals of a group. This common feature is, then, what is essential with reference to the governing value of the representation, and it also adequately exhibits the individuality of the group. . . .

At this point, suppose we take a look back. The logical distinctiveness of an empirical science is to be understood in terms of the relationship the content of its concepts bears to empirical reality in its unique and distinctive form. The fundamental difference between natural science and history is that natural science forms concepts with a general content, whereas history forms concepts with an individual content. Or, the former generalizes and the latter individualizes. But this does not mean that the particular has *no* significance for natural science and the general *no* significance for historical science. Not only are the concepts of the general and the particular relative, but no science at all is possible without general concepts. Nevertheless, the vague formulation that history requires the "general" says little about its method of concept formation. Moreover, there is certainly no sense in which the idea of a universal method based on natural science can be justified in this way. First, the "general" does not always refer to a concept with general content. And even in the case of general concepts, what is important is the position they occupy in the totality of a science and the principle that consolidates their elements into a unity.

Above all, we must distinguish the following four kinds of generality in history.

First, the *elements* of all scientific concepts are general. Only natural science forms from these elements concepts that themselves have a general content. History forms from them concepts with individual content.

Second, history cannot represent all individuals, but only those that are essential with reference to a *general value*. Nevertheless the relevance to this value does not make the content of concepts general. On the contrary, the general significance of historical objects attaches precisely to their individuality.

Third, historical science never regards individuals in isolation, as the generalizing sciences do, but in a *general nexus*. Again, this is not a concept with a general content, but rather an individual reality. The incorporation of an individual into the "general" whole to which it belongs cannot be confused with its subsumption under a general generic concept. In the last two cases, therefore, we cannot even speak of natural scientific components within a historical nexus of ideas.

Only in the fourth and last case, when history comprehends a *group* of individuals so that each qualifies as equally significant, does history form concepts with a general content. But even in this case, it does not employ a natural scientific *method*, for concepts that are relatively historical do not have the purpose of articulating the "general nature" of the objects subsumed under them. Their content is intended rather to represent the historical individuality of a group of objects that all become historically essential by means of the same characteristics. Thus they are "historical" concepts – in other words, formed in an individualizing fashion through value relevance – not only because their general content, in comparison with an entity even more general, is particular and is regarded explicitly with reference to this particularity, but also because precisely these and no other components are linked by means of a "teleological" principle to form a unity, as a result of which the conceptual elements are connected in a *coherent* fashion.

In view of the foregoing, it should be clear what we mean both by natural scientific components in history and by relatively historical concepts. We should emphatically reiterate that these amplifications

of the concept of the historical as we first set it up are indispensable
to the logic of the historical sciences. It would never occur to us to
maintain that natural science is concerned *only* with the general and
history *only* with the individual. Even a cursory glance at representations in natural science and history shows that this would be mistaken.
Natural science always proceeds from the unique and the individual,
and history is continually in need of general group concepts. The only
point was to show what significance the general and the individual
have in the natural sciences and the historical sciences. However, a
logic of the sciences will never ignore the fact that in *all* scientific
disciplines, the general and the particular are *connected* with each
other in the most intimate fashion. . . .

7. HISTORICAL SCIENCE AND MENTAL LIFE

Nevertheless, we have still not finished.[10] In addition to logical and
formal differences, there are *material* differences that no one will
deny, and logic must obviously be concerned with them as well. In
fact, the theory of historical science will be *complete* only by examining
both principles of differentiation. We know why we were obliged to

[10][In the two paragraphs immediately preceding section 7, Rickert makes the
   following observations: "Thus we come to the following result. It is not only the
   case that in our prescientific forms of knowledge there are two conceptions of
   reality that are different in principle, the generalizing and the individualizing.
   Corresponding to them, there are also two forms of the scientific treatment of
   reality. In their ultimate objectives as well as their final results, they differ from
   one another logically and in principle. That should not be understood as the
   principle for the *real division* of scientific labor. A logical classification or
   articulation is not a real division. The *formal* opposition of nature and history
   cannot and should not serve as the actual division. This is because the latter is
   linked with *substantive* differences in the material, not with logical differences.
   Here we are concerned only with the conceptual differentiation of two different
   general orientations in the sciences that quite often, or even always, may actually
   function conjointly. But their conceptual differentiation would still be necessary
   even if, with respect to their ultimate *objectives*, two kinds of scientific
   conceptualization could not be distinguished from each other in the way we have
   shown. Even if no science is possible without the help of the general, the
   fundamental logical difference between natural science and historical science
   remains unaffected, in spite of all the relativity of natural scientific and historical
   concepts. In both disciplines, the path sometimes moves through the particular, at
   other times through the general, and the general is always employed as an
   instrument. But the goal of one discipline is the representation of the more or less
   general; the goal of the other, the representation of the more or less individual.
   All borderline cases and intermediate forms can alter nothing with regard to the
   logical opposition between these two *orientations*.
      With these considerations, we can conclude our investigation of the *purely logical*
   forms of historical science and their relation to those of natural science."]

begin with purely logical oppositions. Now that we are acquainted with them and have developed the differential logical structure of conceptualization in both history and natural science, we are compelled to consider the question of whether and to what extent a methodologically significant *connection* between the *formal* and the *material* differences of the sciences is demonstrable. Only by answering this question can we obtain a *substantive* concept of history that must be more limited than the previously established formal concept and that we can eventually link with what is generally understood by a "historical science."

We now turn to this new problem. Suppose that on the basis of the logical distinctions developed in the foregoing, we now show that the actually existing material differences between the sciences – which we intentionally disregarded at first and which are usually employed to distinguish the sciences from one another – can also be understood as logically necessary. This demonstration does not signify a softening of our position; nor does it even represent a "concession" to the usual way of proceeding in these problems, which is not rigorously logical. On the contrary, it forms the necessary conclusion of our logical theory, its real *confirmation* and culmination. This is because it is only by considering material differences that we can show how our logical concepts can be made *fruitful* for the entire theory of science. As regards the opposition of formal and material – and this point must always be stressed – it is a question not of "either/or" but of "both/and." To give precedence to form, as we were obliged to do, is not to *ignore* content completely.

We have already considered the material differences between objects in the distinction between nature and "spirit." This distinction becomes most obvious in the consideration that history is in fact primarily concerned with *mental* or *psychic* processes. Of course, if one takes the "materialistic" philosophy of history seriously, it might seem as if this were placed in doubt. In truth, however, this doctrine has virtually nothing to do with the question of whether historical objects are psychic or physical. Even if it were true that all historical movements are determined by "material" interests – in other words, by the aspiration for things that preserve and advance corporeal existence – *endeavors* oriented to "material" goods remain volitional acts, and thus mental processes. A "materialist" history is concerned with them as well. Thus we are obliged to pose the following question: How is the fact that the material of history is *mental life* – even if not exclusively, but at least in part, and often primarily – relevant to the logical structure of historical conceptualization?

The first and most general concept of the historical had its source in the concept of the limits of the natural sciences. This is why, from a logical point of view, we were obliged to reject "human science" as the name for history. In addition, value-relevant and individualizing conceptualization also seemed indifferent to the distinction between mind and body. The *first* concept of the historical individual was even developed by comparing two material objects and was then applied to mental individuals without requiring the addition of anything new in principle. In the further course of our investigation, we were also able to develop logical principles without considering the substantive characteristics of the psychic. When reference to examples made the discussion of human mental life unavoidable, a concept formed in this way was still not *exclusively* applicable to representations of psychic existence. We must now, however, attend to the fact that most historical sciences are predominantly concerned with mental processes. This raises two questions of logical importance.

From this fact, can we perhaps derive further previously unnoticed distinctive logical features of the historical method that would force on us another definition of the concept of historical science? And, assuming that this question is to be answered in the negative, is the predominance of the psychic in the material of history quite arbitrary methodologically, or can it be understood on the basis of the logical nature of historical conceptualization? The second question is not resolved with the first. Even if further logical properties specific to historical representation cannot be established on the basis of the concept of the psychic, it is still possible that mental life has properties as a result of which it *requires* a historical representation by means of a value-relevant, individualizing conceptualization to a greater extent than holds true for physical existence.

Even if we begin by contesting the view that completely new logical *principles* definitive for historical representation can be established on the basis of the concept of real psychic existence, this does not mean that we overlook the fact that a fundamental difference obtains in the *investigation* of mental and corporeal material and that this difference would have to be taken into account by the parts of methodology concerned with the determination and the *critical analysis* of the *factual material* of history. Bodies are immediately given to us all through sense perception. As regards the totality of psychic processes, on the other hand, our direct knowledge based on sense perception is limited to our own mental life. In representing a real mental process, therefore, the historian lacks access to the object of immediate experience. However, does anything of significance for establishing the logical ideal of a historical *representation* follow from this?

We know why the difference between the physical and the psychic just mentioned implies no fundamental methodological differences for the natural scientific or generalizing mode of analysis. A natural scientific concept never attempts to comprehend the individuality of an object. This is why the psychologist who generalizes on the basis of his own directly accessible mental life can develop material for the formation of concepts that are valid for *all* psychic existence. At most, the inaccessibility of third-person mental life, as a result of which it cannot be directly experienced, creates difficulties for this psychologist in that he cannot bracket the individual on the basis of a direct comparison. On the contrary, it is often only by means of a complicated chain of inferences that he learns whether this or that psychic characteristic is generally distributed or purely individual. In historical conceptualization, on the other hand, are matters not fundamentally different? It is precisely from the perspective of its individual qualities that the historian represents third-person mental life. Thus he is concerned with what is inaccessible to immediate observation under all conditions. This is why it seems that the historical representation of psychic processes is actually linked with difficulties that differ in principle from those that would be posed by the representation of directly observable bodies. In the final analysis, therefore, does not the concept of "human science" [*Geisteswissenschaft*] acquire a fundamental logical significance, even if – or precisely if – what we understand by "mind" [*Geist*] is nothing other than the temporal course of real mental existence?

Because this question is of interest for us only insofar as it bears on the problem of whether additional essential *logical* modifications should be introduced into the opposition developed earlier, between generalizing and individualizing conceptualization, our answer can be negative. Consider the difficulties posed for the historian by the inaccessibility of third-person mental life. Disregarding the importance they acquire for the process of research and *investigation* – which is irrelevant to our inquiry – they are essentially included among the factors that follow from the disparity between source material and factual material that is necessary to all history. *Logically*, therefore, they signify nothing more than the *incompleteness* of the factual material of history, which can almost always be confirmed. It is true that the historian needs the capacity – as this is often put – to "place himself in" the mental life of another person or to "recreate" other individualities in his own experience. In this case, he practices a variety of theoretical activity known neither to the physical scientist nor to the generalizing psychologist. This activity, of course, poses interesting problems concerning the mutual "understanding" of individuals. But this consideration does not show that the distinctiveness of so-called historical understanding has any importance in principle for the *logical* structure of historical *representation*, which is our only concern here. . . .

Thus we only have to answer the other question. Can the fact that psychic realities are more frequently represented in the unique and individual development than holds true for corporeal realities be understood on the basis of the logical nature of historical conceptualization, or must this remain logically fortuitous?[11]

But, so it will be asked, can we even pose such a question in light of the foregoing considerations? Suppose that the distinction between the physical and the psychic that is necessary to the natural scientific interest is unimportant for history. And suppose that the concept of the spiritual that history would have to form in order to retain the concept of a unified world that can be represented historically remains undefined. In that case, does the claim that history is primarily concerned with "spiritual" or "mental" processes qualify as an unequivocal proposition? Is it not rather the case that without a *line of demarcation* between the physical and the psychic – and one that is also acknowledged by history – our question about the basis of the privileged status of mental life loses its sense?

This is in fact the case. Even if we ignore this point and provisionally propose to retain the natural scientific distinction between the physical and the psychic, it would immediately be clear that we could never understand why that which falls under the concept of what occupies space should be less significant for a historical representation than that which does not occupy space, which holds true for everything that is psychic. As regards the psychic in this sense, an individualizing representation can be no more necessary than it is for the physical. Thus we must try to identify a distinction between body and "spirit" that differs from the one usually employed in the generalizing sciences. Only in this way can we hope to understand why it is actually the case that mental life is more often represented in an individualizing historical fashion than holds true for corporeal existence.

If we begin with empirical reality that has not yet been analyzed by natural science, we can clearly differentiate in it processes in which a way of acting on the basis of alternatives is expressed – in other words,

---

[11]Not infrequently, the following exposition, which develops the concept of the "historical center," has been virtually ignored in the criticism of my views (recently, this holds true even for Troeltsch). For this reason, I should like to point out that it is of *decisive* importance for my *total conception* of history. Without it, what I understand and mean by "history" in the *stricter* sense – that is, the sense that is *more* than formal-logical – remains unintelligible.

acknowledgment or refusal, approval or disapproval, desire or abhor-rence, affirmation or denial: in short, *taking a position on a value* – from processes that are indifferent to all values. This difference is of fundamental significance for us in the following respect: Without encountering a contradiction, we will always characterize all realities that – in the sense just indicated – take a position or valuate only as mental processes, and never as corporeal processes. The converse of this proposition is, of course, not true: The act of valuating cannot be ascribed to everything that qualifies as mental or psychic. If, for example, we claim that we only "conceive" something, we exclude valuating from mental life but include conceiving. So there may be much more in the domain of real existence that does not valuate, and yet still should be included in mental life. In consequence, this concept of the mental would be too narrow. It is sufficient, however, if the only point is to know what *always* qualifies as mental – and thus not corporeal – with a view to posing an unambiguous question about the relationship between mental life and history.

In these considerations, we even have an indication of the direction in which the question must be answered. Since the concept of value is connected with the concept of the historical in such a way that the only reality represented historically is reality as related to a value, and since the concept of the mental is linked with the concept of value in such a way that only mental beings[12] are valuating beings, then *the concept of value also establishes the relationship between the mental and the historical.* Moreover, the value-relevant moment of historical conceptualization must make it clear why real mental life stands in a different and more intimate relationship to historical science than does real corporeal existence. So from the *formal* concept of historical method, we finally arrive at the *substantive* character of the historical *material*.

Of course these remarks alone do not yet say very much about the nature of such a relationship. In the first place, it seems that the objects of history are connected with a psychic existence insofar as they are objects for a *subject* that distinguishes their essential from their inessential aspects with reference to a value. It could be shown that even the scientific subject must take a position and valuate; thus it must also be a mental being in the sense explained. Even though this consideration is quite important for the objectivity of the sciences, there is *no* science that lacks such a relationship of its objects to a mental being that forms concepts. If this fact were decisive for the methodical character of a scientific representation, natural science

[12] *[Seelische Wesen:* This expression, which is used repeatedly throughout chapter 4, section 7, designates a creature that has a mind, or a being to which the mental acts of willing, thinking, judging, valuing, and so on can be ascribed.]

would also have to be described as a human science [*Geisteswissenschaft*] on the grounds that it is also inconceivable without a "mind" [*Geist*] that distinguishes the essential from the inessential. So if our purpose is to discover the special connection that obtains between historical method and mental life, we should begin by completely disregarding the cognitive *subject* of science and concern ourselves exclusively with the *objects* of history. In other words, we should consider only the question of why it is primarily real mental existence that is found in the *factual material* of history.

In every case in which reality is related to a value, the objects wi which we are acquainted fall into two fundamentally different class those for which this relationship is merely possible, and those that r only *signify* something for the value by virtue of their existence also *take a position on this value*. Objects belonging to the first class be mental as well as corporeal. Objects of the second class, on other hand, which are essential because of the position they tak the value, are necessarily mental. We should consider this point

Suppose that in an empirical reality to be represented individualizing fashion or in the factual material of history, were such beings who also take a position on the values that g their individualizing representation. In that case, these beings have to occupy the *central focus* of the material represented. In words, all other objects would not only qualify as historically ess insofar as they become historical individuals with reference governing values of the *subject* of the scientific representation – t the historian; they would also qualify as historically essential inso their individuality has a significance for the real mental *objects* volitions and actions are represented. Thus history would link other objects to the governing values of the representation, and i would connect them with the mental beings represented, the be that take a position, valuate, and are present in the *material* of his

In this way, a concept of historical representation more *limited* the previous concept is developed. As long as we did not reflect specific historical material, we were concerned solely with *one* kin historical object. But if we presuppose mental objects of the kind indicated, or historical personalities that *valuate*, they must be dis guished from other objects. In particular, all bodies in such representation become essential only in the following way: becaus what links them to the governing values of the cognitive *subject*, historian, as well as because of the way they influence the volitio and valuational *objects* – that is, the mental processes of the histor personalities represented – or because of the manner in which th are the object of the volitions and actions of these personaliti

Consider, for example, a history of Italy that is governed by the perspective of the value attached to art. Here it must above all be the volitions and actions of *artists* that are essential. It is their individuality that is significant from the standpoint of the governing value, and all other real existence will be connected to this *mental* phenomenon of volition and action.

In order to make the paramount significance of mental beings within the historical material explicit, we propose to designate as *historical centers* all historical objects that themselves take a position on the governing values of the representation and that must always be mental entities. Then we will see that if such centers are present in the material of the representation, history necessarily relates everything else to them. According to the foregoing, however, it is only *possible* that there are such centers in the material of history. Even by this point, therefore, our concept of history remains *substantively* undefined. Indeed, in light of the foregoing exposition, it does *not* seem necessary that such mental entities are *always* present in the historical material. Finally, it is not clear why these entities have to take a position concerning precisely *those* values that govern the historical representation. In other words, it is not clear why they are always historical centers. Thus we must move beyond the mere possibility, which is all we have established up to this point, and show why some sort of mental life *necessarily* belongs to all historical material.

This will be managed without difficulty as soon as we consider the only conditions under which a reality can *give us occasion* to represent it in an individualizing fashion, and when we further reflect that not every arbitrary value can become the governing perspective of a historical representation. The results of this consideration will then be, first, that every historical object must be related not only to values in general but also to a real valuating – and thus mental – entity; second, that the presence of these mental entities in the material of history is not logically fortuitous; and, third, that we have occasion to represent a reality in a historical or individualizing fashion only under the following condition: Among these mental entities, there are some that themselves take a position on the governing values of the representation. In consequence, there is in fact *no historical representation without a real mental center.*

At this point, we do not need to show why an explicit justification of this fact – which is probably self-evident to every historian – is not superfluous from the standpoint of methodology. This is the only way it is possible to understand the logical structure of the historical "human sciences." Finally, it is also the only way we can see why the concept of the human sciences has been so tenaciously held to be important for methodology.[13]

In regard to the necessary relationship of every historical object to a valuing mental being, we will return once more to the prescientific conception of reality characteristic of practical life, from which our definition of the concept of the historical individual began. The agreement between historical conceptualization and the prescientific conceptualization of the active and volitional person consisted in the fact that for both, the individuality of things acquires significance. The fundamental difference between the two lay in the fact that the historian does not take a volitional and valuational position on things, but rather relates them to a value by considering them theoretically. Thus although historical objects are also detached from every valuating, volitional, and active being in the sense that they can no longer be objects of a direct valuation, the values to which they are related cannot – as this might be put – "remain suspended in space." In other words, they cannot merely "hold validly" as "pure" values. On the contrary, if we are concerned with a *historical* science of reality, they must be values appraised by a real volitional, valuating – and thus also mental – being. But this implies that to qualify as the object of a historical individualizing representation, an entity must not only stand in a general logical relationship to values, but must also have a *real* connection to an actual valuating being. It follows that there is a certain sense in which the concept of a psychological life and the concept of a historical individual that is conceived in a value-relevant fashion are inseparable.[14]

This insight is not sufficient for our purpose, however. Valuating mental beings always appear as mental beings in the historical *material* as well. It seems that the preceding considerations have not yet made this understandable. To demonstrate the extent to which this is

[13]In view of this statement of the problem and the ensuing attempt to solve it, I cannot understand how Bernheim (*Lehrbuch der historischen Methode*, 5th and 6th eds., p. 3) can maintain that I "did not adequately recognize the logical connection between the historical object and the principle of the historical mode of thought." I think, rather, that precisely the *logical* connection between human science [*Geisteswissenschaft*] and historical science – as well as the logical connection between cultural science and historical science considered in the next section – is clarified for the first time in this book. That is because it could be understood only on the basis of insight into the value-relevant character of individualizing conceptualization. I must also stress this point in opposition to critics such as Troeltsch, in order to repudiate the view that I was concerned *only* with formal differences. The contrary is the case. I have considered material differences just as scrupulously as the formal. It was only necessary that I *begin* with formal differences since it is a *logic* of the historical sciences that is presented here.

[14]This will be shown more precisely in section 9.

necessary, we should not reflect on a representation that is restricted to a *part* of a historical development. On the contrary, we must consider the most comprehensive historical nexus or the "ultimate historical whole," as we have called it: the whole that still possesses a historical individuality for the governing value perspectives of the representation, and to which all objects, which are merely its parts, can be interrelated as constituents. For example, one might think that historical biology is not at all concerned with mental life. But that holds only as long as we confine ourselves to one of its aspects. The historical whole of biological development includes man – insofar as he represents its "peak" – as a mental entity too. Otherwise we could not speak of "progress." And, as we have seen, the entire sequence must be related to man to qualify as a *historical* "development."[15] In the same way, psychic realities, with which all historical individuals must be brought into a real connection, also belong to every historical whole. Thus it follows that in a comprehensive historical whole, all historical objects stand in some sort of historical connection with mental entities.

There is, of course, a special case that creates difficulties in this context. The real mental being to which historical development is related – and that, in consequence, necessarily belongs to the real historical nexus as a constituent – may possibly be a *single* individual, namely, the historian. This seems to be an exception to the foregoing position, which requires that we abstract from the cognitive subject. But suppose we examine this case more closely. If no mental entity other than the historian is present in the historical material to be represented, the historian comes into question not *only* as a cognitive subject but also as an *object* in a historical nexus with the other individuals. As a constituent, therefore, he is necessarily incorporated into the most comprehensive object of historical representation, or the whole of the value-relevant sequence of development. This entails that in the ultimate historical whole, there is always at least *one* mental entity.

Finally, why should this mental entity always constitute the historical *center* as well? When the historian himself is not only the cognitive subject, but must also be included in the most comprehensive historical nexus of the objects represented, the answer to this question is obvious. This is because the governing values of the representation are necessarily those on which the historian takes a value position. We have mentioned this possibility only to show that there is *no* conceiv-

[15][This thesis is defended in Rickert's discussion of concepts of historical development (*Die Grenzen*, chapter 4, section 5), material that is not included in the translation.]

able case in which a mental entity fails to appear in the historical material. In fact, the historian almost always represents developmental sequences to which he himself does not belong as a historical constituent, sequences in which only other mental entities are present. Why should these mental entities include those who themselves take a value position on precisely the values that govern the historical representation?

This is in fact the decisive issue. Here too, however, the answer is not difficult. Suppose that the values of the narrator himself, on which he takes a value position, are not held by any of the mental beings that belong to the most comprehensive historical nexus. Nevertheless, to understand these beings, he must at least be able to "get the feel" of their values. This is because whenever a reality stands in no relationship either to us or to valuing beings whom we can understand, we will see that reality solely as "nature." That is, in science, we will try to subsume it under a system of general concepts. For a historical representation, this leaves only two possibilities open. On the one hand, the values of the mental beings that belong to the historical material are the same values with reference to which historical individuals are formed for the narrator as well. In that case, the matter is simple, for it is self-evident that these "spiritual" beings will also be historical centers. In a history of art, for example, the value of art with reference to which historical concepts are formed for the historian is the same value on which artists take a real value position. Thus the artists in question must necessarily become historical centers. Or, on the other hand, the values of the mental beings are not those of the narrator, as will be the case for events that are spatially or temporally remote from him. Then he must get the feel of these mental beings to the extent of being able to understand them. As a result, suppose that the unique and individual actions and passions of these valuating mental beings have become interesting to him. In that case, as long as he conceives these mental entities in a strictly historical fashion – in other words, as long as he proposes only to relate them to values theoretically – he can do no more than the following: In distinguishing the essential from the inessential in a representation of these beings based on value relevance, he is obliged to employ the values on which they take a real value position. This is because it would make sense to employ for concept formation values totally different from those found in the historical material itself only if the objects were not to be represented historically in a value-relevant fashion on the basis of a standard of value but were, rather, to be valuated. And we know that this cannot be the task of the historian who proceeds in an "objectively" scientific way.

So at least as regards those historical representations that are fundamentally restricted to a theoretical value relationship, and thus in no sense take a practical or extratheoretical value position as well, it is clear why we cannot speak of a purely fortuitous coincidence between *those* values that govern the representation and those that determine the valuative conduct of the mental beings represented. In a representation that is purely scientific in the sense at stake here, the values governing conceptualization are always to be derived from the historical *material itself.* That is, they must always be values in regard to which the beings or centers themselves – the objects of the representation – act in a valuative fashion. To understand this result, it is necessary for us always to keep in mind that it holds exclusively for the *logical ideal* of an "objective" historical representation. Thus it cannot hold true for a historical science that goes beyond the theoretical value relationship to the practical valuation of its material.

Therefore we come to the following result. First, every historical individual is related to real beings that valuate and thus are mental. Second, these mental beings must be included among the objects from which the ultimate whole of the historical representation is constituted. And third, these beings must also be the mental historical centers, with which all other objects are to be brought into a real historical nexus in a value-relevant fashion. So the *stricter* concept of history, which in the foregoing was obtained as a mere possibility, has become the *substantive concept of history in general.* At the same time, we approximate much more closely what the empirical sciences regard as history in the stricter sense than was possible by means of the purely formal concept of history. The linguistic usage that is tied to substantive rather than logical differences will call "historical" only those representations in which mental beings constitute their center.

As we now see, this is quite legitimate. For this reason, we should not dream of contesting the view that history in the strict sense, as a special science, must always be concerned with mental objects *too*; *to this extent,* therefore, it can be called a human science. At the same time it is again clear why a logical investigation cannot *begin* with the concept of human science as a science of real *mental life.* The fact that history is a science of mental entities does not determine its logical structure, for mental processes can also be represented in a natural scientific or generalizing fashion. Rather, the converse is true: On the basis of the logical structure of historical science – in other words, from the nature of an individualizing and value-relevant conceptualization – it can be understood why history primarily takes a certain kind of mental life as the object of its investigation.

Thus we can understand quite well how it happened that almost all theories of historical science attempted to obtain the decisive criterion for its differentiation from natural science by means of the substantive opposition of body and spirit. The foregoing discussion explains the broad currency of views of this sort and even lends them a *relative* justification. All students of the disciplines that do not fall within the natural sciences – the theologian, the jurist, the philologist, the historian, and the economist – feel that, in comparison with natural scientists, they belong together. If we inquire into the reason for this, we will always be disposed to regard the concept of the "spiritual" – in other words, the concept of the psychic – as the bond that ties the nonnatural scientific disciplines together into a unified whole. In fact, their objects are and must be predominantly mental. Thus it is easy to understand why anyone who proposes to survey the entire domain of scientific activity and its differences would divide the sciences into natural sciences and human sciences, or sciences of mental phenomena. Finally, suppose that in the attempt to develop a theory of the human sciences, the volitional and *valuing* subject is taken as the starting point. Because natural science – including psychology, but in contrast to history and the other "human sciences" – must always detach its objects from every valuing subject, the starting point chosen is not false. It can even bring much to light that is valuable for the characterization of history and its opposition to natural science.

The detailed pursuit of this matter would carry us too far. Moreover it is not needed, for even at this juncture the following point must be obvious: Despite the necessary connection between history and mental life, whoever wants to understand both the *logical* and the *substantive* differences between natural science and history will not succeed by *beginning* with the mental and the concept of human science. We no longer need to show that in this way, the logical oppositions of method are more obscured than clarified. Even if we construe the concept of "mind" so narrowly that only volitional and valuing beings fall under it, we must always emphasize that like any other reality, they can also be subsumed under the concepts of natural science or treated in a generalizing fashion. From a logical standpoint, therefore, wherever the understanding of the nature of *historical* science is at stake, the term human science remains as vacuous as ever.

In addition, it should also be explicitly pointed out that nothing can be achieved even if we employ the concept of the spiritual as a specific *kind* of psychic phenomenon in order to define the substantive concept of history. In that case, the concept will be too narrow in a certain respect and much too broad in another. The concept is too narrow in the sense that only the historical center must be a being that takes a value position, and thus a mental being as well. Even the historical center is never represented by history in its "spirituality," which is achieved exclusively by conceptual isolation. In other words, it is never represented as a mental being, but rather always as a complete mental and physical reality. The concept is too broad in the sense that not *all* volitional and valuing mental beings are also objects of historical science. Thus another concept of mind would have to be formed even if it is only the central material of the historical sciences that is to be defined by its means. As a result, the fact that a necessary relationship between mental life and history obtains to the limited extent that valuing beings are always psychic beings, shows just how *little* can be learned from these considerations, even for the problem of defining a substantive concept of history.

If the word "mind" is used in a sense still more restricted than that just indicated, its meaning becomes arbitrary. In a methodological investigation, therefore, it would be most advantageous to drop the concept of human science [*Geisteswissenschaft*] in which "mind" [*Geist*] continues to be understood as a real psychic being. There is only one reason why the expression has become entrenched: Formerly what was understood by "mind" was different from what is meant today. It actually stood in opposition to what is merely psychic. Nothing but misunderstandings can result from the retention of expressions that not only have forfeited their earlier meaning but are even expressly employed in a sense different from that of their former use. The danger of such misunderstandings is particularly acute in the case of the word "mind." This is why the polemic against the term "human science" is more than a verbal quibble. We can terminate the controversy only when we are again in the habit of understanding by "mind" something different from the psychic. In that case, it would be especially important to distinguish this concept from what J. S. Mill has in mind when he speaks of a "logic of the human sciences." Indeed, this word should be used only on the assumption that everyone knows quite well that the spiritual [*das Geistige*] is juxtaposed not only to the corporeal but also to the purely psychic. The concept of the spiritual as the psychic remains totally inadequate under all circumstances for the characterization of historical method, as well as for the definition of the historical material. This will become quite clear when we find out what actually constitutes the material of the so-called contemporary human sciences.

8. THE HISTORICAL SCIENCES OF CULTURE

Suppose we want to determine those aspects of reality for which a natural scientific, generalizing mode of treatment can never suffice, and thus which *material* not only makes a historical, individualizing representation possible but also demands it. In other words, suppose we want to arrive at a complete *substantive* concept of history on the basis of a more precise determination of the logical principles explicated in the foregoing. In that case, we are obliged to employ the concept of the *values* that govern historical concept formation. The issue of which material becomes historically *essential* and which does not depends on these values. In particular, a more precise determination of their content must identify the content of the historical *center*. This is the preeminent issue for – to the extent that this is possible in logic – a substantive concept of the historical center also implies a substantive concept of the historical in general.

It is obvious that the further development of this line of thought is possible only by ascertaining *facts* that can no longer be deduced as logically necessary. The circumstance that a value as such governs historical representation made it understandable that the historical center is always a valuing entity. Thus it is also a mental entity and in this sense "spiritual" [*geistig*]. But even this point could be determined only by reference to the fact that valuing beings in the empirical world as we know it are never *merely* corporeal beings. This demarcation, which is basically not much more than negative, was the *first* step along a path we will now pursue further. If we propose to restrict the concept of history, *which is still too broad*, then we must successively adduce the various facts from which something germane to the substantive concept of history can be derived.

The *second step* we have to take along such a path follows from the consideration that every putatively scientific historical representation must relate its objects to a value that is a value *for everyone*. In the first place, this refers to all those for whom the historian's representation is intended. But this *generality* of the value can have a twofold sense. It is either the value that is really esteemed by everyone, and thus accepted by them; or it is demanded of everyone as a value that should be esteemed and accepted. In other words, it can have either a *factual* or – as we propose to put it – a *normative generality*. Provisionally, however, the concept of the normative in our case should still be differentiated from the idea of a supraempirical element of *objective* "validity." Even as regards the normative, we will remain within the domain of the factual in the following sense: We will call values "normatively general" when their recognition is in fact *required* of all members of a certain community.[16]

---

[16]At this point, I do not intend to consider the different kinds of "validity" of values in any more detail. This issue arises only in Chapter 5. On this matter, see also my *System der Philosophie*, I, pp. 132 *seq.* Here it should also be noted that general

Suppose we consider what follows from this as regards a more exact determination of the governing values of the historical representation. A look at the facts shows that every general value germane to historical science must be a value that is either acknowledged by or required of *human beings*. In the case of normatively general values, this is obvious. And even values that are in fact acknowledged as general can only be values that human beings recognize. For the historian to identify them, they must be open to empirical determination, and this is possible only in the case of human beings. It follows that human beings will always stand in the center of the reality that is the object of a historical representation. We have a historical interest in a reality only if it is truly connected with mental entities who themselves take a position on general human values. And human values, as far as we can tell, are held only by human beings. Thus we have obtained a concept of the historical center – and therefore a concept of history as well – that already comes another step closer to what empirical science in fact regards as "history." The principal object to which existing historical scholarship relates everything else is always the development of *human mental life*.

Even this concept is still too broad, however. The next and *third* step on the path to the definition of the concept of history is taken when we reflect on the following fact: General values – and this holds true for values that are in fact generally acknowledged as well as for normatively general values – obtain only among human beings who live together in some sort of *community*, in other words, *social* beings in the broadest sense of the term. We know that there are no isolated individuals at all in empirical reality. Moreover, human mental life that has developed to the point of recognizing general values can only be a life with other human beings, or a social life.

As regards factually acknowledged general values, the concept itself implies that they are values of a human community. Even when we regard a value as normatively general, however, it is always demanded of a real community of human beings. Concerning the word "community," we should think not only of social groups whose members are situated in spatial and temporal proximity, but also of communities that are held together solely by an "ideal" bond, for example, the communities consisting of all those who take a position on science, on art, and so on, and whose members may be widely dispersed in both space and time. If we call the general values of such communities "social values," we can say that the values governing a historical

values should not be confused with general concepts of these values. What is meant by "generality" in this sense – namely, the fact that it is valid for everyone – can itself be something individual.

representation are always human social values. Here again, it follows that there must be human beings in every reality that is a possible object of a historical representation. By virtue of the individuality of their volition and action, they constitute in-dividuals with respect to social values. It also follows that the mental life of a human community, which is significant because of its singularity, stands at the center of every historical representation. Even individuals as apparently isolated and detached as Spinoza should be seen as social beings with regard to the scientific community or the *societas philosophorum* to which they belong, and must belong in order to acquire a historical significance.[17]

Thus the central historical process is always either the development of a single human mental life in an individual social nexus or else an individual social whole whose individual constituents are combined into groups. These individual constituents need be brought only under a relative historical concept because each single constituent is historically essential by virtue of the same volitional acts and the same conduct as all the others. In that case, all other objects are related to these social individuals because they stand in a real historical relationship with them.

Consider, therefore, the principles of value-relevant historical concept formation and the three foregoing facts: the fact that valuing beings are mental beings; the fact that general values are human values; and the fact that for the historian, general human values are social values in the most comprehensive sense of this term. On this basis, we arrive at a concept of history that from a substantive standpoint, already is quite often regarded as exhaustive and is used to distinguish history from natural science. Nature, on the one hand, and human social life, on the other – these are the two groups of facts, so it is supposed, into which the two main groups of sciences are divided. Now we see how such a view acquires a relative *justification* in our investigation.[18]

[17]The concept of the social can also be taken in a narrower sense. In that case, social goods such as marriage, the family, the state, and the nation are juxtaposed to asocial goods such as art and science. On this point, see my *System der Philosophie*, I, pp. 370 *seq.* We cannot consider this issue here. Asocial goods such as art and science are of relevance to *history* only insofar as they are situated in a real social nexus. Philosophy, which attempts to interpret their *transhistorical meaning*, can – indeed, must – conceive them differently.

[18]Critics who find that I have not given the *substantive* characteristics of the material of the historical sciences in the stricter sense their legitimate place have paid insufficient attention both to these and to the ensuing remarks, and to my concept of the historical center as well. Otherwise the charge of "formalism" would not make sense. Of course, the facts on which I base my position here are so trivial that

Only one further point should be noted. This concept of the historical is frequently linked with the idea that "social" life cannot be represented "individualistically." Here again the atom is confused with the individual, and the social totality is confused with the general class concept. That is why we deliberately speak of an "individual social nexus" and of "social individuals." Such a verbal juxtaposition can sound paradoxical only to someone who does not see that the real historical nexus of a society is always something individual and that it is precisely the subsumption of individuals under a general concept that would detach them from the social and historical totality in order to constitute them as abstract atoms. As we have seen, generalizing concept formation necessarily remains connected with a more or less isolating – and, in this sense, atomizing – concept formation.

Nevertheless, even the concept of history we have now obtained is still not sufficiently precise for our purposes. Indeed, the decisive feature is still missing, for on its basis we still do not understand why the purely natural scientific treatment of human social *mental life* should be less *satisfactory* than such a treatment of another real object; in other words, why a generalizing sociology cannot answer all the scientifically essential questions the life of human society poses for us, and why there is also an individualizing history of human society. So to arrive at an even more limited concept of history, we must define the concept of the general value that governs the historical representation more precisely.

In this context, the following point is crucial. The factually general recognition of values with reference to which objects are supposed to become historical in-dividuals cannot rest exclusively on a so-called natural drive. That is, it cannot coincide with the propensity of any given individual, as is the case, for example, in goods such as the appeasement of hunger or satisfaction of the sexual drive. Regardless

one might suppose it is not worthwhile to make them explicit. What is at stake here, however, does not concern new and interesting *facts*. Indeed, it would fare badly for my line of thought if the facts I adduce were not trivial or self-evident. Here as everywhere in a logic of history, my task has been to demonstrate the *connection* between the characteristics of the factual material of history, with which everyone is familiar, and the logical structure of their historical representation. Not everyone is familiar with this connection. The "formalism" with which I am reproached lies in its analysis. None of my critics has been able to explain how a logic of history can employ a procedure that is not formal in this sense and still remain logic. The opposition to my formalism can be explained only by the fact that although we have "theories of the human sciences," we have no logic of the disciplines that do not fall within the natural sciences. The purpose of this book is to establish the basis for such a logic, and this is the sole perspective from which it should be judged.

of how "general" the values may be that are linked with these goods, their realization in goods remains, at least in part, an affair of single individuals. To the extent that this is the case, a formation of individuals that is valid for everyone can never develop with reference to these values. It is only social organizations, created by the members of a society for the satisfaction of their needs, that in their individuality have a significance for everyone conjointly. Thus we can say that the general values governing historical concept formation also must always be a common concern of the members of a community. In that event, the difference between factually general and normatively general values disappears, for under these conditions factually general values must also appear as requirements for all members of the community. In this sense, they can be seen as normatively general values, which is the case, for example, for the values of the church, the nation, law, the state, marriage, the family, economic organization, religion, science, art, and so on. Thus only human beings who become in-dividuals with respect to goods of this sort and the values attached to them are possible historical centers for the science of history. This is because only a representation that gives an account of them can presuppose acknowledgment of its governing values by everyone for whom the representation is intended. In consequence, only such a representation can make a claim to general validity.

Suppose we try to find a common *name* for these values that are attached to goods of this sort, values we have only illustrated thus far. In that case, we will best reconsider the concept of *nature* in order to see what, in addition to the purely logical or purely formal concept of history, stands in *opposition* to it. Here again, we can proceed only from a concept of nature that includes psychic as well as physical existence but that still has a sense different from the sense "nature" bears when it designates reality with respect to the general. Suppose we also consider that by nature we understand all real objects in which we bracket every value relationship – the necessary consequence of subsumption under general concepts. We are not introducing a novel concept of nature. On the contrary, we are simply making explicit the value indifference of the concept of nature already established, which comprehends reality with reference to the general.

Thus there are two groups of concepts that can appear in *opposition* to the concept of nature as understood in this way. Earlier we mentioned pairs of concepts such as nature and art, and nature and morality, as well as pairs of concepts such as nature and God. We could also include nature and mind under this second type – where "mind," however, would not be understood as the empirical material of psychology. *The* common feature of both pairs of concepts would lie in the fact that they juxtapose to the natural as the value free, something that has value as a supranatural, supraperceptual, transcendent entity. It is obvious, however, that here, where we are concerned with determining the principles of an empirical science, metaphysical oppositions such as nature and God or nature and "mind" cannot be employed. In contrast to the supraperceptual, the historical is also "natural." Thus only *that* group of concepts remains that includes the pairs nature and art, nature and morality, and so on; and the name for what is juxtaposed to nature in this way can only be culture. This expression, therefore, will be important for us.

This word, originally used for the cultivation of the soil, is now conventionally employed as the name for *all* those goods that the members of a community take seriously, or whose "cultivation" can be required of them. For this reason, the normatively general social values we have discussed should be designated as *cultural values*, and the opposition of nature and culture finally makes it possible to develop conclusively the *substantive* concept of historical science in opposition to the *substantive* concept of natural science. Culture is the common concern in the life of peoples. Thus it is also the good with reference to whose values individuals acquire their *historical* significance as something that everyone acknowledges. In consequence, general cultural values that are attached to this good govern historical representation and concept formation in the selection of what is essential.

In this context, we will leave open the question of whether there is a relationship between cultural goods and supraperceptual and transcendent goods whose necessity can be demonstrated by philosophy. As an empirical science, history is not concerned with this question. Here the only issue is to demarcate a domain of normatively general entities that are objects of valuation and cultivation from *those* realities we regard as indifferent to values – indeed, realities we must regard in this way if we propose to conceive them as "nature," that is, as mere instances of general concepts that can be replaced by other such instances.

But if normatively general cultural values are the governing principles of every historical representation, we have gone one step farther in the definition of the concept of the historical *center*. In the first place, it is self-evident that *those* persons become preeminently important for history who themselves have taken a real value position on the normatively general social values of the state, law, the economy, art, and so on,[19] persons whose individuality has acquired

[19]In a sense that later will be further specified, instead of "taking a position" we can also say the following: Those persons (whether as individuals or as groups) are included in the historical centers of a historical material of the past in whom the

essential significance for the real course of history in this way. All other real existence remains historical only to the extent that its individuality has an influence on human cultural activity and its results. But this concept of the historical center is still not entirely sufficient for our purposes. The "general" historical nexus is of relevance not only insofar as every historical individual is linked with a more extensive social whole of which it is a constituent. On the contrary, we also have to consider that history – to the extent that this is possible – always has to represent the development of its objects, that is, *sequences of change*, whose successive stages are fundamentally different from each other.

A community of the following sort is, of course, conceivable. In their volition and action, its members take a position on values to which they ascribe normative generality. They may even work unceasingly for the realization of normatively general goals without noticing any essential changes in the character of their activity and its results as time passes. In this case, it seems that history is limited to the representation of a continuous state. Even in such a case, however, the focus of the interest would concern the question of how the continuous state was gradually attained as the result of a unique development. Indeed, if there really were no longer *any* sense in which changes were essential, such a community would no longer have a "history" that still required a distinctive representation. This is because everything of significance in the end product – which no longer undergoes development – must already have been present in the history of its previous unique development. Regardless of this consideration, it is doubtful whether there are many *constant* cultural communities in the sense under consideration here. And in any case, culture, in the sense of the word that has become conventional today, obtains only if, at least earlier, the life of communities has occurred in such a way that the activity of each stage presupposes the activity of the previous stages, or continues to build on their foundation in such a way that an essential and individual *difference* between the various stages can be identified with respect to general values.

In other words, real culture exists only where value-related or historical-teleological *development* either exists or has existed. Thus we see an even more intimate connection between culture and history. It can also be clarified in another way by employing a concept that has been the subject of much discussion. We speak of "natural peoples" [*Naturvölker*] and juxtapose them to "historical" peoples as well as to

cultural values of their time were "truly vital." This is why they become historically essential.

"civilized" or "cultural peoples" [*Kulturvölker*]. Again we can leave undecided the question of whether there are absolutely unhistorical beings who have no culture at all. But if a people really exhibits no historically essential changes in the entire course of its known development, then in fact we could subsume it only under general concepts of recurrence. In this respect, therefore, we could conceive it only as "nature," in the logical sense. A people exhibits historically essential changes only if it manifests a historical development with reference to its cultural values. On the basis of this consideration, we see that there is only one respect in which it makes sense to speak of natural peoples. We also see the relationship between this concept and the concepts of cultural and historical peoples. As a result, it is again clear that historical peoples must always be cultural peoples, and culture can exist only in historical peoples. The concepts of culture and history condition each other reciprocally. In a certain sense, they are interdependent: It is cultural values alone that make history as a science possible, and it is historical development alone that brings forth real cultural goods to which cultural values are attached.

Now we have finally defined the concept of the *central processes of history* to the extent that this seems necessary for our purposes. The governing perspectives of every historical representation must be values of normatively general validity. These values are realized in the goods to which they are attached only within a historical development. As the historical center, the material that should be historically essential with reference to such values must include the development of human cultural life, to which the other aspects of this material can be related.

Obviously this concept of the historical material as the concept of historical cultural life is also *formal* in a certain respect. It comprises only the members of a historically developing community who have volition and act. The actions of these members become essential by virtue of their individuality when they are related to their own normatively general values and also to the values governing their representation, where the latter values are in agreement with the former. Therefore, the specific *content* of these values and actions remains undetermined and does not concern a logical investigation as such. As was previously the case, the different cultural values mentioned here and the objects that correspond to them should be regarded only as examples. The concept of history that remains formal in relation to culture will suffice to answer the questions we still have to pose. The fact that we call the concept of history obtained in this way both *substantive* and *formal* cannot be a cause for misgivings. It is substantive – and, in this sense, more than formal – in comparison with the *purely* logical concept of reality considered from the perspective of its individuality. But it remains formal in comparison with the concept of a representation that is concerned with a historical material substantively defined in terms of *specific* cultural goods and cultural values. Only in what follows can we show the extent to which the normatively general governing cultural values of an "objective" historical representation must remain formal, in the sense indicated, under all conditions. At this point, we are concerned only with ascertaining the *name* that must be most appropriate for the governing values of history and, in consequence, also for the material that is historically essential with reference to these values. Concerning this point, there can no longer be any doubt. . . .

. . . As a result, we can conclude the purely logical exposition of the structure of concept formation in the historical cultural sciences. The distinctive problem of this book, which was formulated in the Introduction, seems to be solved. We have identified the logical nature of the kind of scientific representation that begins at the limits of concept formation in natural science, as regards both its *method* and the most general character of its *material*. We have also seen the extent to which this representation can fill the lacunae in our knowledge of the real world that must always be left by natural science, no matter how comprehensive it may be. The elucidation of these theses was the chief purpose of our enterprise.

9. NONREAL MEANING CONFIGURATIONS AND HISTORICAL UNDERSTANDING

Nevertheless, perhaps our exposition – which, for the reasons that have repeatedly been given, we have deliberately made as formal as possible – does not yet clarify in all respects the concept of *culture* as the material of history, in the stricter and more conventional sense. Thus it may require an *addendum*, especially in the interest of reaching an agreement with endeavors in our area of research that do not have a logical and formal orientation. Even the allusion to Hegel's concept of the spirit[20] points to an aspect of our problem that we cannot entirely ignore if we want to reach a satisfactory conclusion. For this reason, certain addenda are in order that elucidate for methodology the character of the value-relevant historical *material* and the charac-

---

[20][This is an allusion to a paragraph omitted from the translation (*Die Grenzen*, pp. 525–6), in which Rickert employs Hegel's concept of spirit, or *Geist*, in order to show why, at one time, the term *Geisteswissenschaft* was not altogether inappropriate as the name for the historical sciences of culture.]

ter of the representation by historical science that is *substantively* appropriate to it.

In the foregoing, we intentionally limited ourselves to *that* historical material that falls within the domain of the real event. That approach was justified, even necessary. The interest of history – which, in the sense indicated, can actually be called the science of reality – always remains focused primarily on the temporal course of *real* processes as its genuine material. It is real facts at specific points in space and time that are "historical" in the broadest sense. We began with this concept of the historical. It is true that we can define its content more precisely, but we can never choose to relinquish it. At the same time, however, we have seen that the historian does not represent the real event for the sake of its reality, but only to the extent that it is linked with something that points beyond its *mere* real existence. In the foregoing, this was expressed by saying that historical reality must be theoretically related to values in order to become "essential" for the historian. We have also characterized the sort of values that govern historical selection by calling them cultural values. Examples of the different provinces of culture included law, morals, ethics, religion, art – in short, what Hegel calls objective or absolute spirit. In light of the foregoing definitions and assuming that real processes in mental life are intended, such spiritual configurations [*Geistesgebilde*] belong not only to the historical material in general but also to the historical *centers* of the historical representation, whose governing values are linked with the cultural goods just named. To this extent, everything is clear. But we can mean something completely different by "spiritual configurations," something *nonreal* that we have already encountered in an earlier context. Now that we are concerned with a more precise substantive definition of the historical material, this becomes important for us.

We have repeatedly pointed out that the "noncorporeal" does not necessarily have to be a real psychic entity. On the contrary, there are configurations that are neither corporeal nor mental events. Thus they simply cannot be conceived as empirical realities that occur temporally. Nevertheless, we are all directly acquainted with them, which is why they also cannot be relegated to a metaphysical beyond. In every respect, this domain is *nonreal.* In it we would have to include, for example, the "meaning" of a word or the theoretical "content" of a judgment. Every thinking person who "understands" such a configuration at all, understands it as *the same.* Conversely, we will later see that a nonreal "object" necessaily belongs to "understanding," assuming that the word is not to lose its exact meaning. At the outset, it is important to see that the real mental acts of understanding – or of "meaning" as well – are *different* in every individual, in spite of the identity of the object of understanding. In other words, they can at best *resemble* one another – to the extent that realities can in general resemble one another. But they can never be *identical*, like the common object of understanding. Earlier we posed the question of whether such nonreal configurations – directly "experienced" *in common* by many individuals – are found *only* in the domain of the theoretical or the logical. It is not difficult to show that there are other nonreal entities. Everything Hegel calls objective or absolute spirit can be understood in the following way. As regards its content, it falls within a sphere that is certainly not corporeal. But insofar as it is directly experienced in common by many individuals, it cannot be called a real psychic entity either. Thus it must qualify as nonreal, as long as we do not propose to admit realities that are neither corporeal nor mental. Thus there are also atheoretical objects of a quite distinctive character, and there is good reason to designate them as nonreal if physical and psychic existence is the only thing that can be called real.

This point now becomes important. On the assumption that such configurations are nonreal, that which constitutes the "spiritual" sort of culture as *culture* – namely, its value relevance – also seems to be a nonreal world. But if this is the case, it seems we cannot call the material of history "culture," for the historical sciences propose to represent real events, not nonreal objects. Or is it perhaps false that the historian always attempts to understand real temporal events? Is history – precisely insofar as it is a cultural science – possibly a science of nonreal configurations? That is, in addition to its real material, does it also have a nonreal "material"?

To clarify these matters, suppose we examine the concept of culture from another perspective. In fact, the concept has an ambiguity that we must eliminate, at least to the extent that the precise definition of our concept of the historical cultural sciences requires this. In this connection, we will also encounter some other widely discussed problems in the theory of history, and we will finally settle accounts with the ideas responsible for the fact that many still hold to the concept of human science as definitive for history. Above all, it will also be shown how little our *logical* investigation need *conflict* with *those* theories of historical science that proceed from differences in the *material* of scientific representations and give prominence to concepts such as historical "understanding," in contrast to that of scientific "explanation." Indeed, it must follow that we can approach problems such as those of historical "understanding" philosophically and move toward their solution in our way *only*: by conceptually distinguishing in "culture" real historical existence from the nonreal configurations that are linked with it. Even in the question concerning the nature of understanding, we cannot manage without the concept of the nonreal.

In the definition of the historical material, we had to proceed from the *values* that govern historical concept formation. Only on this basis could we arrive at the concept of culture under which the material of history falls. Even this consideration makes the aforementioned ambiguity of the concept of culture understandable. It is an ambiguity that has proved fateful for many theories of the so-called human sciences. The term "culture" shares this ambiguity with a number of concepts. They do not designate mere realities as such. On the contrary, they refer to real processes that because of their value relevance, have a "significance" or a "meaning" that transcends their real existence. Values as such are never real. On the contrary, they hold validly. In other words, the values themselves cannot be real, but rather only the goods in which they are "realized" and in which we discover them. In the same way, the *meaning* reality acquires with reference to a value does not itself fall within the domain of real existence. On the contrary, it obtains only in relation to a valid value. In this sense, the meaning itself is unreal. In consequence, by culture we understand, first, real historical *life* to which a meaning is attached that constitutes it as culture. In addition, we can also understand by culture the nonreal "content" itself, conceived as the *meaning* of such a life that is detached from all real existence and is interpreted with reference to cultural values. In "meaningful life" itself, both of these senses interpenetrate. In the theory of such a life, they must be distinguished.[21]

As an example of the distinction between real being and nonreal meaning, we again need to consider only the real psychic act of judging, on the one hand, and its nonreal logical content, on the other. Only the latter is "true" or has theoretical value in the proper

[21] In my essay "Vom Begriff der Philosophie" (*Logos*, I, 1910), I considered the interpretation of nonreal "meaning," in the most comprehensive sense this concept can have, more thoroughly. I also tried to articulate this concept more precisely in my *System der Philosophie*, I, pp. 277 *seq.* There I distinguish "subjective" or "immanent" meaning from "objective" or "transcendent" meaning. Only the conjunction of both constitutes the total domain of nonreal meaning configurations. For a more detailed orientation, I must refer to these studies. As regards the domain of theory, the concepts at stake here were already fully developed earlier in my book *Der Gegenstand der Erkenntnis*. Subsequently it was only a matter of extending these results so that they could be transposed onto the atheoretical areas of culture and applied there. There is the closest of connections between the exposition of this section and my general philosophy of value and meaning.

sense of the word. To this extent, it is completely independent of the psychic being that apprehends it, a being that is neither true nor false because it is merely real. Real acts of theoretical meaning and understanding never coincide with (immanent or transcendent) logical "meaning." It is only this logical "meaning" that can be true or false, that is, an object of theoretical value or significance. Now we must not only apply this distinction to real science as a historical process, that is, to human beings who engage in research and pursue understanding and to their scientific works. We must also apply it to the other goods of culture, that is, the atheoretical goods that the development of history exhibits. In the case of the word "art," for example, we should consider not only real works of art and the human beings who either create or comprehend them, but also the nonreal aesthetic "meaning" the historical processes bear. If we generalize this distinction, in every case we obtain the following result: on the one hand, culture as the reality to which a meaning is attached; on the other hand, the nonreal meaning or "spirit" that is conceptually detached from reality. In other words, art and science – and even religion, law, politics, and so on – designate, first, meaningful realities and, second, configurations that are no more real than the valid content of scientific truths. For this reason, we will always explicitly refer to the latter as *nonreal configurations* of cultural *meaning*. Without exploring the differences between these configurations in more detail, we do this to scrupulously distinguish them from the *historical realities of culture* to which they are attached.

If we maintain this position, we can already eliminate the difficulty mentioned earlier, according to which it seemed doubtful how far history is concerned with reality if it is to be a cultural science. Suppose we claim that all history represents the unique development of human culture. Then we do not have in mind meaning configurations conceived in conceptual abstraction as nonreal objects, but rather the *meaningful real* processes that are the bearers of these configurations and with whose real development the historian is concerned. In this way, the concept of the historical science of culture is freed of every ambiguity. As a science of reality, history does not consider the nonreal content of culture in conceptual isolation, but rather the unique temporal course of meaningful cultural realities.

This has another consequence that we should especially stress in opposition to those who pejoratively characterize our theory of historical science as "purely formal," allegedly because it does not do justice to the substantive character of the historical material. Such objections, which we have already mentioned, can easily be completely refuted on the basis of the standpoint we have now reached. Suppose history is not defined as we have done it: by employing the concept of the individualizing and value-relevant *method* in order to analyze its logical structure. On the contrary, suppose, as is usually the case, that history is defined on the basis of the concept of its *material*. In that event, we would have to proceed from the following considerations in order to distinguish history from natural science. On the one hand, there are realities that we regard in terms of their purely real existence. On the other hand, there are realities that we conceive as bearers of nonreal meaning configurations: in other words, realities that refer to something that goes beyond their real existence. If we consider the difference in the methods to be employed in a scientific representation, it can be shown *on this basis as well* that the bearers of nonreal meaning configurations constitute the "primary" material of *individualizing* history in the strict sense. As regards nonmeaningful realities, on the other hand, regardless of whether their real existence is physical or psychic, our only interest is "natural scientific." In other words, we limit ourselves to representing them in a *generalizing* fashion, at least as long as they are not brought into a real historical nexus with meaningful bearers of culture, thereby acquiring the status of secondary historical in-dividuals.

These methodological differences between the sciences, which are now linked with a *substantive* opposition, are not incompatible with our theory. Rather, they necessarily follow from it, and their necessity can be understood only on the basis of our theory. These considerations again show how unjustified it is to claim that our account is limited to the purely "formal" and therefore "external" characteristics of the historical sciences of culture and that we are unable to appreciate the distinctive "inner" – that is, substantive – features of its material. On the contrary, as in the case of the development of the concept of the historical center, it is also clear here that it is precisely our way of defining the concept of the historical material by means of the method of value relevance that must lead to the philosophical understanding of the *connection* between the *substantive* and the *formal* characteristics of the different sciences.

This should especially be stressed in opposition to the critique of our work by Troeltsch, which we have already mentioned.[22] A response to this critique is all the more apropos since Troeltsch expressly "presupposes" the "essential correctness" of our logic of history. He wants only to "advance" from this logic, since it is "only a beginning and not an end," an enterprise with which we are obviously

---

[22]"Ueber den Begriff einer historischen Dialektik, Windelband-Rickert und Hegel," *Historische Zeitschrift* (vol. 119), 3rd series, vol. 23, 1919, pp. 373 *seq.*

in complete agreement. But it seems that Troeltsch does not fully appreciate the premises of our theory that are already available for its further development, precisely in the sense of its substantive elaboration. He focuses exclusively on concepts that were deliberately developed in a purely formal fashion, the concepts from which we were obliged to *begin*. He does not pay sufficient attention to the manner in which – even in the development of our own line of thought – the path leads from these concepts to the distinctive substantive characteristics of the historical material. Thus in his critique, our concept of the historical *center* in particular, as well as everything connected with it, remains as good as unnoticed. This is precisely the point at which a critique would have to begin in order to show that one could not "advance" on the basis of our endeavor.

Concerning our theory of history, Troeltsch makes the following claim: "*Invariably*, it is not the *object* that is decisive, but rather the *interest* that first differentiates the object from the continuum of the experience of reality, and that discloses and forms this object only by means of the method that is linked with this interest."[23] That does, of course, hold true for the *beginning point* of our investigation. In a logically oriented theory of history, we were obliged to "disclose" the logical structure of the object by means of the method. Indeed, this was the real intention of our enterprise. But it is not correct that for this reason, as Troeltsch claims, there is "*no* sense in which" the object is developed "from the inner nature of the material itself" or that the interest of the investigator is "always" decisive. On the contrary, we have focused on both the method *and* the inner nature of the material of history. If we *began* with method in a logical introduction to the historical sciences, that cannot be described as a "violation." *At the outset*, of course, the methodological "external determination of purpose" had to be decisive for us so that no doubt should remain concerning the most general *logical* oppositions. Troeltsch himself does not contest these oppositions. On the contrary, he explicitly acknowledges them. From the moment we turned to the concept of the historical *center*, however, the main aim was to show how the external methodological determination of purpose *corresponded* exactly to the "inner" nature of the central historical material.

In any case, we question "the distinctiveness of the object of historical life" no more than the historian does. The fact that we are concerned with *logic* is the only consideration that distinguishes us from scholarly specialists. The *connection* between the substantive distinctiveness of their material and the formal distinctiveness of their

---

[23]Ibid., p. 376. Here and in the following, I have added the emphases.

method remains concealed from specialized scholars. We could not *stop* at this point. We knew that, in the interests of logic, the distinctive formal characteristics of method should, in the beginning, be placed in the foreground. But we did not limit ourselves to these characteristics, as one might suppose from Troeltsch's critique. On the contrary, we tried to do justice to the "interpenetration of object and method" by explaining why it is cultural realities, and above all their mental centers, that *require* a value-relevant, individualizing representation by history. We were able to do this by showing the following. Consider the logical ideal of history as a science, which perhaps can never be realized. From the perspective of this ideal, the historian will best do justice to the distinctive character of his material in a thoroughly "objective" fashion *only* if he is led in the selection of what is essential by *the same* values that provide the basis for the meaning of the cultural life of the historical centers: in other words, the human beings who appear in his material.

The point of our theory lay precisely in this consideration. The distinctive central *material* of historical science – which, in its essence, is meaningful cultural life – is historically represented in such a way that the values that endow it with meaning at the same time provide the governing principles of concept formation with the help of which historical science appropriates its material. This point clearly showed how the methodological purpose, at first "externally" imposed, is necessarily connected with the "inner" nature of the historical object. *Now* that we have reached this point, we can also articulate some ideas first developed in another context. The object or the material of history, in the usual, stricter sense of the word, has the following *substantive* characteristic: It is *primarily* concerned with cultural realities that are meaningful and mental. *For this reason*, a *representation* of this object requires a value-relevant, individualizing concept formation. The domain of nonmeaningful "nature," on the other hand – in other words, everything whose existence is independent of value and meaning – intrinsically conforms to a system of *general* concepts.

The opposition between nonmeaningful, merely real processes and meaningful processes, to which our inquiry, proceeding synthetically, has gradually led us, is the *only* valid *substantive* opposition that actually provides a basis for classifying the empirical sciences with reference to their materials. We have another reason for stressing this point. This circumstance also best explains why the usual division of the natural sciences from the human sciences will not disappear. When the word "mind" is used with any seriousness at all as justifying the term for a classification of the sciences, what is almost always meant, without being altogether clear about what is intended, is not really the opposition between the psychic and the physical. In methodology this opposition is relatively useless. One rather has in mind realities that are not *only* realities, and thus they are not only psychic realities either. On the contrary, they are characterized as "higher" because they have a meaning, which purely psychic existence does not necessarily possess. For this reason, they cannot be exhaustively treated by the natural scientific method. That is because the conception of these realities as instances of general concepts of nature, or as special "cases" of natural laws, would abstract from all the values linked with their individuality, and thus from all the meaning connected with these values as well. Therefore our distinction, which could be fully elucidated only in a logical or formal fashion, also resonates with other theories of the historical sciences, theories that, like our own, oppose a universal natural scientific method, even though they juxtapose the "human sciences" to the natural sciences.

For example, the distinction between meaningful and nonmeaningful realities actually forms the real core of Dilthey's theory of the human sciences, especially as it is developed in his last writings.[24] Thus even in the foregoing we could point out that there can be no question of a fundamental opposition between Dilthey's ideas and those set out here. It is only that Dilthey, as we saw earlier, unfortunately did not succeed in providing a *clear conceptual* analysis of the essential feature of his principle of demarcation. This is because he too always remained too preoccupied with the difference between bodies and mental processes. There is no sense in which this difference is methodologically crucial. It becomes essential only insofar as mental life takes a position on value and meaning, and in this way can constitute itself meaningfully. Bodies, however, cannot do this, a circumstance that is certainly not sufficient to justify the division into natural sciences and human sciences. Dilthey confuses the nonreal, meaningful content of culture that is situated in the realities of history with the real psychic existence that actually occurs in the mental life of single individuals. Thus it remains concealed that it is not the real spirit [*Geist*] but, rather, the nonreal meaning that forms the genuinely decisive factor in *substantively* distinguishing history from every natural science. Indeed, Dilthey simply does not see that two domains that lie in conceptual spheres as different from one another as the real and the nonreal are to be distinguished here. As a result, that which, in spite of this, is valuable in his theories, remains ad hoc and

---

[24]See Arthur Stein, *Der Begriff des Geistes bei Dilthey*, 1913. The second edition appeared under the title *Der Bergiff des Verstehens bei Dilthey*, 1926.

unsystematic. It stems more from a powerful historical "instinct" than from conceptual clarity concerning the nature of history. . . .

Now that we have been able to show that the opposition between nonmeaningful and meaningful existence is decisive for the chief substantive difference in the material of the sciences, we can again see why the expression "cultural science" is more appropriate as the name for the nonnatural scientific disciplines. By "culture" everyone understands those realities that have an intelligible meaning for us because of their value relevance. It is also in complete conformity with linguistic usage if we designate as cultural life primarily the mental life of the past insofar as it is of "general" significance, in the sense explained. In addition, the word "culture" suggests, on the one hand, that this mental life is not conceived as psychologically isolated in history, in other words, conceptually separated from the physical. On the contrary, it is conceived as existing in a real connection with the corporeal world as well. On the other hand, the value factor we think of in the case of culture calls to mind the connection that obtains in every historical center between value relevance and meaningfulness. At first we saw that in an "objective" historical representation of culture, the selection of its material is governed – to the extent this is possible – by the same cultural values that also determine the meaning content of the cultural life represented. If we now claim that the historical centers of culture are always a real meaningful process, this is basically the same point we made in discussing the development of the method when we spoke of a theoretical relationship between historical objects and general cultural values. In that context, perhaps it could still seem as if the cultural value had been transposed from the outside onto the historical material. Here we see that this perspective, which at first is external, again corresponds exactly to the inner nature of the material, which is cultural life.

For the rest, the main point remains the following: Culture is a *value* concept, and the nonreal meaning configurations in the historical material of culture as well as the governing cultural principles for the selection of this material lie in the sphere of that which is something like a value. The content of meaning can be interpreted only with reference to values. The value character of the meaning configurations that appear in the material of history also determine the method of historical concept formation: Because of the value content possessed by the meaning configurations of culture, the individualizing representation of the real event, with which they are linked or that embodies them, becomes a scientific necessity. Accordingly the generalizing method of natural science is unable to do justice to the substantive content of the material.

Finally, consider the intrinsic "unity" or the indivisible "totality" that "spirit" [*Geist*] allegedly possesses in contrast to nature, which is always divisible. This has often been discussed, and we have alluded to it repeatedly. It should also be stressed that this is not characteristic of the material of history with reference to its *mental* reality. This problem was already discussed in the development of the most general concept of the historical in-dividual, to the extent that there we showed how the relationship to a *value* consolidates the essential aspects of an object into a totality that is not to be divided. Here, where we are less concerned with the method than with the inner nature of the material of history, the following point should be noted. To the extent that this material consists of meaningful realities, its unity or totality also occurs only by means of the *meaning* configuration of culture that it embodies. Namely, every meaning as such excludes a certain kind of segmentation. In other words, only as a *whole* does it retain its character as meaning, even when it is possible to speak of its "segments." In the domain of value-free reality, the relationship of the parts to the whole is also completely different from what we find in the domain of value and the nonreal. . . .

Now that we have disclosed the dual significance of the concept of culture in order to safeguard the concept of cultural science from misunderstandings, and have also seen what the essential demarcation criterion must be in an articulation of the sciences with reference to their *materials*, we need not discuss the nature of nonreal meaning configurations any further. As regards the *method* of historical concept formation and representation, nothing else fundamentally different from what we have already discerned can be derived from the distinctive character of meaning, once its value character is established. However, a certain reproach is frequently raised against our investigation: Instead of discussing determinations of the content of historical objects, it considers the logical structure of their representation. Regardless of how unjustified such a reproach may be, perhaps we should at least indicate how the concept of culture – more precisely defined by the concept of the *central mental bearer of meaning* – provides access to the treatment of other much discussed problems concerning the so-called human sciences, problems that are, of course, more germane to the process of research than to the representation of its results; and how a philosophical clarification of these questions as well is possible only on this basis.

In this account, we will limit ourselves to points on which objections can be raised against our theory of individualizing concept formation in the cultural sciences. An exhaustive treatment of the problems that arise in this context is not possible within the limits of this book, which explicitly disregards the question of a logic of historical *investigation*.

As regards the difference between real existence and nonreal meaning in the material of history, it is above all the following consideration that is methodologically important. The nonreal actually stands in opposition to psychic existence to the extent that, unlike real mental processes, it never need directly pertain to a single individual alone. On the contrary, it can always be "experienced" in common by many – indeed, in principle by all – real subjects. For this reason it should also be called "general." Thus in addition to the four kinds of generality differentiated earlier, we have a new concept of generality in history, and we have reason to ask what this "fifth generality" signifies for individualizing historical concept formation. After this is determined, we will reexamine the peculiar character of the historical material – and especially that of the historical centers – from a new aspect. Finally, we will try to understand what is meant when it is said, with respect to this peculiar character, that a "re-creative understanding" is a procedure distinctive to historical science.

At first, however, we will examine the intrinsic significance of the "generality" of nonreal meaning configurations. Here it will be best to employ an example. We will choose an object that is simpler than most of the processes with which historical science is concerned when it represents the culture of the past. Nevertheless, it seems complex enough to exhibit the different aspects of the issue. This will make it possible to transpose the concepts we obtain in considering this example onto the actual material of history.

Let us assume that a number of people are gathered in a church for a worship service. The realities we identify include, first of all, bodies such as the building with its pews, pulpit, and organ; and also a plurality of psychophysical individuals – the clergyman, the organist, and the members of the congregation who listen to both the sermon and the church music. But it is obvious that what is actually present is not yet *exhausted* by such a complex of real physical and psychic objects. Indeed, in these realities, insofar as they are *merely* real, we simply do not yet have what we can call the worship service of a *congregation*. In this context, we will disregard completely an interplay of any divine or supernatural factors whatsoever. Because they would always remain inaccessible to any treatment by an empirical science, we have to do this. We will focus only on what cannot be denied even by someone who sees in the worship service the expression of a crass superstition.

In that case, we are obliged to claim the following: The people gathered in the church constitute the "unity" of a congregation only because they understand the *meaning* of the sermon and the sacred music that the preacher and the organist bring to expression by means of words or tones. This meaning consists neither in the real sounds of the words or organ tones with which it is connected nor in the mental realities by means of which it is grasped. On the contrary, it is a nonreal configuration built from theoretical, religious, and aesthetic factors, and perhaps from others as well. Without exception, however, they are nonreal. The different real individuals "experience" this meaning in common as the same. It is on its basis alone that the members constitute *one* congregation. Perhaps no one of them grasps this meaning in an absolutely complete fashion. Some may find the preacher too difficult to understand, and others may be unmusical. As a result, only one aspect of the entire meaning configuration that belongs to the worship service will be accessible to them. However, the real psychophysical individuals gathered in the church become the members of the religious congregation only *to the extent* that they participate in the nonreal meaning configurations expressed by the sermon and the music; or – as this may also be put – only to the extent that the meaning of the words and tones somehow becomes "truly vital" in their mental life.[25]

This meaning, which is more or less completely realized in the different members of the congregation, can also be called the "spirit" of the congregation, assuming that we want to use this word for the totality of nonreal meaning configurations. In that case, the spirit comprehended by the different members in common is a type of that "generality" with whose distinctiveness we are now concerned.

We will now apply the concept obtained in this way to problems we have already mentioned. Entities such as the "zeitgeist" and the "folk soul" must be regarded as wholly problematic as long as they are understood as psychic realities. This is because only what takes place temporally in single individuals is mentally real. Thus a real general zeitgeist or a real general folk soul cannot exist, except as a thoroughly problematic metaphysical reality. The problems posed by such concepts, however, assume a new aspect when entities such as the "spirit" of a religious community described earlier are considered. Without being corporeal, they are vested in many individuals in common. Thus they also lie beyond the only opposition between general and particular we have considered so far. It is true that the conceptually abstracted *meaning* of historical culture is not a general reality. But it does not coincide with the individual mental life of

[25]In the ensuing, we will determine more precisely what this means.

single individuals either. Suppose one proposed to speak of a general zeitgeist or a general folk soul as a nonreal meaning configuration in which many persons participate in common, even if only more or less completely. This is the sense in which we could speak of the general spirit of the congregation in the church that was more or less completely experienced in common by the individuals participating in the worship service. In that case, this sort of concept of a folk soul or a zeitgeist, even though it may remain imprecise in some respects, is at least not open to the doubts raised earlier.

Still more can be said on this point. There are also historical *realities* that insofar as they represent the bearers of such meaning configurations, history can bring under special group concepts. We have already touched on their logical structure in our discussion of *those* general concepts in history that are not relatively historical, and thus are also not natural scientific components.[26] In other words, they do not *only* contain what is found among absolutely *all* the members of a historical group. On the basis of the presuppositions indicated, terms such as "Greek," "German," "Renaissance," and "romanticism" are, first of all, to be understood as names for concepts of unreal meaning configurations that can be more or less completely grasped in common by many persons within a people or an age. Then, however, history would also have to consolidate the *real* events into groups that in the manner indicated, are the bearers of these meaning configurations. In this way, a history of the *real* Greek "spirit" and the real German "spirit" or of the real Renaissance and real romanticism would be produced.

At this juncture, the only point is to show how the problem of a general folk soul or a general zeitgeist can be conceived in a way that does not lead to a metaphysical conceptual realism. The question of how to represent this generality *historically* remains for subsequent discussion. First, we will continue to focus on the nonreal meaning itself that is attached to a historical reality. Like an empirical reality of the past, it is "discovered" – in a way that will not be further discussed here – on the basis of the historian's interpretation of extant source

[26][This refers to a discussion omitted from the translation: *Die Grenzen*, pp. 439–42. In discussing the extent to which generalization has a role in the formation of historical concepts, Rickert claims that not all general factors in history qualify as natural scientific components of the historical sciences. For example, historical concepts such as "the Renaissance" do not designate common properties that characterize all individuals who lived during the Renaissance. On the contrary, the content of such concepts is exhibited only by a relatively small number of individuals. This is why historical concepts such as "the Renaissance" and "the Enlightenment" cannot be regarded as natural scientific components of the historical sciences.]

materials. As we will see, there are reasons why we can often ascribe a greater accessibility to this meaning than to the real historical processes that were its bearers, and since we see the essence of historical concept formation in an individualizing method, this meaning poses a special kind of problem for us. Because the nonreal meaning configurations, which can be detached from historical realities, are always "general" in the sense indicated, it seems that the concepts of these meaning configurations must also have a general content. But they can be neither absolutely historical in the sense indicated nor relatively historical as general group concepts are. Everything we have set out thus far holds true exclusively for concepts of *real* historical processes. How does the historian grasp the nonreal? Does he perhaps employ a *generalizing* concept formation?

There are no circumstances under which the answer to this question can turn out in such a way that it again renders the main result of our inquiry problematic. To the extent that history is a science of the *real*, everything remains the same as above. But this is precisely the point at issue: Can history be regarded *only* as a science of the real? In the event this question were answered in the negative – which seems to be unavoidable in light of our concept of cultural science defined by reference to the concept of unreal value and meaning – our theory must be *supplemented*. The following needs to be shown: first, how the difference between generalizing and individualizing concept formation retains its decisive significance in the representation of detached *nonreal* meaning configurations as well; and second, how individualizing representation is structured as the only form of representation that is truly *historical*, that is, that represents *real* events with reference to the nonreal meaning configurations adhering to these real events. Only when this is clear will we be able to see how history does not lose its character as an individualizing cultural science in spite of the circumstance that, in part, it also employs concepts such as that of a general zeitgeist, a general folk soul, or other general meaning configurations. Finally, this will also clarify the concept of "recreative understanding," which is most intimately related to the nature of nonreal meaning configurations.

As long as we restrict ourselves to conceptually detached meaning, everything is basically quite simple. Like the meaning of the sermon or the music in the church, this meaning is "apprehended" or "experienced" in common by a plurality of individuals, perhaps by all. It is legitimately called "general" insofar as it is distinguished from real mental processes, which are always individual and which directly pertain only to single individuals. But does it follow that its *content* is also general in the same way as the content of a class concept or a law of nature, so that it must be represented in a generalizing or "natural scientific" fashion?

A closer examination of this matter will show the following: Regardless of the extent to which deeply engrained habits of thought make it seem "self-evident" to many that nonreal meaning as such is general and only nonmeaningful reality is individual, this kind of generality simply does not pertain to nonreal meaning. On the contrary, within the domain of nonreal meaning, a distinction must be drawn with respect to the generality and the individuality of the concepts we form of it. General cultural values possess generality of content insofar as they govern historical representation as principles of selection. We have seen how, in spite of this, an individualizing representation of reality takes place by their means. However, nonreal meaning configurations – which are attached to real historical processes in such a way that the latter are the bearers of the former, with the result that these unreal meaning configurations themselves belong to the material of history – do not coincide with these substantively general values. It is true that they are experienced in common by many or by all. But it does not follow that their *content* is general, like that of a general value or a law of nature. On the contrary, this content is distinguished from the governing value principles of historical representation in the following respect: Like the real, it is filled with content, and thus it also bears a distinctive and individual character.

This can easily be elucidated by returning to the illustration of the "general spirit" of the congregation in the church. Moreover it will be best if we consider the church building too, which, with respect to the congregation, should also be called "general." The following, in any case, is certain: *In common* with all the others, the different individuals "experience" the same building, the same organ, and the same pulpit. But the content of these experiences is not general. On the contrary, the building, the pulpit, and the organ all bear a distinctive and individual stamp. The same holds true for the content of the meaning configurations that are attached to the words of a particular sermon or the sounds of a particular piece of music and that are more or less completely grasped by the members of the congregation. Like the church building, they are general insofar as they can be experienced by all in common. In other respects, however, their content has a specific and individual character. It is true that their individuality does not really exist. Thus it is differentiated from the individuality of psychic or physical realities in the following respects: It is not the limitless, "infinite" individuality of a real heterogeneous continuum, and it also seems to depart from the individuality of such a continuum in that it seems to lack the unrepeatability or uniqueness of everything that is merely real. But this does not mean that it fails to qualify as an individuality. On the contrary, it at least stands on the same logical footing as the value-relevant irreplaceability and uniqueness of every real in-dividual.

The same claims must also hold true for the content of meaning configurations that belong to the material of history to the extent that they are either connected with historically essential real cultural processes or are realized in these processes. Especially in opposition to the substantively general values of culture that govern historical representation as principles of selection, they are formed in a thoroughly distinctive and individual manner. In spite of the fact that the "generality" of the nonreal [*irreale*] Greek "folk soul" and the unreal [*unwirkliche*] romantic "zeitgeist" can be more or less completely experienced in common by many people, in their totality they remain individual, even as detached meaning configurations. In other words, they differ from all other meaning configurations. Thus they conform to a general concept no more than this holds true for a real individual. On the contrary, to the extent that they are relevant to history, their individuality is comprehended by historical concepts. Thus regardless of how more or less completely their representation is structured in detail, as long as it remains the representation of the "Greek" folk soul or the "romantic" spirit, it must be placed in a fundamental logical opposition to every generalizing natural science. However, as long as this issue concerns meaning configurations detached from all real existence, we cannot speak of an individualizing *historical* concept formation in order to juxtapose it to a generalizing theory of meaning configurations as *natural scientific*. In the first place, meaning that is understood in an individualizing fashion as *only* nonreal also remains *unhistorical*. Moreover, the general concept of a value or a meaning is not a general concept of *nature*. Now, however, we must *extend* the concepts of individualization and generalization in such a way that they also apply to concepts of *nonreal meaning configurations*. In principle, nothing stands in the way of the following attempt: on the one hand, to represent the concrete meaning in its substantively complete individuality, for example, the meaning that everyone directly experiences in listening to a particular sermon or a specific piece of music; on the other hand, to try to develop a generalizing theory that explicates in their generality the values that constitute the meaning.

Indeed, we cannot stop here in the extension of our theory of generalizing and individualizing. Even in concepts of nonreal meaning, the individual does not necessarily stand in an *absolute* opposition to the general. On the contrary, just as in historical and natural scientific representations of the real, there can be concepts with the most diverse gradations of *relatively* individual and *relatively* general content that refer to nonreal meaning. However, this idea need not be pursued in any further detail, for it would only be a matter of the simple application of principles we have already set forth in the discussion of historical components in natural science and natural scientific components in history.

We can also leave undecided the question of the extent to which there really are individualizing sciences of conceptually abstracted meaning configurations. Finally, we need not consider how a generalizing theory of unreal meaning would have to proceed in order to take systematic shape.[27] It needs to be stated only that this theory cannot assume the form of any "psychology," including psychology as a "human science." Indeed, such a theory has no psychic material at all.

In this context, the only remaining important point is to show how, with respect to its content, the domain of the nonreal becomes *indifferent* to the difference between the individualizing and the generalizing conception as soon as we take the concept of the individual in a sufficiently comprehensive fashion so that it can refer to nonreal meaning configurations as well as to real physical and psychic processes. Even this consideration must make clear why the "generality" of nonreal meaning – a conception that is quite legitimate – in itself poses no difficulties in principle for our theory of individualizing historical concept formation. It can never be the problem of history to provide a generalizing theory of the nonreal meaning attached to the historically essential material. On the contrary, here, as in the case of real processes, the historical interest is oriented to specificity and individuality. At most, a general "theory of principles" for history – which itself would not proceed historically but, rather, would inquire into the metahistorical principles of historical life – would be conceivable as a generalizing theory of the meaning of culture. Something of this sort may be in the mind of those who speak, with little sense, of psychology as a human science.

It will be claimed, however, that by itself, all this still means little. History is concerned not only with the nonreal content of the meaning of culture in its individuality but also with the temporal course of meaningful cultural *reality*.

We need not investigate the *extent* to which history must consider

---

[27]This is the central problem of method in philosophy as the theory of value. I have treated it in detail in the first part of my *System der Philosophie*.

the real in order to remain history. There are certainly representations that qualify as history even though they do not have *much* to say
about real historical events. Consider, for example, a "history of
philosophical problems." It is true that the names of the philosophers
are noted, and we are told where and when the different philosophical ideas appeared. But in the main, the interest of the scholar can
remain concentrated on the nonreal meaning of the philosophical
position itself. Even if what is important to him is to pursue the
diversity in the philosophical content of problems and problem
solutions through different periods, the real bearers who have
actually developed these ideas may play only a subordinate role.
Analogously, a history of art is conceivable that is primarily an
account of the aesthetic content of works of art. In such an account,
therefore, the personalities of artists or other realities signify nothing
more than relatively indifferent loci for the realization of unreal
aesthetic meaning.

But we will not examine these representations in any more detail.
For the most part, what qualifies as historical science bears a fundamentally different stamp. In historical science, the representation is
primarily concerned with real bearers of meaning. As we have seen,
insofar as historical centers are at issue, this is always a matter of
human mental life that is somehow actually "lived" in values or
meaning configurations, a mental life that in this way itself becomes
meaningful. At least that is one way to express this point. In the
ensuing, we will explain this sense of the word "live" more exactly.
Bodies are also bearers of meaning. But in bodies, meaning is not
really "vital." Moreover, as long as no one comprehends it with real
psychic acts, meaning lacks "historical efficacy." Thus the historian
turns his interest to these acts and to meaningful real mental life itself.
Now we have to explicitly clarify how he represents it in an individualizing fashion as meaningful, real, mental life.

To make progress in this task, we must consider not only the
distinctive character of the material of history in contrast to that of the
natural sciences. We must also take into account another difference
that has been the subject of much discussion. This difference is
characteristic for the *conception* of the material by the scientist insofar
as it distinguishes, or so it is supposed, the historian as subject from
the natural scientist as subject. We know that there have been
repeated attempts to differentiate two groups of sciences or two kinds
of representation within the same science in such a way that one
"explains" its objects and the other "understands" them. The concept
of historical understanding, which is often linked with that of
"reexperiencing," has actually been made the focal point of a theory

of the human sciences. In this context, it is usually regarded as self-evident that the object of understanding or reexperiencing is the real mental life of historical personalities or mass movements. Because psychology deals with the reality of mental life, the attempt to make a "psychology" the foundation of historical science again comes into play, and this time apparently with justification. However, it is not a natural scientific, explanatory psychology but a science of human mental life based on understanding and reexperiencing. This science is supposed to provide the general "principles" that the historian needs for the representation of his material. We have already mentioned this idea, and at this point we return to it to *supplement* our exposition on the basis of the substantive concept of history we have now obtained.

As soon as we consider that, in fact, meaningful mental life necessarily belongs to the material of history, we will understand even better than before what is of validity in those theories that differentiate the sciences according to whether they explain nature or understand spirit [*Geist*]. At the same time, however, we will also be able to see more clearly than before where the *limits* of this validity lie. In other words, we will be able to see why, now as before, the significance of "psychology as a human science" conceived as a "foundation" of historical science remains thoroughly problematic, and also why the theories in question can be fruitful only to the extent that they do not terminate with the distinctions between nature and spirit or explanation and understanding considered for their own sake, but rather take these concepts in a special sense, which, in the end, amounts to what *our* theory regards as decisive for the nature of history. Above all, we have to ask, What alone can we conceive as *historical* understanding and reexperiencing, assuming that this is actually supposed to characterize the procedure of historical science, which is concerned with meaningful mental life? And how does the concept of historical understanding and reexperiencing, as correctly understood, fit into our theory of individualizing concept formation in cultural science?

To answer this question, it is advisable to distinguish, as in the foregoing, not only the concepts of nonreal meaning and meaningful reality, both of which fall under the concept of "spirit," but also the concepts of *understanding* and *reexperiencing*, which are usually conflated as well. Only in this way can we hope to reach clarity concerning the rather complicated problems at stake here, and thus finally liberate ourselves from every form of psychologism.

To begin with, therefore, we will completely disregard the "reexperiencing" of psychic existence and ask, To what extent is there any justification at all for calling history a science based on understanding [*eine verstehende Wissenschaft*], and thereby distinguishing it from the explanatory sciences?

The expression "to understand" has many meanings, which will not be enumerated here, and theories of understanding are as heterogeneous as the meaning of the word itself.[28] To stress only one aspect of this matter, the expression is linked, on the one hand, with the concept of the faculty of understanding, and, on the other hand, it is used precisely for the grasp of nonrational, atheoretical meaning – for example, the meaning attached to works of art. Since it is obvious that the historian also has to "understand" atheoretical material – indeed, for the most part historical existence occurs in a thoroughly "irrational" fashion, even though this does not make it "unintelligible" – in this context we should not think specifically of the faculty of "understanding." On the contrary, we should employ the term

---

[28]Since the appearance of the second edition of this book, which contained only a few remarks on historical understanding, this concept has been widely discussed, especially in connection with Dilthey's investigations, which to some extent provide more stimulation than ultimate enlightenment. However, no generally accepted view of the matter has been reached. Both philosophers such as Simmel and Spranger as well as specialized scholars such as Max Weber and Jaspers (*Allgemeine Psychopathologie*, 1913; second edition, 1920) have taken up this problem in an interesting and instructive fashion. Even this circumstance suggests an addendum to my theory of history. For reasons stated in the Preface, however, here as elsewhere I must forgo a detailed discussion of the comprehensive literature, which includes the Bern *Habilitation* thesis of Arthur Stein as well as an unpublished study by Karl Mannheim. Only the following point may be noted here. If a satisfactory theory of understanding does not yet exist, the reason, as far as I can see, lies primarily in the fact that the problem of value and meaning in this concept – which I already stressed in the second edition of this book (with an inadequate grasp of the individual factor) – has not received sufficient attention. As is so often the case in "psychologically" oriented endeavors, a clear distinction between the concepts of the real and the unreal is almost completely absent here too. At any rate, the problem of *historical* understanding cannot be solved in an exclusively psychological fashion, that is, by an investigation of real mental life. If the nonreal object of understanding is overlooked, this must lead to one of the following: either to "psychological" assertions that imply covert interpretations of meaning or value; or where this danger is avoided, as in the case of Troeltsch, to a disposition to treat the question metaphysically. Not infrequently, psychology is also transposed into metaphysics. I have taken pains to avoid all psychology as well as all metaphysics. I have also resisted the flight into a refuge of ignorance, which some may find tempting in the discussion of a matter that is apparently quite obscure and is in any case difficult to clarify. Much remains unexplained, as I know quite well. Here there are only the beginnings of an attempt to understand "understanding." But even the most modest initial effort at conceptual clarification seems to me scientifically more valuable than reveling in the profundity and the obscurities of understanding in the human sciences. . . .

"understanding" in a more comprehensive sense. But we should not conceive it too loosely either. Thus we should not regard it as equivalent to just any arbitrary account of historical materials. In order for the word not to lose its full and methodologically useful meaning, understanding must be taken as knowledge of a special kind of scientific material. What is involved here can be negatively expressed by claiming that understanding always concerns *more* than the comprehension of real entities that can be described, or also explained, as merely real. Positively expressed, this means that what does not have *value* and *meaning* in some sense or other remains "unintelligible." Thus – assuming that it is accessible to science at all – it can only be described or explained just like the value-free and nonmeaningful realities of nature, in the most comprehensive sense of the word. This is the only way we can surmount the generally prevailing imprecision concerning the concept of understanding.[29]

The grasp of a nonreal meaning configuration is what is usually *meant* by understanding. In any case, as a methodological term it is advisable to use the word in this sense. This is based on a further consideration. We have pointed out the distinctive "unity" of the nexus or the "totality" characteristic of nonreal meaning in contrast to merely real existence. The distinctiveness of the understanding of an object, in comparison with the explanation of that object, is also determined on this basis. This is the only way the expression "understanding" acquires a thoroughly precise meaning. Meaningful wholes can be understood only *as* unities or totalities. As I have already noted, however, this does not deny that the concepts of these totalities are composed of their elements, or that meaning configurations are more or less completely understood. The object of understanding as a nonreal meaning configuration always remains a whole or a unity. Realities, on the other hand, are decomposed into their parts for the purpose of explanation. Or, in explanation, the path leads from the parts to the whole; in understanding, it proceeds in the opposite direction, from the whole to the parts. At this point, one might link the differences in the *material* discussed earlier with the

[29]As an illustration characteristic of this prevailing imprecision, consider the following claim by Dilthey in the *Festschrift* for Sigwart (1900): "We call that process *understanding* in which we acquire knowledge of something that is inner on the basis of externally given perceptual signs." What is an "inner" process? Everything depends on this question. We know how vacuous the concept of an inner process is. And even if we disregard this point, the problem of understanding cannot be solved with the concept of an inner process that has the status of a *psychic* process. The signs that are "externally" given must make it possible to acquire knowledge of more than a real "inner" process. Otherwise they will remain unintelligible.

distinctiveness of the method employed in providing a scientific *representation* of this material. For many areas – even if not, perhaps, for all – this certainly holds true. In that case, one can make the following claim: In the explanation of the real, one holds the parts in one's hands and must be satisfied with putting them together again to form a whole. Ultimately, however, this is not a genuine whole. The spiritual bond we want to understand is always a nonreal meaning configuration. It is either attached to a reality or embodied in it. This is the only way reality is constituted as a genuine whole, in other words, a whole that is more than the real aggregate of its real parts.[30]

This is the legitimate core of those theories that call for an interpretive psychology [*eine verstehende Psychologie*] for historical science, in opposition to a natural scientific psychology, and point to the unity of a "psychic structural nexus" that can never be explained by the natural sciences, but only understood by the human sciences. The "inner" as the purely psychic does not possess this unity. As we have already seen, the unity in the *material* of history, which consists of meaningful realities, is based not on the reality but on the meaning embodied in it. Here again, therefore, we should pay careful attention to the point that the distinctiveness and necessity of the logical structure of a *method* of understanding as well will become clear only when we consider that it is never the unity of a real psychic existence but, rather, that of a nonreal meaning configuration that is to be understood, or that the failure of a natural scientific explanation of the historical material – and thus the legitimate requirement that knowledge of it depends on an interpretive method – is due not to the psychic character of this material but to its meaningful character.

Suppose we take the opposition between explanation and understanding in this way. And as regards the theories that speak of the inexplicable unity of historical objects, suppose we limit ourselves strictly to their legitimate "core" as just indicated. In that case, the difference between understanding and explanation must remain irrelevant to the difference between mental and corporeal existence. On the one hand, there is no reason why there should not be a value-free and nonmeaningful mental life that is explained by analyzing it into its parts, or why we should not want to represent mental life as a real, purely "natural" temporal process that takes place independent of the value or meaning that attaches to it. On the other hand, bodies can also be understood, assuming that, like works of art, for example, they express an aesthetic value or meaning. Moreover, if we restrict ourselves to realities that are immediately given, then, with

---

[30]It may also be possible to deal with the problem of the "organism" on this basis.

the exception of our own mental life, *only* bodies directly present themselves as objects to which an understandable meaning is attached. Thus there is still no necessary connection between the dichotomy of explanation and understanding and that of nature and spirit unless we understand by "spirit" only nonreal *meaning* configurations. The idea of psychology as a human science again becomes thoroughly problematic.

On the other hand, these considerations clearly exhibit the extent to which the concept of understanding as knowledge of a meaning is necessarily related to *our* theory of the historical representation of cultural processes and their centers. As we have seen, history is always concerned with value-relevant existence. Meaningful mental life is a special type of the value-relevant event as such. To this extent, therefore, it is quite correct that understanding is a part of the historical science that represents cultural life. This is because value-relevant and meaningful existence, in the sense of these words under consideration here, can be "understood" only *as* value relevant and meaningful. But it cannot be "explained" in this way. Indeed, if we proposed to restrict understanding to nonreal value and meaning detached from real existence, for our purposes the concept of understanding would require, at this point, no further discussion beyond the results already established. We can always call the comprehension of nonreal meaning "understanding" and thereby distinguish it from the explanation of psychic and physical material that is merely real.

At the same time, of course, these considerations also show why this most comprehensive concept of understanding still does not have a sufficiently *determinate* relationship to the distinctiveness of a historical representation. In the first place, the following point is clear: Just as isolated configurations of nonreal value and meaning are indifferent to the methodological distinction between the general and the particular, so the concept of an understanding of these configurations, in its most comprehensive sense, must also remain independent of the difference between generalizing and individualizing concept formation. On the one hand, we can speak of a generalizing understanding of nonreal meaning, namely, when our object is to subsume the manifold of meaning configurations under a system of general concepts of value and meaning. This is one of the problems of philosophy. On the other hand, when our objective is to comprehend a distinctive, concrete, substantively complete meaning configuration in its distinctiveness and concreteness, we will have to call this an individualizing understanding. For example, it is possible to develop a general theory of the meaning of religious sermons as well as to understand the meaning of a particular sermon by Schleiermacher. Here again, there are the most diverse degrees of generality and specificity imaginable in generalizing and individualizing interpretive representations. The general theory of the meaning of sermons has a specific and individual content in comparison with a theory of religious meaning configurations in general. And even the latter exhibits specific and individual features when we consider an absolutely general theory of all cultural meaning. However, none of the general theories includes history. Thus only a theory of *individualizing understanding*, and not a theory of understanding as such, is a part of the methodology that is definitive for historical science.

Even with the concept of individualizing understanding that arises in this way, however, the problem in the theory of history to which these considerations have led us cannot be clarified in a satisfactory fashion; nor, in the final analysis, can it be solved. Indeed, the extent to which individualizing comprehension – or, as we must now say, the individualizing understanding of *detached* nonreal meaning configurations – should be included in historical science in the authentic sense of the word, remained questionable. We are primarily concerned with the historian's representation of *real* meaningful mental life. If we want to call this representation as well "understanding," we cannot restrict the expression to the comprehension of detached nonreal meaning configurations. On the contrary, we are obliged to say that the historian wants to "understand" real mental life itself.

Is this view also justified? Certainly. But the understanding of real historical material can never be concerned with a *merely* real – and thus value-free and nonmeaningful – mental life. In its pure reality – given that we want to assume it actually exists – mental life remains just as "incomprehensible" for us as a purely real material object, such as a stone lying in the street. Otherwise, there is no objection to the use of the expression "understanding" for the comprehension of real, meaningful mental life. In that case, the real is an object of understanding in the sense that and to the extent that it is the "bearer" of a nonreal meaning. This makes good sense, and it is surely what is usually meant when we speak of the understanding of real psychic existence. In quite the same way, we do not understand an artwork insofar as it forms a purely real complex of canvas and color, but rather in the sense that and to the extent that it presents itself as the bearer of a nonreal aesthetic meaning. Thus we finally arrive at the question that must be the primary consideration for history in regard to the issue of understanding: If the historian investigates and conceptualizes real, meaningful, mental life, to what extent can this be called an individualizing understanding of the meaningful, central material of history?

The answer to this question poses difficulties that the program of an interpretive "psychology" does not recognize. Moreover the complete resolution of these difficulties would far exceed the limits of the problem we have set ourselves in this book. The problems that arise now do not so much concern the structure of historical *representation* or concept formation as they do the nature of historical *research* and *investigation*, that is, the process by which the historian works out the historical "facts" from the source material available to him. Throughout, we have disregarded this question and restricted ourselves to the conceptual representation of the factual material presupposed as given. We will not give an exhaustive answer to the question of how the historian acquires knowledge of the mental facts from which he forms his concepts, a consideration that already restricts the range of our problems.

However, even if we limit ourselves to the question of the representation of the factual material that is presupposed as given, we now encounter an area that will probably always resist *complete* clarification by means of logic. That is because history, in the representation of meaningful mental life, goes beyond what can be called *concept formation* in the strict sense. This holds true to the extent that it attempts to approximate not only the individuality but also the "perceptual reality" of immediately "experienced" and unconceptualized mental life. We already mentioned this point in our discussion of the historical analogue of conceptual *determination* in natural science. Accordingly, we will pursue the ideas developed there only to the point where we can at least see the issue that lies in the representation of the meaningful mental life of the past as a *problem*. We will discuss the question of the discovery of the mental factual material in the historical sources only to the extent that this is necessary to gain an insight into the logical structure of the *representation* of the given mental material.

Suppose we begin with the material whose historical representation is at stake, namely, the meaningful mental life of the past and its substantive distinctiveness. We will be able to grasp the nature of this material only if we always keep in mind that it consists of *two* factors. In the immediate "experience" of this material, these two factors interpenetrate. For logical theory, however, they must be rigorously distinguished from each other. This is because they lie in two completely different conceptual spheres. This says no more than what was earlier expressed in the term "meaningful mental life." Mental life is a reality; however, the meaning that is embodied in it or that it

realizes lies in the domain of the unreal. It is the aim of the historian
to conceptualize both the real and the unreal: the real as he actually
identifies it, as a unqiue, individual temporal process, and the unreal
as he understands it in its individuality.

If we conceptually distinguish the real and the unreal in this
manner, we can say that in many cases, perhaps even most, the
difficulty the historian encounters in *finding* his material in the
available sources concerns the real more than the unreal. With the
sole exception of the material of an autobiography, which constitutes
a unique and complicated case, the real mental life the historian hopes
to grasp in its actual individuality is never his own, but is rather always
the mental life of *another* person. And according to the assumption we
made earlier, nothing psychic that really transpires in other individuals can ever be *directly* accessible to the historian. In other words, it
cannot be immediately "experienced" as real existence. But it lies in
the nature of nonreal meaning configurations that they can be
immediately grasped or understood by many individuals, in principle
even by all, wherever sources for them are available. That is, as
regards *the meaning of the mental life of other persons, we may perhaps
acquire direct access to the individuality of its nonreal meaning, but never to
the individuality of its real existence.*

In the interest of always holding firmly to this difference – which
we have to keep in mind to see where the *difficulty* lies for the historian
in the representation of the meaningful mental life of the past – we
will make the following terminological distinction. Provisionally, we
will call only the comprehension of the unreal *meaning* of the mental
life of other persons "understanding." The comprehension of the *real*
mental existence of other persons, however, we will call "re-creation."
As a result, the problem that lies in what is usually called re-creative
understanding or interpretive re-creation – and that cannot even be
unequivocally recognized as a *problem* as long as these two concepts are
conflated – can be posed more clearly. Historical understanding,
therefore, must be a matter of the interpretive re-creation of the
meaningful mental life of other persons. As we can now claim, it is
both "re-created" in the individuality of its real existence and "understood" in the individuality of its nonreal meaning. The historian may
not only regard his material as something "unified." The re-creative
understanding of the meaningful mental life of the past may even
seem to him to be *one* integral act of his scientific knowledge, which he
then designates with an expression such as "empathy with the mental
life of another person." But regardless of the extent to which this
holds true, it is certain that the understanding of the nonreal meaning
embodied in mental life and the re-creation of the real psychic process

that transpires in time are not *identical.* In spite of this, how are both *integrated* in re-creative understanding, and how is this much-discussed activity of the historian "possible"? This is the genuinely "critical" question for a logic of the so-called human sciences.

We will best advance in the clarification of this problem if we begin by limiting ourselves to the question of whether there is any sense in which the mental life of another person can simply be "re-created." In other words, without understanding its meaning, can its real existence be grasped in such a way that the result is not merely concepts of psychic processes whose general elements comprise what we have in common with other individuals, or the respects in which we are the same? Or can it be grasped in such a way that through re-creation, we can also become acquainted with that in the mental life of another person that we ourselves are not able to experience directly as reality? It is obvious that precisely this issue is important for the theory of history. This is because the historian is not concerned with a generalizing psychology. On the contrary, he wants to represent the mental life of historical personalities or mass movements in its individuality.

Conceptual knowledge of the mental individuality of another person certainly does not seem impossible in principle. Even if we assume that only the reality of his own psyche is directly given to the historian, we still know that we can also represent individual entities by means of general concepts as soon as we combine the concepts as conceptual elements in such a way that their totality constitutes the content of an individual concept. The historian will also proceed in this way in the individualizing representation of another psyche. We need not pursue this matter. In the foregoing, we thoroughly discussed the question of how the representation of the individual is possible by means of the general. At the same time, however, we also noticed something else. The historian does not limit himself to what we call concept formation in the strict sense. On the contrary, he goes beyond it. Like the necessity of individualization itself, this was a consequence of the concept of history as the science of the unique and the individual as they really occur. Everything real is not only individual but also perceptual. Therefore, although history as a "science of reality," in the sense under consideration here, can never grasp perceptual reality completely, it at least attempts to *approximate* it more closely than is possible by a mere consolidation of general conceptual elements – which are essential or necessary on the basis of value relevance – into an individual concept.

Thus we will speak of a "re-creation" of the mental life of another person only where history is more or less successful in transcending the purely conceptual content of its representation. In the foregoing,

this is why we linked the moment of historical science that is focused
on the perceptuality of the real with those theories that proceed from
the assumption that the historian has the problem of making the
realities of the past "vital" again. It is true that this idea was not
satisfactory as a *point of departure* for a theory of history. But it must
find its place somewhere, and we have now come far enough in our
investigation that we can indicate where it is.

Only one further point should be noted first. As regards the question
of the scientific accessibility of the mental life of another person to
re-creation, in this context we will not inquire how the historian comes
to the supposition that real psychic processes exist in other individuals.
For history, this never becomes a problem. History presupposes
psychophysical individuals, in other words, bodies that have a mind,
in the same way that this holds true for the historian himself. But
history also presupposes that the mental life of these individuals has
a *content* that differs from what the historian directly encounters in his
own case. In consequence, this is now our question: To what extent can
the historian advance beyond a purely conceptual representation to a
substantive grasp of the real mental individuality of another person,
and in what sense can we, therefore, speak of a re-creation of real
individualtiy and a historical representation based on it that at least
approximate the perceptual reality of the individual? . . .

This problem could never be solved if the world of *experience*
coincided with the *real* world, or if our empirical knowledge were
limited to empirically *real* existence, that is, to corporeal and psychic
processes. Then we could go no farther than to subsume the mental
life of other persons under general concepts that we can form on the
basis of our own immediately given psyche. In fact, the psyches with
which we are empirically acquainted have real "windows" no more
than do monads. Thus as long as our knowledge of the noncorporeal
is nothing more than knowledge of a psychic entity that is the private
possession of every person, we could not speak of a re-creation of the
real mental individuality of another person that signifies more than a
comprehension mediated by general conceptual elements.

But this is not the way things are. The noncorporeal exists not only
as real *psychic* existence, but also as nonreal *meaning*. Moreover, the
latter does not lie in a problematic transcendent domain of metaphysics. On the contrary, we encounter it on the basis of experience just as
directly and certainly as we encounter the bodies of our surroundings
or our own psychic existence. Nevertheless, it is neither psychic nor
physical. We can all "understand" this nonreal meaning that is
attached to physical or mental processes. It would be absurd to doubt
this in precisely that science whose meaning we are attempting to

understand. But meaning as *detached* from mental and corporeal existence is neither our own nor that of some other person. For in the strict sense of these words, what is my own and what belongs to another person refer only to mental or corporeal realities. At best, nonreal meaning can be ascribed to me or another person only in a metaphorical sense, insofar as it has become "vital" either in my mental realities or in those of another person. Meaning also has a property that can never be ascribed to psychic existence: It can be directly grasped by us in common with other persons as *the same* nonreal meaning and, as we have seen, not as an entity that has a general content but, rather, in its *individuality*, in the same way that we all perceive the same body as an individual. Because we understand the nonreal individual meaning of the real mental life of another individuality, this opens up the possibility that meaning erects the *bridge* that leads us from our own mental life to that of another person, even in its *real* individuality. From this perspective, we proceed to the problem of re-creative understanding. . . .

. . . What does it mean to *re-create* the real mental life of another person if one only has direct experience of his own mental reality and if, in spite of this, history is not limited to the indirect comprehension of the psyche of a historical individual on the basis of general concepts of mental realities? This is the issue on which everything obviously turns. Through its *nonreal* "window," how does one psyche see the *reality* of another, and not merely the nonreal meaning that both have in common?

In order to make progress, suppose we once again explicitly link the difference between understanding and re-creation noted earlier to the difference between nonreal meaning and real mental existence. And in this connection, suppose we first clarify the concept of interpretive re-creation by means of an example that can be drawn from everyday experience. In the theory of history, we can also make use of an event with which everyone is acquainted in prescientific life, for Simmel is undoubtedly correct when he claims that "although the premises and the methods, the interests and the subject matter may be very different, ultimately our understanding of the Apostle Paul and Louis XIV is essentially the same as our understanding of a personal acquaintance."[31] Thus let us consider how we "come to an understanding" in a conversation with our fellows. We hear words – that is, acoustical sounds – to which a meaning is attached. We do not *directly*

[31]*Vom Wesen des historischen Verstehens* (Berlin: Mittler, 1918), p. 4 [See Georg Simmel, "On the Nature of Historical Understanding" in *Essays on Interpretation in Social Science*, trans. Guy Oakes (Totowa, N.J.: Rowman & Littlefield, 1980), p. 98.]

"experience" the mental life of the other person, but rather only bodies and meaning configurations. We need them to learn something about the other person's psyche. They are an "indirect path." In what sense?

Suppose someone tells us something the meaning of which we understand completely. To this extent we can also make it "our own." At the same time, however, it may strike us as quite "alien."[32] This would certainly be the case if a German, after the World War, expressed his satisfaction with the "Peace" of Versailles. What happens inside us? In this way at least one aspect of the problem of interpretive re-creation can be clarified. In our terminology, what is at stake here can be formulated in the following way. We "understand" the nonreal *meaning* of the alien words, but we cannot "re-create" the real, alien *mental* processes of the person who expresses this meaning. In such a case, we say that although we have understood the *words* completely, the other *person* remains "unintelligible" to us, meaning thereby that we are unable to re-create his real mental life. There are circumstances under which the matter may be left at that. In this sort of case, the *difference* between understanding nonreal meaning and re-creating the real mental life of another person – as we propose to use these expressions – becomes clear. The understanding of meaning succeeds, the re-creation of the mental does not.

Suppose, however, we do not regard our contemporary as "insane," and therefore as permanently "incomprehensible." Then we can attempt to penetrate his real mental life on the basis of the meaning of his words that we have understood. In other words, we can ask what must have occurred in his mind that was responsible for the fact that he could really intend and express these words with precisely this meaning that we have understood. In such a case, it will at least become evident how we use the understanding of nonreal meaning to build the *bridge* from our own mental life to another mental life that is not directly accessible to us. To see how that is possible, suppose we make just one further terminological distinction explicit. Implicitly we have already made repeated use of this distinction. Because of the ambiguity of the word "live," however, peculiar terminological difficulties arise in its formulation.

Suppose we *only* understand an "alien," nonreal meaning – that is,

---

[32] The expressions "our own" and "alien" are used here with deliberate imprecision. In the strict sense, they can apply only to *real* processes, which are either included in our own real individuality or in that of another person. Real processes can also be described in this way metaphorically when they are related either to our own real individuality or to that of another person. To this extent, a meaning configuration *detached* from every reality is neither alien nor my own.

a meaning intended by another person. That means we do not yet have knowledge of this meaning as it is *really* vital in a mental life, or as a psyche *really lives* in it. These expressions are not very appropriate, but it is not easy to find better ones. To make them unambiguous, the qualification "really" should be noted. *Every* understanding of a meaning can also be called an "experience." To this extent a meaning that we understand always becomes "vital" in our mental life. For this reason we must distinguish two varieties of the process in which a meaning "becomes vital" and designate only one of them as the process in which the meaning "*really* becomes mentally vital." We will use this term only in cases in which we are not limited to *merely* understanding meaning.[33] In our example this means the following: We may understand the meaning of the words that refer to another mental life without also seeing how the person who speaks these words *really* lives their meaning in his own mental experience. This is what we mean when we say that although we understand the meaning of the words, the person, nevertheless, remains "alien" and "unintelligible" to us. In that case, all we know is that the meaning we understand is in fact really vital in the mind of the other person, for he intends it. But we are not only unable to experience directly the mental life of the other person in which this meaning is really vital. This never happens. We are also unable to re-create it. This can be expressed in the following way. Although we have a complete understanding of the meaning as a nonreal meaning, we only understand it in this way. It is *really* vital only in a mental life that is completely *unknown* to us. For this reason, we are unable to re-create it.

In this case, the nature of re-creation consists in the fact that we do not merely understand meaning as nonreal meaning. On the contrary, we also attempt to "empathize" with a mental life in which this meaning is really vital, a mental life that really lives in this meaning. That can happen if we ask the following question: Assuming we spoke

[33]In my *System der Philosophie*, Volume I, I used the concept of "vital life" [*des "lebendigen Lebens"*], in opposition to the *merely* real and organic life [*vitalen Leben*], in order to do justice to the sense of value and meaning that resonates with the contemporary feeling for idiom in the case of the word "vital" ["*lebendig*"]. A vital life refers to a life filled with meaning, not to a meaningless life. In this context, on the other hand, the point is rather to stress that meaning *really* becomes vital in mental life. Here, therefore, there is a sense in which the focal point lies on the reverse side. . . . Real life can merely be life. It is self-evident, however, that a mental life that "really lives" in a meaning configuration is at the same time always a "*vital* life," in the sense of the word employed in my *System der Philosophie*. As a result, no misunderstanding will arise. What is important here is only the distinction between the "mere understanding" of a meaning configuration and the "real life" that is in it.

these words and merely understood their meaning, how would *our* mental life have to be constituted for these words to be really vital in it? In this case we will say that we are "transposed" into the psyche of another. In this process we use the following pieces of knowledge: on the one hand, our understanding of the nonreal meaning of the alien words and, on the other hand, our knowledge of our own real mental life, the only thing concerning which we have direct knowledge. From the *composite* of these two pieces of knowledge, we construct the mental life of another person, in which the meaning of the alien words – which has not really become vital in our own mental life – really lives. Thus it must be clear what the step from the nonreal meaning that is merely understood to the meaning that is really vital in another psyche signifies. It is true that the meaning as such always remains nonreal. Now, however, it is conceived as having become really vital in the mental life of another person in such a way that we think we know on the basis of the experience of our own mental life that this meaning can become vital in a mental life as such, and thus also in the mental life of another person. In other words, unlike us, the other person is not limited to the mere understanding of this meaning.

On the basis of these arguments – in which we have still not considered the individuality of the other psyche and have examined only a special kind of meaning because it is a good idea to treat the different aspects of the problem separately – we propose to distinguish *three* concepts from one another and to define them in the following way. First: the *mere* "understanding" of a nonreal meaning that, in its abstraction from all real existence, is neither our own nor an alien meaning. In other words, it is not yet understood as a meaning in which a real mental life, our own or another, really lives. Second: real, primordial "life," in a sense with which we are directly acquainted as the genuinely vital interpenetration of *our own* real mental existence and real meaning. Third: the "re-creation" of the meaningful mental life of *another* person, which we never really experience as an interpenetration of nonreal meaning with the real psyche. Thus we have no *direct* knowledge of it either. But because we have understood the meaning that really lives in this mental life as nonreal meaning – on the basis of our knowledge of mental life in general, which is grounded in our own mental life – we can construct the mental life of another person in such a way that we acquire *mediated* knowledge of it as an interpenetration of nonreal meaning and real mental life that can be re-created.

If there is no objection to the use of the expressions "really experienced" and "genuinely vital" meaning, in opposition to meaning that is "merely understood" and that to this extent, remains "lifeless," at least there will no longer be any ambiguity about these three most general concepts: the mere understanding of meaning; one's own meaningful mental life, which at first was really experienced; and the meaningful mental life of another person, which is not originally experienced but is rather re-created. We will also see how it is in principle possible for the re-creation of the meaningful mental life of another person – in which the nonreal meaning configurations that have been understood really live or have lived – to come about on the basis of a mere understanding of nonreal meaning configurations that are expressed in or attached to a psychic process, even though they were never really originally experienced in our own mental life. Nonreal meaning, therefore, can form the bridge between our own real mental life and the real mental life of another person. This is because, as nonreal meaning, it can be ascribed neither to us nor to another person. . . .

If we adhere to these deliberately pedantic and comprehensively developed distinctions and connections, which are indispensable for the purpose of clear concepts of the real and the nonreal, they must also clear the path for the solution to problems in the theory of *history*. To gain a better insight into the processes that are called *historical* understanding and *historical* re-creation, we need only transpose these distinctions and connections from the experience of contemporary everyday life, from which they were obtained, to the observations the historian makes on the basis of his source material of the past. In detail, of course, such a transposition would require quite complicated reflections and stipulations about gradual differences in the certainty of understanding, as well as in the dimensions of the individualities that are objects of understanding and re-creation. The foregoing discussion, however, establishes that it cannot be impossible in principle. That is because the historian, in this sphere of his activity, is also invariably concerned with an attempt to re-create – on the basis of the understanding of nonreal meaning – the other mental life in which this meaning was once really vital. We will limit ourselves to pointing out the considerations that lead to a theory of historical understanding, insofar as this is necessary to exhibit the general principle required by methodology. Fundamentally this is all quite simple, and a few remarks will suffice.

It is only that we must always keep in mind the status this part of the discussion occupies in the context of our inquiry. It is an *addendum* to the theory of individualizing concept formation in history that was developed earlier. This also holds true in the following respect: In historical science, re-creative understanding also signifies nothing more than an *addendum* to the *purely* conceptual representation. It goes beyond concept formation in the strict and authentic sense only as an addendum. We know why this is the case. As we have repeatedly seen, there are many cases in which history is not content to synthesize general conceptual elements into individual historical *concepts*. On the contrary, it attempts to advance until it reaches the comprehension of historical reality in its *perceptual reality*. This is related to its character as a science of reality. It will not be satisfied with the products of mere concept formation and their relatively considerable remoteness from reality. At this point, we have to subsume the historical grasp of the perceptual quality of reality that develops from this dissatisfaction under the concept of re-creative understanding.

In this context, we should not only keep in mind that the interest in perception remains limited to one part of historical representations. We should also note that even here, it leads to only one *part* of the historian's concerns. That is, to a certain extent, re-creative under-standing *presupposes* genuinely historical concept formation; in other words, knowledge of the unique development of the historical event with reference to its physical and psychophysical reality. This is why we call it an addendum. Without this basis, it would lack any point of reference and any firm scientific footing. Thus the historian must already know something about the complete psychophysical reality of the persons he represents before he undertakes to understand the meaning of their mental life. For this reason, the part of his representation we will examine now always concerns *filling* with perceptual content historical concepts that have already been formed, or clothing the purely conceptual scientific "skeleton" with historical material that has been perceptually re-created, and can also be perceptually re-created for the reader. Thus in the ensuing remarks, we should also keep in mind this supplementary, relatively subordi-nate character within historical science to avoid the mistaken impres-sion that any of our earlier results are being retracted or even qualified.

Assuming the ideas previously developed are sound, what is still wanting requires only a few remarks.

First, the following is a self-evident consequence of our exposition. Suppose the historian proposed to limit himself to the comprehension of individual mental realities as *merely* real, temporally occurring processes: in other words, without regard to the nonreal meaning that is linked with them. In that case, for this historian there would simply be no re-creation of past mental life in its perceptual individuality. The psychic existence of earlier times would be only indirectly accessible to him, on the basis of general concepts. That is, he could represent its individuality in one way only: by employing general conceptual elements to form concepts with an individual content. This is the negative side of the matter.

The positive side proves to be just as simple. Suppose that in spite of this, the historian manages to achieve more than an individualizing concept formation that is relatively quite remote from reality. This can be a consequence only of the following consideration. From the extant source material, it is not only the knowledge of real historical facts that is accessible to him. On the contrary, sometimes he has access to a profusion of nonreal meaning configurations that he understands in their distinctiveness and individuality. As meaning configurations that are merely understood, even here they must be called free-floating. This is especially the case here, where their real bearers, in which they were once genuinely vital, are no longer really alive. To this extent, they are not yet "historical" in the authentic sense of the word, which always includes the idea of a reality. However, the historian connects them with the real historical centers – that is, the historical personalities or masses about which he knows the following on the basis of his sources: at one time, the meaning configurations that he has merely understood, really lived in them. He thereby attempts to re-create the meaningful mental life of the past in the manner that we were able to document with reference to the experiences of contemporary life.

This is all that can be meant when it is said that history should again "bring to life" eras that have become "lifeless," or that it should "recall the past to mind." With regard to real mental life that once existed, this always signifies an *individualizing re-creation of the real on the basis of an individualizing understanding of unreal meaning configurations*. Thus the *principle* of *historical* understanding and re-creation becomes clear. This may suffice as a way of supplementing the earlier remarks on the proximity of history to reality, remarks that inevitably remained quite general as long as we had not yet considered a specific historical material. As a result, the main purpose of our exposition – to show how *re-creative understanding also finds its place in our theory of individualizing concept formation* in its history – is realized.

We need not consider any further *the particulars* of how this part of historical activity as the transconceptual, perceptual, or "intuitive" grasp of the factual material of history takes place, and the extent to which, in every such case, more than *mere* perception or *mere* "intuition" is involved. By this point it must already be clear how in historical representations that attempt to give a transconceptual grasp of the past, purely conceptual elements are most intimately connected with elements that fill out these concepts with perceptual material, and how the perceptual *pictures* of the mental life of the past, intensified to the point where they can be re-created, are possible in this manner, pictures that put us under their spell when we read the works of the great historians. We have no misgivings about extending the concept of historical comprehension so that it also includes these quasi-pictorial historical concepts in which the material of perception is embodied. Under these conditions, we must speak of historical concept formation in a narrower, stricter sense and in a more liberal sense. It is obvious that the different factors on which this difference rests are to be distinguished only in the *theory* of history. Actually, historical representations will usually employ more or less picturelike concepts that embody the material of perception. These concepts exhibit both the stricter and also the more comprehensive senses of the conceptual, linked in one unified entity. But this poses no fundamentally new problems for the general nature of individualizing historical representation. . . .

We do not need to pursue *the supplementary remarks* of this section – much of which could be presented only as suggestions – any further. As noted, they had only one aim. As regards the problem of a taxonomy of the sciences, consider *legitimate* efforts in this direction that proceed not from formal logical oppositions but on the basis of differences in the material. In a theory of history, they underscore the concepts of human science and the re-creative understanding of the spiritual. Our purpose has been to show how these endeavors find their place and their elucidation within the context of our ideas as well – indeed, how they can be logically elaborated and fruitfully developed for the purposes of methodology only on the basis of our position. At this point we will briefly summarize all that has been established concerning these issues.

If we want to speak of the "human sciences" [*Geisteswissenschaften*] in methodology, what we mean by "mind" [*Geist*] cannot be merely real psychic existence. On the contrary, we must also include its immanent nonreal meaning. This is the only way to reach the central historical material. Even given this stipulation, however, we will still not find the term "human science" particularly appropriate for achieving conceptual *clarity* about the nature of history and its subject matter. For this purpose, the word is too ambiguous, and precisely in the direction that leads to philosophically questionable confusions. First, "mind" refers to real psychic existence in general. Second, it refers to "higher" mental life, in other words, a mental life with higher values. Third, for "mind," many intend a supernatural or spiritual world. And fourth, the expression can also be used for unreal constructs detached from all real existence. It is especially important to distinguish these *four* concepts in the effort to gain insight into the nature of the *material* of the historical sciences and its significance for the methods of historical concept formation.

To these considerations we should add that even quite recently, "mind" [*Geist*] has once again begun to take on the character of a fashionable slogan. It is in the nature of such slogans to be ambiguous and thus confusing. On the whole, nothing of specific import can be identified with their use, which is why they appeal all the more to feeling and surmise. This is the basis of their popularity, and reason enough to be on our guard against them in science. So let us ungrudgingly leave "mind" to those who are less interested in the conceptual rigor of thought than in making an exciting impression.

It obviously remains true that in characterizing one *part* of historical activity, we *can* speak of a re-creative understanding of the "spiritual" [*der geistigen*] world. But the concepts of understanding and re-creation are also too imprecise and general to provide a fully autonomous and *exhaustive* characterization of the nature of all historical representation. As regards understanding, it is important, first, that the object of understanding in history is always something more than merely real; namely, it is value relevant and meaningful. And second, to remain within the domain of history, the value relevant and the meaningful are compreheded not in a generalizing fashion but in an individualizing fashion, even though their content may be only relatively historical. Finally, even the concept of the "re-creation" of historical individuality acquires its precise significance for the theory of the historical sciences only on the basis of the concept of the individualizing understanding of meaning.[34] Historical re-creation is always concerned with the reconstruction of the individual mental life of the past that was meaningful because the goods of culture were expressed in it. Thus without our concept of the *value-relevant and individualizing science of culture* whose central material is constituted by the meaningful mental life of cultural human beings, both the concept of human science and that of re-creative understanding remain without any logically useful meaning. So once more it must be clear where the focal point of a logic of history lies, and why we had to *begin* not with the historical material but with the form of the historical concept to reach a philosophical understanding of the nature of history. . . .

[34][Rickert's discussion of the individuality of the meaning configurations that are objects of understanding (*Die Grenzen*, pp. 578–88) is not included in the translation. This part of the text is concerned with the individuality of the object of re-creative understanding, and thus with the individuality of nonreal meaning configurations.]

5

Philosophy of Nature and
Philosophy of History

I remain convinced that I am on the right path when
I seek in what *should* be the basis for what is.
Rudolf Hermann Lotze

INTRODUCTION

From philosophical standpoints, the question to which we now turn can be regarded as the most important. In the foregoing, we have shown only that *if* history as the representation of the unique development of human cultural life is to exist, it has to proceed according to the method we have set out. We were also able to point out the conditions that must be satisfied for history to be objective or have the status of a science in the same sense as natural science. But it has not yet been established *whether* these conditions are also fulfilled. We cannot let the matter rest here. If history did not possess scientific objectivity, the significance of the limits of concept formation in natural science that we have exhibited would be problematic in the following sense: They would not be the limits of only natural science, but, rather, the limits of science in general.

At this point, therefore, we are again led to a question touched on in the Introduction: Within what "weltanschauung" does historical science have a logically incontestable significance? Must philosophy acquiesce in a naturalism that conceives the real world as an eternal recurrence that is indifferent to all distinctiveness and individuality, with the result that only a subordinate role falls to the historical? Or is there not a conception of the real in its totality that sees history as a process of development to which we can ascribe a "meaning" that lies beyond all nature? In consequence, do the distinctive and the individual in the real process acquire a significance in its distinctiveness and individuality by virtue of the relation to meaning, so that historical thought has the same theoretical justification as natural science? The problem of the scientific objectivity of historical representations can be solved only by answering these philosophical questions.

Nevertheless, in the ensuing we will not leave the framework of the foregoing discussion. On the contrary, we will remain within the limits of the *theory of science*. The problem we still have to solve imposes only one condition: that we no longer restrict ourselves to the determination of the cognitive goals that in fact obtain and regard concepts as means for their attainment. On the contrary, we are additionally obliged to inquire into the theoretical significance concepts in natural science and history have independent of the goals set by human volition, and thus the extent to which we can speak of a scientific objectivity of the different forms of knowledge.

1. NATURALISTIC PHILOSOPHY OF HISTORY

Since our main task is to arrive at a judgment concerning the relationship between the objectivity of historical representation and the objectivity of natural science, we should first see what can be said about the scientific status of concept formation in history from the perspective of *natural science*.

An advocate of naturalism will be prima facie inclined to deny scientific objectivity to the method of history. If, so he must reason, history represents the real with reference to the distinctive and the individual, and if the principles of concept formation in history are value perspectives, the historian is necessarily left with vacillating and individual opinions. This is because the question of what qualifies as a historical individual depends on what he regards as a value, and the ordering of "teleological" or value-relevant developments, in the sense under consideration here, is always the result of individual caprice. In opposition to this, natural science advances to timelessly valid laws. Whereas history always remains confined to human precepts, natural science makes it possible for the scientist to transcend himself by enabling his transitory spirit to grasp the eternal in a law of nature. From these premises, one of the following consequences can be drawn: Either there is only *one* science, the science of nature, in which case history cannot be called a science at all, or it is possible to constitute history as a science only by providing it with a natural scientific – or at least value-free – foundation.

For the present, we will not consider the first consequence. We propose to investigate only the question of whether natural science is able to alter historical science insofar as it does not conform to the natural scientific ideal of scientific objectivity. If this cannot be done by transposing the method of natural science onto history itself, then there may be a naturalistic *philosophy* of history that can at least provide a natural scientific validity for the governing principles of concept formation in history. On this basis, history could be elevated to the status of an objective science. An attempt of this sort can be undertaken in two different ways. First, it is possible to ask whether we can dispense with values as the governing principles of concept formation in history and replace them with a value-free philosophy of history. And second, should this prove unfeasible, it is possible to ask whether values can be established on the basis of the concept of nature itself. In that case, these values would define culture in an objective fashion. Or as "natural values," they would no longer jeopardize the objectivity of concept formation in history.

We already touched on the possibility of a philosophy of history that is completely value free when our investigation led us to the concept of a general law of development that allegedly forms the basis for representations of different individual sequences of development. In this concept, we found the only logically intelligible sense that can be ascribed to attempts to bring history and natural science closer together.[1] At this point, therefore, we must inquire into the presuppositions on the basis of which such a law of development might be established. Then we will see what its discovery could mean for the objectivity of historical science.

Consider the requirement that the historian should compare the different historical sequences of development with one another, underscore what they have in common as that which is essential, and then employ this result for the organization of the historical material. This requirement may seem quite plausible to many. However, if such a comparison should really be undertaken independent of previously established cultural values – and in this context that is the assumption on which everything depends – then considerable difficulties may lie in the path of the execution of such a program. What are the historical sequences of development that history must compare with one another? This question cannot be answered from a value-free, natural scientific standpoint. Are we perhaps expected to consider every human community whose development can be followed through a certain span of time? The historian will never agree to this. Not all communities are "historical" in the stricter or more substantive sense of the word explained earlier.

Rather, in the attempt to work out a comparative history, the idea appears as quite self-evident that the developmental law that is the object of the inquiry is to be discovered by a comparison of different *peoples*. But what is a "people"? Without the help of a cultural value,

[1][Rickert considers this possibility on pp. 468–9 of *Die Grenzen*, which are not included in this translation.]

can we say where its development begins and where it ends? In other words, does the purely natural scientific, value-free conception possess a means both for unambiguously comprehending the developments of peoples as self-contained entities of a totality and for differentiating them from one another?

Let us even suppose this were possible. Then a new question arises. Consider what is common to the development of *all* peoples. Can history take this and *only* this as the general law of development that provides a basis for its representations? History must also make a selection among peoples, and for this purpose it again requires a governing principle. Of course, it seems quite "self-evident" to natural scientific historians that they should concern themselves only with peoples who have a culture. That is because they are invariably guided by cultural values as well, even if they are unaware of this. But from the value-free standpoint of natural science, it is by no means self-evident what a people with a culture is. The historian in search of general laws of development, like every other historian, is led to the question of what culture really is. Without value perspectives, he cannot answer this question. In principle, therefore, even a comparative "history" that attempts to discover laws needs all the presuppositions that constitute the reason why the advocate of naturalism contests the scientific character of the history that, in our sense, proceeds in a "teleological" or value-relevant fashion.

But perhaps cultural values serve only as a preliminary orientation. As soon as a law is discovered, it holds true independent of these values. If we suppose this position is correct, we immediately encounter a new difficulty, assuming that a *law* of cultural development is actually obtained. It will not be discovered by the analysis of a single developmental sequence. Here the empirical comparison of several developmental sequences is the only logically admissible means. But the number of different peoples with a culture that are to be compared with one another, and whose development is known from "beginning" to "end," proves to be quite small. No natural scientist would regard himself as justified in drawing an inference – that is more than a mere conjecture – from the observation of only a part of such a small sample to a conclusion about all the other peoples. Here, therefore, a "complete induction" – that is, the investigation of every single case – would be an inescapable requirement. And even in this way we would not arrive at a real law of the kind natural science seeks. At best, the result would be an empirically general model. But does this not presuppose that we already know the fundamentals of the history of all peoples with a culture *before* we proceed to establish the general model of development, and therefore that all history is

already written before "objective," scientific, historical research in this
sense begins?

An empirical law discovered to hold for a sample of cases can be
employed as the governing perspective for the investigation of the
unknown cases only where a large number of single cases is involved.
In the representation of the small number of peoples with a culture
that can be compared with one another, we can never achieve more
than uncertain conjectures. These conjectures can easily lead to the
result that the historian begins the investigation of his subject matter
with unfounded *prejudices*. Thus they are hardly qualified to endow
historical representations with the "objectivity" that is wanted. One
might, of course, formulate laws such as that according to which
prehistory, antiquity, early and late Middle Ages, and recent and
contemporary history follow one another in the development of every
people. The validity of such a "law" might be maintained, and this
schema could also be supplied universally. But because it expresses no
more than the fact that what comes earlier precedes what comes later,
it can hardly be regarded as an important scientific insight. Other
schema that claim that every people must first experience a stage of
youth, followed by a stage of manly maturity, and finally ending in a
stage of old age fare no better. Whatever holds true in claims of this
sort proves to be either so vacuous or so self-evident that it does not
need to be made explicit. The problems with such claims begin only
when we ask about the sense in which it is possible to speak of the
"youth" or "old age" of an entire people – in which there are always
old as well as young persons – and whether concepts that are valid for
the single individual retain their scientific significance when they are
transposed onto the developments of peoples. Is there a young or an
old *culture* in the sense in which an organism flourishes or withers?
That cannot be regarded as self-evident. Perhaps it only has the value
of a picture.[2]

It is not logically impossible, however, to formulate a general law of
cultural development and then attempt to determine how far one can
go with it in the specifics of providing a historical representation. For
this reason we cannot leave the matter as it now stands. Thus let us
assume that a developmental law were discovered that is valid for the
cultural development of all peoples. Would this law also make the
governing cultural values of concept formation in history superfluous?

[2]In this regard, the success of Spengler's work shows how astonishingly easy to
satisfy many are in the demands they impose on concepts in the philosophy of
history. This book is not only quite unreliable in its details; its conceptual bases are
also completely unclear. All that it contains in the way of "imagination" should not
deceive anyone on this point.

The general law can never do more than provide the space within which the historical representation of distinctive and individual developments takes place. Moreover, this space must be filled with what is characteristic of specific historical developments, and with this alone. Thus the developmental law would replace the governing value perspectives in history only if it could also serve as the principle of selection in the representation of purely individual historical material. However, we have seen that the nature of the nomological – like the nature of natural scientific generality as such – consists precisely in the fact that it is indifferent to the specific and individual characteristics of objects, which fall under general laws as instances. As a result, it is not clear how a general law of development should be used to distinguish the essential from the inessential in the *individual* factual material, in which history goes beyond what is common to the developments of all peoples. Accordingly, laws can never be employed as the governing principle for the representation of a unique historical sequence of development in its individuality. It is invariably only values that can have this function, for it is only with reference to values that the individual can become essential.

It will be claimed, however, that this cannot be correct, for there actually are historical representations that have attempted to employ a developmental law as the governing perspective. And even if they are substantively false, do they not at least formally exhibit the intended logical structure? As a result, does not their mere existence constitute a counterexample to our claim?

It is easy to show why this is not the case either. Suppose that somewhere the impression arises that a general law of development is the principle for the selection of what is historically essential in the representation of a unique individual development. In that case, the content of the alleged law of nature will always be regarded as what *should* be realized by the development. In consequence, all the principles of value-relevant concept formation in history that we have encountered can be employed. But then the "law" is not a *natural* law at all, but rather the formula for a *value* principle. Therefore, such a procedure is inadmissible from a purely natural scientific standpoint that shuns every value relation.

It will be useful to elucidate this point in more detail with an example. Earlier we could characterize the social dynamics of Comte as the model for a naturalistic philosophy of history. This holds true insofar as history should be explicitly constituted as a natural science that is supposed to discover the natural laws of human development. Now we can show that as regards his *intention*, a law of nature is indeed present in Comte's "law" of the three stages. In fact, however, the equivocation between a law that says what *must* happen and a principle of progress that says what *should* happen has found its typical expression in this "law." Only as a result of this confusion could the impression arise that this law produces a generalizing philosophy of history that is formally natural scientific. Consider the *value* that "positive" science had for Comte. Within the framework of his weltanschauung dominated by the ideals of the *Polytechnique*, it was the means for the realization of his plans for social reform. In the last of his three stages, Comte based the total development of human culture on the *value* of positive science as its authentic *purpose*. And then, by means of the addition of the other two stages, he established a general formula for the gradual realization of this cultural goal. Thus even if Comte's "law" were valid, the basis on which he attempts to ground history would not be the concept of nature but rather the *cultural concept of natural science*. In other words, it is only "positive" science as a cultural good that governs the organization of the historical periods and the selection of what is essential in Comte's work. As a result, he does not thereby formally establish a natural law of history. On the contrary, he undertakes to interpret its *meaning*.

Thus we see that in his sociology, Comte advocates naturalism only in intention, but not in practice. Precisely because it is undertaken on the basis of "positivist" principles, there is no respect at all in which his historical representation formally differs from the logical character of all historical representations. In his work, sociology also follows the unique and individual development of human culture and represents it in concepts. The individual content of these concepts is consolidated with reference to the cultural value of positive science to constitute the in-dividual as a "teleological" or value-relevant unity, in the sense explained earlier. And at the same time, the recognition of this cultural value is expected of everyone. Such a historical conception can be called "unhistorical" insofar as it also employs its value perspectives for the direct valuation of historical processes. Thus it does not represent cultural development "objectively" in the sense of an empirical science. But this circumstance makes no difference as regards opposition to the natural scientific conception. In particular, for Comte as well, the connection between the different stages of history is value relevant. Indeed, he explicitly deduces the second stage as the teleologically necessary transition between the first and the last. In this regard, the positivist schema of development falls under the same logical category as attempts made in the idealist philosophy of history to define the meaning of the entire history of humanity by means of a formula, as undertaken by Fichte or Hegel, for example. The similarity can even be pursued into its details. Like

Fichte, only in slightly different terms, Comte also has the development of humanity progress from the instinct of reason to the science of reason, and ultimately to the art of reason. And for Comte as well, there is an intermediate stage that becomes the age of consummate wickedness.

Obviously the considerable differences between the *contents* of teleological formulas of development should not be overlooked. In this regard, however, it remains questionable whether positivism can be distinguished to its advantage from a philosophy of history as developed, for example, by Hegel. Comte was completely confused about the logical nature of his "sociology," and he believed he was proceeding in a natural scientific fashion, whereas in fact – to employ our language – he was following a course that was relatively historical. Aside from these considerations, because of the poverty and inadequacy of his value schema, Comte's work is vastly inferior to the constructions in the philosophy of history produced by German philosophers. As in the case of Hegel, Comte's idea of the plan and meaning of history is basically grounded in his own philosophy of value. But whereas Hegel was able to comprehend a truly vast profusion of cultural life with his metaphysically anchored "spiritual" principle of value, Comte's intellectualism and his positivist ideal of knowledge restrict the scope of cultural goods, so that as attempts to write history on this basis become more consistent, cases of one-sidedness and other violations inevitably become even more pronounced.

We need only consider the influence that Hegel, on the one hand, and Comte, on the other, have exercised on the empirical science of history to see that there can be no doubt about the significance of at least the *effect* achieved by these two thinkers. German historical science owes more to Hegel than can even be hinted at in a few words. Comtean positivism, however, was not further developed in a consistent fashion until Du Bois-Reymond's famous lecture, which held that Rome collapsed because the Romans failed to discover gunpowder. Here the absurdity of the enterprise that conceives the development of positive natural science and technology as the real *meaning* of the *total* development of human culture is obvious even on the most fleeting examination.

We need not pursue this matter any further, however. In comparison with the fundamental question, it is marginal. Our only purpose was to show that although Comte's sociology claims to proceed in a natural scientific fashion and to establish "historical laws," in fact it uncritically accepts all the presuppositions on whose account the scientific character and objectivity of a history that proceeds in a teleological and value-relevant fashion are disputed by the partisans of natural science. What holds true for Comte can also be easily proven for other advocates of generalizing sociology as a philosophy of history: All their alleged laws more or less clearly contain formulas for the *advancement of values*. It is only in this way that the representation of historical sequences of development is possible. In this respect, of course, Comte has also exercised considerable influence. On the whole, however, he owes it to his logical confusions.

Finally, Lamprecht's theory of cultural ages can serve as a typical example of the lack of conceptual rigor that must flaw every philosophy of history that pretends to employ a natural scientific method. In theory, this historian opposes all teleology and value relevance. In practice, not only does he proceed teleologically in the scientifically legitimate sense: Like every historian, he relates unique developmental sequences theoretically to empirically confirmable cultural values. He also goes far beyond the purely historical and logically indispensable use of values in the representation of historical material. Following celebrated prototypes, he attempts to comprehend the governing values of his concept formation in *one* formula, which he calls "the principle of progressive psychic intensity." On the model of speculative philosophy of history, the entire historical past is to be compressed into this principle. As one of the many precursors of Spengler, he also undertakes to predict the *future* on its basis, for he knows quite well that "the motion of history must (!) exhibit a constantly increasing psychic intensity."[3] Thus his formula has the same logical structure as Comte's "law" of the three stages. We can easily understand why Comte arrived at such an "ideological" violation of the historical facts. But it is difficult to understand how a historian of Lamprecht's time could still believe that historical life must invariably proceed from the hypothetical age of animism through conventionalism, typism, symbolism, individualism, and subjectivism to as yet unknown ages of the constantly "increasing intensity of sociopsychological life."

One would have thought that the view according to which it is the problem of the empirical science of history to grasp the "meaning" of history as a *whole* in *one* formula of this sort had been scientifically repudiated long ago. Finally, when it is claimed that the objectivity of historiography as Ranke practiced it can be surpassed on the basis of these speculations, this seems utterly ridiculous. At best, only a *philosophy* of history can make the attempt – from the standpoint of precisely defined *ideals* – to construe conceptually the entire course of historical life as an endeavor to realize these ideals. It will always

[3][The exclamation point is Rickert's.]

remain aware, however, that in this enterprise it is proceeding no longer historically but, rather, philosophically. The empirical science of history cannot become a philosophy of history, and least of all can it believe that it will advance to an ideal of greater historical objectivity in this way.

As regards the question of a value-free naturalistic philosophy of history, therefore, we reach the following conclusion: Either general laws of development really are laws of nature – in which case they cannot be employed as governing perspectives for the selection of the material in the representation of unique sequences of development; or putative laws of development are in fact value principles – in which case either a construction in the *philosophy* of history or a purely value-relevant and individualizing representation of historical events can be produced on their basis. In the latter case, historical representation falls under the concept of historical science as set forth here. Thus, should the use of values in science prove illegitimate, history – that is, the representation of unique sequences of development in their distinctiveness and individuality – must be completely stricken from the ranks of the sciences.

So if we want to ground history as a science from the general standpoint of natural science, only one possibility remains open: to discover its basis in "natural values." For this purpose, it is above all theories of naturalistic evolutionism, which have become fashionable in the more recent "developmental-historical" biology, that come into play. This matter can also be easily clarified on the basis of our concepts developed earlier.

Consider ideas that have led to successful scientific results in limited areas. There is a prevalent tendency to see in such ideas a principle that must prove fruitful for the treatment of all possible problems, especially philosophical problems. Corresponding to this tendency, it has been proposed to employ "Darwinism" to finally endow the philosophical disciplines with the natural scientific basis that is so earnestly desired. The biological concept of development seemed particularly well suited for the solution to value problems. Thus the idea of a Darwinian ethic has emerged. Work has been done in aesthetics on the basis of Darwinian principles. Elements of a Darwinian logic and epistemology have appeared in what has been called pragmatism, and even earlier. We were even obliged to witness the attempt to provide a Darwinian justification and foundation of religion in the book by Kidd, which proceeds to extoll religion as a first-rate weapon in the struggle for existence among peoples. So why not make naturalistic evolutionism into a philosophy of history as well, and by this means establish "natural" cultural values?

In attempts of this sort, the following line of thought usually seems to be more or less clearly in evidence. Darwin's theory – this refers primarily to the principle of natural selection – has not only eliminated the old "dualistic" teleology and made possible a "purely causal" explanation of all processes by incorporating organisms into a mechanistic nexus of nature. It has also established the true concepts of progress and perfection. Before Darwin, there is a sense in which all values were suspended in space; that is, they had no necessary connection with reality. Thus it was necessary to denigrate nature to gain a meaning for life. The natural was regarded as the principle of evil, or man appeared as an alien in nature. Now, however, we see that natural laws themselves necessarily lead to improvement. This is because natural selection in the struggle for existence invariably leads to the destruction of the imperfect and allows only the perfect to preserve itself. Where the law of nature holds, things invariably become increasingly well adapted and more functional. As a result of natural development, therefore, what comes to be is always what should be. Suppose, however, that by using the principle of natural selection, a reliable criterion is given for what qualifies as a positive value. In that case, it must also be possible to represent the historical development of different peoples or of the entire human race with reference to this value perspective, and then to claim that it has the status of natural scientific objectivity.

What are we to think of such theories? If we assume they are correct, it immediately follows that the concept of natural progress by means of selection is useless for providing a naturalistic basis for *history* as a science. Here not only are processes of development related to a value; in addition, the temporal sequences of their different stages necessarily coincide with an increase in their value. In other words, we have a typical example of the sixth concept of development discussed earlier.⁴ But we must call this sort of conception of the historical process "unhistorical" insofar as it is incapable of doing justice to the distinctive individual significance of different stages of development. Rather, every stage can be regarded only as a precursor of the following stage. It has value only insofar as it collapses to make room for a more highly developed stage. So in the final analysis, everything can possess what is at most a secondary historical significance. If, therefore, a natural scientific *law* of progress could really be established, then, like every other natural law, it would inevitably destroy the primary historical significance of

⁴[*Die Grenzen*, pp. 424 and 430–1, which are not included in the translation. This concept represents development as progress, an increase in value.]

objects. Moreover, in the complete realization of this conception, the different stages of development would be devaluated as generic representative cases of a sequence of general concepts. They would be ordered according to the principle of increasingly high levels of adaptation, and nothing would remain of the historical distinctiveness they possess as historical individuals, in the sense previously explained.

And even that is not all. The idea of progress based on the concept of selection has another aspect that makes it completely useless as the principle of concept formation in history. If the better adapted were the more perfect and the law of adaptation really were an unconditionally general law of nature, a continually advancing level of perfection would inevitably be produced *everywhere* as a necessity of nature. Every part of reality would always attain a continually increasing level of value. On this assumption, the world, at every moment and in each of its parts, would be the best of all possible worlds conceivable by natural science. Given such a sweeping optimism, however, it would be impossible to distinguish those objects that are more closely linked to the governing value perspective from other objects. In other words, with regard to the concept of natural perfection, *every* reality would be *equally* essential. But this is tantamount to the claim that *nothing* is essential any longer. The value that naturalistic evolutionism believes it can establish proves to be thoroughly unsuited for governing the process of value-relevant concept formation in history.

In another respect, however, precisely this result seems to be questionable for our enterprise as well. There cannot be two mutually inconsistent modes of value conception. So if the laws of nature really were laws of progress, it is obvious that every other sort of value that lacked a secure foundation in natural science would have to be abandoned in favor of the "natural values." And because natural values are useless as the principle of concept formation in history, every possibility of forming generally valid historical concepts would be eliminated.

Suppose we examine the justification for speaking of natural values more closely. Then it can be shown that all attempts to derive values in general – or even cultural values – from naturalistic evolutionism stand or fall with the assumption that natural *adaptation* is also *perfection*. Precisely from the standpoint of natural science, there is no sense in which this holds true. Perfection is a *value* concept. The *natural scientific* significance of the theory of selection, however, rests on the following consideration: By a kind of reversal of the teleological principle, it comprehends every apparently teleological development as a *value-neutral change*. In spite of this, can the theory of selection still regard change as improvement? In other words, does it make sense for the theory of selection to see a higher level of value in the inevitable natural process of adaptation?

There is, of course, a hidden teleological moment in the concept of "adaptation" that we cannot detach from the concept of the organism as such. As we were able to show, however, this no longer has anything to do with a value concept. The only issue here is the reversal of the causal conception that proceeds from the end and regards all preliminary stages as its conditions. The process of adaptation qualifies as perfection only from the standpoint of the beings that adapt, ascribing a positive value to their mere existence precisely because it is *their* existence. This, however, is exactly the narrowly teleological perspective that natural science proposes to give up in order to arrive at a unified explanation of all bodies, in other words, to comprehend organisms also in such a way that they are at least no longer in conflict with a general mechanistic theory of bodies. For a consistently developed natural science, therefore, every change must appear as totally indifferent to every positive or negative value. For this reason it can also never regard the inevitable natural process of adaptation as an advance to a higher level of value. To represent the product of adaptation through natural selection as equivalent to perfection or positive value is to confuse the *preservation of existence* with the *preservation of value*. Precisely from the perspectives of natural science, therefore, this position must be rejected. For natural science the functional purposiveness of an organism signifies nothing more than the ability to maintain its existence. Suppose one holds that everything that is dysfunctional with respect to the preservation of existence will be eliminated by natural selection, and thus that only the functionally purposive will continue to exist. This has absolutely nothing to do with the claim that a development that falls under the principle of selection always leads to a higher level of perfection. Consider the concept of purpose that natural science is obliged to retain so that it can continue to speak about organisms and their development. There are no circumstances under which this can be a value concept. Here only the concept of *telos* as a value-free *terminal* stage has a place.

How does it happen that, in spite of this, many regard the antithesis of this position as quite self-evident? The deception that grips us here rests on the following consideration: In the case of certain organic entities, we cannot resolve to abstract from the values that we *habitually* associate with their existence. That is why we see in them purposes that have a positive value. These values obtain *prior to* any natural scientific investigation. Not only do we maintain them; we also interpolate them into the concepts we employ to explain the genesis of the objects to which these values are ascribed. This is how it could happen that the "antiteleological" principle of selection became the principle of progress. It leads, or so it is thought, to what has positive value for us today, namely, to the human being. Accordingly, the principle of selection itself is a value principle. But whenever we cease to posit the human being as a good with which a value is connected – and this is the position natural science is obliged to take – every basis for regarding the principle of selection as a principle of value collapses. A standard of value has not been derived from the concepts of natural science. On the contrary, human values that were already positively esteemed are *transposed onto* the concepts of natural science.

Since we are human beings, it obviously makes sense that everything human and humanlike has a positive value for us. In history we cannot abstract from the distinctive significance of the human either. It rests on a value relation, and it endows the human with meaning. However, if we regard a developmental sequence as progressive because it leads to the human being, we are no longer thinking – in the modern sense – in natural scientific terms. And least of all are we thinking antiteleologically, in the sense that Darwinism claims to think. Thus for a consistent natural science, there are no "higher" or "lower" organisms either, assuming this means that the former have more value than the latter. At best, "higher" or "lower" can mean as much as "more or less differentiated." Moreover, the differentiation process as such has nothing at all to do with perfection and a higher level of value, even though the differentiated can frequently qualify as the appropriate *means* for the realization of goods to which values are attached. In the first place, we often esteem the simple more highly than the complex. Second, the differentiated acquires significance *only* as the instrumentally useful, that is, as the means to an end. Thus it has a value only if the value of the end is already established beforehand. However, as we have shown, the purposes we assume in natural science cannot be regarded as value configurations. Every belief in "natural progress" or in "natural values" rests on a naive anthropomorphism that is unjustified from the standpoint of natural science. One cannot first situate man in a sequence along with other living things, and then immediately place him in prominence above them as the "highest" being. That is an insupportable contradiction.

Before we knew anything about Darwinism as a "philosophy of history," K. E. von Baer[5] had already ridiculed its anthropomorphism in an exquisite fashion by conceiving evolutionary history written

---

[5]*Ueber Entwicklungsgeschichte der Tiere, Beobachtung und Reflexion*, I, 1828, pp. 203 *seq.*

from a bird's-eye view. The denizens of the air naturally find man quite flawed. They regard the bat as the most advanced of the mammals, and they reject the idea that living things that are unable to find their own food so long after birth and never fly should be more highly differentiated than they are. The Darwinians, who believe that they have advanced far beyond Baer's teleology, fail to see how anthropomorphically teleological their own thought is when they celebrate the "progress" from protozoans to man and regard the principle of natural selection as a value principle. Regardless of the circumstances, progress remains not only a teleological concept but also a teleological value concept. Within the limits of natural science, only the developmental concepts of becoming, change, and value-free development can come into play. In these cases, what we have in mind are conditional-teleological relationships. However, none of the developmental concepts that are linked with a value perspective – such as the concept of progress – has a place here. This is why biology as a natural science will never produce a philosophy of history whose allegedly natural values can provide the governing perspectives for the individualizing concept formation of history.[6]

In the interest of completeness, we should also stress that these same considerations also hold when naturalism appears in the aspect of a psychological theory. The attempt has been made to demarcate cultural life from mere nature by means of psychological concepts. It goes without saying that, in principle, there is nothing objectionable about such a cultural psychology. From a methodological standpoint, it belongs to the generalizing sciences of culture, the logical structure of which we have indicated. Here too, however, it is not clear how a rigorous distinction between nature and culture should be possible unless some sort of value concept of culture is *presupposed*. If we do this, we can, of course, attempt to identify the differences between the mental life of peoples with a culture [*Kulturvölker*] and the mental life of primitive peoples [*Naturvölker*], and show, for example, that – in the language of Wundt's psychology – "associative" mental processes predominate among primitive peoples, whereas the mental life of peoples with a culture consists more of "apperceptive" processes. Regardless of how valuable such theories might be, in the way that Vierkandt has employed them in his book *Naturvölker und Kulturvölker*,[7] it can never be claimed that the mental life of peoples with a culture has a historical significance *because* of its apperceptive character. Vierkandt's book, based as it is on a comprehensive body of

---

[6]In my book *Philosophie des Lebens* (1920; 2nd ed., 1922), I have attempted to provide a thorough critique of the biologistic principle of value in its various guises.

[7]*Naturvölker und Kulturvölker. Ein Beitrag zur Sozialpsychologie*, 1896.

facts, contains many valuable discussions and seems to be the most distinguished contribution to the psychology of culture among all the writings that employ the concepts of Wundt's psychology. Yet even Vierkandt would have been able to reach a much clearer position if he had consistently observed the difference between a natural scientific or generalizing psychological mode of conception and that which is historical or individualizing.

The illusion that psychological distinctions have a value that is more than purely psychological rests on the following consideration: When psychic processes can become *means* to an end that has a positive value, then the value this end has is *transposed* onto *these* mental processes. It may perhaps be true that the cultural man can work for the realization of cultural values, or even take a position on them, only if his mental life exhibits certain characteristics that the primitive man lacks. But these characteristics acquire a historical significance only if they are related to cultural values. Without this relation, the meaning that can be ascribed to them is no different from the meaning of any other psychic processes. Thus without the assumption of preestablished values, it makes no more sense to speak of a "higher" mental life – that is, a mental life that has more positive value – than it does to call corporeal structures of whatever kind "higher" in the same sense. Whoever has grasped this point will also see that it provides a reason not to expect much from psychology in regard to the elucidation of value problems. Suppose the impression arises that psychological concepts could contribute something to the resolution of value problems. This is only a consequence of the fact that psychological concepts are actually not *exclusively* psychological. On the contrary, they provide covert formulations of value principles. This can be demonstrated most compellingly with reference to some of the basic concepts of Wundt's psychology. Whoever has read Max Weber's critique – which is just as radical as it is drastic – will no longer be in doubt about this matter.[8]

In every respect, therefore, the attempts to provide historical science with a firm foundation by taking the path of natural science must appear hopeless. It also follows from this that generalizing sociology can never claim to be a philosophy of history. A generalizing science of reality and history are not only mutually exclusive for

---

[8]See "Roscher und Knies und die logischen Probleme der historischen Nationaloekonomie," II, 1905, *Jahrbuch für Gesetzgebung, Verwaltung und Volkswirtschaft*, vol. XXIX, pp. 96 *seq.* This is reprinted in *Gesammelte Aufsätze zur Wissenschaftslehre*, 1922, [For an English translation, see "Knies and the Problem of Irrationality," in *Roscher and Knies: The Logical Problems of Historical Economics*, trans. Guy Oakes (New York: Free Press, 1975).]

conceptual reasons, on the grounds that the former represents the general and the latter represents the individual. They are also mutually exclusive in the following respect: Whereas the former disregards the individual differences of value that are connected with its real material, the latter cannot dispense with values for the purpose of distinguishing what is essential to it from what is not. If real objects are conceived as instances of a general concept, it follows that they are regarded as equivalent to one another. Thus they also all have the same significance for any given value. Any instance can be replaced by any other.

In addition, the concept of a "natural value" is an evident contradiction for a uniform conception of nature. Assuming that values are related to the empirical beings that take a position on them, they are invariably value oppositions too. Therefore, without the *dualism* of positive and negative value, they lose their significance. However, there is no room for this dualism in the "monism" linked with every conception of nature. The more consistently natural science proceeds, the more firmly must it refuse to countenance a "meaning" of life and history that can be interpreted on the basis of values. The generalizing conception takes shape in a necessarily value-free fashion, in exactly the same way that the individualizing conception is necessarily value relevant.

None of this is meant to deny that it is difficult to maintain the distinction between the concept of nature and every value concept. And yet to many, it seems that "nature" is the very essence of every good. For example, when Goethe refers to "nature," he certainly does not have in mind something that is value free. The word "nature," however, is clearly very ambiguous, and nature as the essence of every good is *not* the nature of the modern natural sciences, as we are obliged to understand them. As regards the general principle, Goethe's conception of nature in particular has nothing in common with modern natural science. The great poet always saw nature from a human perspective, or rather from the perspective of Goethe himself; and he transposed the entire value and wealth of his own being onto nature. Thus he thought in a thoroughly teleological fashion and, moreover, in a fashion that is irreconcilable with the mechanistic conception of nature – namely, in terms of a teleology of value. Even the fact that he would have nothing to do with Newton's optics necessarily followed from his way of conceiving nature. It was not a whim, as many people still think. Finally, the modern concept of nature as the "struggle for existence" and natural "selection" would have made the same impact on him as the *Système de la nature*: He would have found it intolerable. In this regard, his position on the theory of development should not mislead us. Certainly Goethe too searched for unity and gradual transition. But he did not want to install man in the mechanism of nature. For Goethe, nature is not a mechanism at all. On the contrary, he proposes to elevate reality as a whole, which he calls nature, to his own personal level. Thus he is radically opposed to the modern doctrine of mechanistic evolutionism. He is delighted to find that humans have the intermaxillary bone too, for only if all of nature is his kinsman can he "gaze into" it "as into the bosom of a friend." It is only then that nature teaches him "to recognize his brothers in the quiet thicket, in the air and water." Even the stones cannot be alien to him – they can be "tumult, brute force, and absurdity." In short, the *Naturphilosophie* of romanticism is rooted in Goethe's conception of nature. The great artist refuses to separate value and reality. Schelling is closely related to him, but not natural science as we understand it today and as we must understand it. In this connection, therefore, an appeal to Goethe's concept of nature would be out of place. At all times, modern science must learn to distinguish between values and realities as rigorously as possible.

In any case, our contention that the concept of nature should be conceived as value free is made only with reference to *the* concept of nature formed by modern science, and we claim that the conception of reality as a nomological periodicity of nature is connected with the rejection of any attempt to define the meaning of the unique development. The world as nature becomes a meaningless process of recurrence. Thus the limits of concept formation in natural science reemerge in the idea of a naturalistic philosophy of history. The concept of nature as reality insofar as it is general excludes the concept of *historical* development. Both historiography as a natural science and also a philosophy of history as natural science are self-contradictions. It is always the case that reality can be conceived only in either a generalizing fashion as nature or in an individualizing fashion as history. To unite these conceptions is an enterprise that is absurd from the outset. A point of unification may lie *beyond* nature and history, but it can never be found *within* one of these two mutually exclusive concepts.

It may be supposed, however, that what is at stake here is not the limits of concept formation in natural science, but rather the limits of *scientific* concept formation in general. Indeed, the more clearly a natural scientist sees that it makes no sense to speak of historically value-relevant development from *his* standpoint, the more decisively must he reject every historical representation as unscientific. For the natural scientist, history necessarily remains dominated by that sort of anthropomorphism whose invalidity has been demonstrated by a devastating plethora of arguments since the Renaissance. It was possible for the Christian Middle Ages to take a legitimate interest in the history of humanity, because it could presuppose that the unique and finite development that takes place between the Creation and the Last Judgment is really the history of the "world" in the strict sense of the term, and because the values to which this process was related existed as absolutely valid and acknowledged in the teachings of the church. To use Schopenhauer's language, however, the arena of history, which was regarded as the center of the universe, has become one of those small illuminated spheres, dozens of which revolve in infinite space around countless others, a sphere on which a layer of mold has created a living and knowing being. Since this has happened, we should at long last part with the idea that the development of the human race has a relationship to objective values that is more than fortuitous. "World history" is nothing but a tiny fragment of the world that is of utterly transitory significance.

Are these really consequences that can be drawn from a natural scientific standpoint? Or is it not rather the case that by virtue of these consequences, the ground of natural science is abandoned, in quite the same way that this holds true in the attempt to obtain "natural values"?

Natural science, of course, is never in the position of being able to understand objective values. But this proposition is not tantamount to the claim that such values do not hold validly at all and thus that history is not a science. If the assumptions on the basis of which natural science rejects a value-relevant historical representation are correct, then it is precisely on the part of natural science that the proof for such a proposition cannot be produced. Judgments about the scientific or unscientific character of a *method* are *value* judgments. Therefore these judgments themselves presuppose a *standard* of value on the basis of which they assess the "objectivity" of the sciences. It follows that natural science immediately exceeds its competence when it declares that only its own procedure is justified. That is a value judgment. The more consistently one maintains the standpoint of natural science – which is intended to be and should be value free – all the more so must one refrain from making any judgment about the positive or negative value of a scientific method on its basis. This is because even a value judgment about a scientific method remains a *value* judgment.

The natural scientist will, of course, *implicitly* presuppose that his method leads to objectively valid results. But even *this* presupposition can never become a scientific problem for natural science itself. Ultimately, therefore, it makes no sense to pass a judgment from the standpoint of natural science on the significance of methods that lie outside the natural sciences. The consideration of theoretical value questions of this sort lies exclusively in the domain of logic. Whoever proposes to resolve them from the standpoint of natural science – the essence of which is constituted by an abstraction from all value perspectives – will inevitably arrive at an empty and negative dogmatism. It will really not do first to proclaim emphatically that all valuation is unscientific and then, with even greater confidence, claim to make scientifically valid value judgments about the significance of scientific methods. For a consistent naturalism, questions like the issue concerning the logical value of methods do not exist. *For naturalism*, of course, there is no history. Naturalism, however, can have absolutely nothing to say about the question of whether history can qualify as a science at all. From the standpoint of natural science, therefore, the scientific objectivity of history cannot be justified, nor are there any well-founded doubts and objections that can be raised against it.

2. EMPIRICAL OBJECTIVITY

If we want to make progress, we should proceed as independently as possible of all presuppositions about the value of the different scientific methods. Since the epistemological standpoint that minimizes commitment to presuppositions can be regarded as that of pure *experience*, we should first ask what follows for history if we consider it with reference to the standard of empirical objectivity.

This sort of objectivity is always presupposed in a scientific context in which the validity of judgments is reducible to purely *factual* truths. This is because facts must be "objectively" stated on the basis of pure experience. At this point, however, we no longer need to consider the view that holds that it is possible to arrive at scientific knowledge by means of a *mere* statement of facts. We have shown in sufficient detail that science always represents the working out and recasting of what is factual on the basis of specific governing perspectives. Empiricism can be understood only as the view according to which not only the material but also the governing perspectives from which we work on it have a purely empirical validity. Here, we are concerned only with the validity of these methodological presuppositions of concept formation. For the rest, we assume that the validity of judgments that state only facts poses no further problem that is essential in this context. We further assume that in both the natural sciences and history, we arrive at knowledge of the material by means of pure experience. That is permissible because the objectivity of *this* knowledge poses no methodological problem that can have a significance for history fundamentally different from the significance it has for natural science.

Thus the focus of our investigation now lies at a different point than in the foregoing. For a natural scientific conception, the mere circumstance that values are the governing perspectives of concept formation in history could already be a stumbling block. From the standpoint of pure experience, however, this circumstance is not intrinsically problematic. That is because values can also be stated as facts insofar as valuational beings actually take a position on them. In particular, their recognition by a specific human community can in principle be established through experience. From the standpoint of pure experience, the use of values becomes inadmissible only when their normative generality in principle goes beyond a general recognition that can actually be confirmed, or if this use should signify as much as an *unconditionally* binding recognition. But on the other hand, it now seems that the objectivity of natural science – which is due to *unconditionally* general natural *laws* – is no longer self-evident. On the contrary, precisely for empiricism it becomes a most intractable problem. Thus we see that from the standpoint of experience, the relationship between history and natural science and the extent to which both are objective can be decided only by establishing whether and in what measure both presuppose unconditionally general and necessary elements. It seems to be irrelevant, however, whether these elements are values and their validity or something else.

If we begin with natural science, then it is clear that our discussion of the empirical generality of natural scientific concepts can easily be brought into conformity with a purely empiricist epistemology. That is because the validity of concepts in this first stage can be based on a direct comparison of objects. Nor is there any sense in which the formal precision of concepts includes a metaempirical moment. Thus it seems that the validity of natural scientific concepts poses a special problem only when they constitute judgments that allegedly express something about an infinite manifold of things and processes – which is, therefore, never directly accessible to experience. But we could show that in most cases even the empirically general and formally precise concepts are to be regarded only as preliminary efforts to form those concepts with which natural science proposes to reduce an extensively and intensively infinite manifold to a unified conceptual system. Thus a consistent empiricism would also have to ascribe to empirically general and formally precise concepts the meaning they have as preliminary stages of nomological concepts. From the standpoint of a consistent empiricism, therefore, the goal we thought we could attribute to natural science is an exaggeration. Concept formation in natural science could rest only on an empirical comparison of objects that comprehends what is common in an infinite manifold as essential and omits individual differences as inessential.

Suppose we assume this position is feasible. In other words, let us suppose that even the concepts of natural laws could be conceived as empirical generalizations. In consequence, we could not speak of natural *laws* in the strict sense, insofar as a metaempirical import is implied. In that case, would there be any sense in which history is inferior to natural science with respect to its scientific objectivity?

Assuming that it is not the certainty of the *material* but only the principles of concept formation that are at stake here, the governing values of historical, value-relevant concept formation need not be less valid empirically than the perspectives natural science draws on to compare different objects in a purely empirical fashion. This is because history is concerned only with the relation of objects to values that are *actually* generally acknowledged, values by means of which the essential aspects of objects are distinguished from their inessential aspects in a manner that is valid for everyone. Thus it is obvious that the word "all" can have only an empirically general significance; that is, it applies to all members of a historical community. However, suppose it is empirically established that a certain group of persons for whom the historian has written his representation in fact has cognizance of shared cultural goods such as the state, art, science, and religion. And suppose that the acknowledgment of these goods as normatively general is in fact expected of all members of the community. Finally, suppose that with reference to the values that attach to these goods, the facts of the past are brought under historical concepts. In that case, the result is a representation that is valid for all members of this cultural sphere. Nevertheless, such a representation certainly does not depart from the ground of pure experience, no more than this holds true when natural science forms a system of general concepts for a specific domain of reality by means of purely empirical comparison.

It will perhaps be supposed, however, that this is not the only question at issue. Despite these considerations, historical concepts remain less scientific. An act of *caprice* lies in the fact that precisely these cultural values – and not other cultural values of other cultural spheres – govern concept formation in history. Or in any case, a historical representation is invariably valid only for the sphere of persons who actually acknowledge the governing cultural values as well. There is no sense in which this conforms to the ideal of scientific concept formation. The general concepts of natural science, on the other hand, obtained by means of comparison and the exclusion of the purely individual, transcend all caprice. They are valid for everyone, regardless of whether the cognitive subjects *previously* acknowledged anything else as valid. In short, concept formation in history requires presuppositions for the acknowledgment of which no one can be logically compelled. On the basis of comparison alone, however, natural science arrives at concepts whose purely logical validity excludes every doubt.

And yet if we examine the matter more closely, then precisely on the basis of pure experience this claim cannot be established. In natural science as well as in history, it is not merely the "substance" or the *material* itself that defines the content of concepts. On the contrary, the cognitive subject makes the decision concerning what is essential and what is not in the domain of the purely factual. In other words, the purely empirical comparison of natural science also requires a governing perspective. Suppose every possibility of regarding such a comparison as a preliminary attempt to develop unconditionally general concepts is rejected. Then there is no sense in which it remains less *capricious* that precisely this perspective and not some other is chosen for the summary comprehension of what is common.

We forget this because the perspectives that govern the comparison frequently have the compelling character of the "self-evident." But this sort of self-evidence, which stems from the interests of *practical life*, can not be ascertained only for the governing perspectives of a historical representation as well; in addition, it has absolutely nothing to do with the logical basis of such a representation. We have shown in detail why natural science can never achieve more than a classification unless it attempts to establish unconditionally general judgments. We have also shown why a *mere* classification is always "arbitrary." Suppose we also restrict ourselves to an extensively comprehensible manifold of objects, as a consistent empiricist must. The intensive manifold of every single object is still infinitely large, and infinite manifolds can be compared with one another on the basis of infinitely *many* perspectives. So it also holds true for comparative natural science that we must always have established *in advance which* perspective we propose to select for the comparison. From a purely empiricist standpoint, moreover, this choice requires the agreement of all those for whom the general concepts are supposed to be valid, in the same way that this holds true for history. In consequence, not even purely empirical natural science can dispense with the assumption historical science must make.

If this is so, it also holds true that from empiricist standpoints, no other kind of scientific objectivity can be required of history. In addition, the historical disciplines are quite capable of satisfying the condition that all persons to whom their inquiries are directed acknowledge their governing perspectives. So with regard to the arbitrariness of the selection, there is no sense in which history is at a disadvantage to natural science. On the contrary, suppose that the historian – with reference to empirically given cultural values that are regarded as normatively general by a certain sphere of persons – limits himself to representing the unique, individual course of the past by employing historical concepts with individual content. From a consistently empiricist standpoint, he attains the highest level of objectivity possible in science. Only the claim that historical concepts have an *unconditionally* general validity remains questionable. For the consistent empiricist, however, this sort of validity has no sense at all. In natural science, this sort of validity depends on the validity of unconditionally general laws; in history, on the validity of unconditionally general values. The consistent empiricist rejects *both*. So, with respect to the objectivity of concepts, it can make no difference to him that an empirically and generally acknowledged value, to which objects are related in such a way that they are constituted as historical in-dividuals, takes the place of the empirically and generally acknowledged perspective of comparison for distinguishing the essential from the inessential.

If we take leave of a purely formal conception of this issue, from the standpoint of pure experience, the situation of the historical sciences is even better. The vast majority of historical works – all biographies, all representations of specific cultural processes such as developmental histories of religion, the sciences, law, art, and so on, and even all histories of individual peoples and states – are governed by value perspectives whose de facto recognition is beyond doubt. If the historian forms his concepts with reference to the values of the community to which he also belongs, it seems that the objectivity of his representation depends exclusively on the accuracy of the factual material, and the question of whether this or that event of the past is essential cannot arise. He surmounts all caprice when, for example, he relates the development of art to aesthetic cultural values and the development of a state to political cultural values. In this way, he produces a representation that – insofar as it avoids unhistorical value *judgments* – is valid for everyone who acknowledges aesthetic or political values as normatively general for the members of his community. On the other hand, suppose that to represent remote cultural developments "objectively" from the standpoint of their historical centers, the historian must first "develop a sensitivity for" remote cultural values. In principle, this can also be achieved by means of a purely empirical determination of facts, when the historian asks which values the historical centers esteem or which meaning configurations they really experience. Consider the question of whether the governing value perspectives employed for this purpose can actually count on an empirically ascertainable recognition in all those cultural communities comprehended by such a representation. This question can be in doubt only in writing a "world history." This last case, however, is not germane to the empirical objectivity of specific representations.

Of course, our line of thought can be convincing *only* if we keep in mind the difference between positive or negative valuation and the purely theoretical *value relation* that is completely independent of this alternative. This is why the objectivity of concept formation in history that is exclusively intended here should not be linked with *that* sort of objectivity that, for example, is juxtaposed to the historical representation that is "subjective" because it is governed by "confessional" presuppositions. Representations of historical events written from different confessional standpoints will never proceed in a purely theoretical, value-relevant fashion. This is why they cannot in fact possess scientific objectivity. Suppose, however, that all value *judgments* are disregarded. Then, for example, in a representation of the reality that is called "Luther," the same aspects that are essential for Protestants must also be essential for Catholics. And so they must also be consolidated to form the same historical concepts. As we saw earlier, a controversy over the value of Luther would simply not be possible without a common conception of reality. Only for a historian who is completely alien to German and Christian cultural life would Luther be of no importance whatsoever, and thus not a possible object of a historical representation. This is because the alien historian does not relate Luther's individuality to any value. But if this historian at least understands some religious value or other, in principle he can also develop a sensitivity for the values to which German and Christian historians relate Luther. In that case, a representation of Luther that abstracts from all value judgments possesses scientific objectivity for him as well.

As we remarked earlier, there can be disagreement over whether it is actually possible for the historian to refrain from value judgments, and also over whether it is merely desirable for him to do this. But this question lies outside the domain of a *logical* investigation. In this context, we only have to ascertain the concept of a *purely* scientific historical representation. By means of the purely theoretical relation of its objects to cultural values, such a representation will express the conception of reality shared by all parties to the controversy. A historical work committed to confessional or political values may be thoroughly justified and indispensable on the basis of religious, ethical, political, or other general cultural perspectives. But it can never be regarded as purely scientific. This is because its valuations will never be valid for all scientists. At best, we could attempt to ground this sort of validity by means of a *philosophy* of history. Here, however, we deliberately disregard this possibility. We are concerned with the empirical sciences of history, and their empirical objectivity cannot be contested as long as the historian limits himself to the representation of real objects that everyone in fact relates to generally acknowledged values.

On the other hand, the justification of the objectivity of *natural scientific* investigations encounters considerable difficulties if a demonstration of the de facto acknowledgment of their governing perspectives is required. As long as natural science works exclusively with concepts of things, perhaps it could be said that everyone must find it practically self-evident which objects are to qualify as the same and which are not. In light of the first two chapters,[9] however, no one will fail to see how difficult it must be to apply pure empiricism to relational concepts as well. In any case, when natural science is required to justify its objectivity before the bar of empiricism, it is in a much more problematic situation than historical representation. History remains the genuine *experiential* science. This is not only because history with its individual concepts approximates the experience of immediate reality – which is always individual – more closely than does natural science. It is also because its governing perspectives can be more easily derived from experience itself. From the empiricist standpoint, therefore, the fact that history requires values as governing perspectives cannot be responsible for introducing a troublesome subjectivity into it. At most, ignorance of the indispensability of these value perspectives for individualizing concept formation will lead the scholar astray in the false pursuit of an ideal of "objectivity" that can never be attained in historical science.

If our only purpose were to demonstrate the legitimacy of a science of unique, individual, cultural development as an empirical discipline, we could now conclude our book. If we disregard metaempirical elements *as such*, then the objectivity of historical science can no longer be contested. However, our investigation was undertaken in the interest of more general philosophical problems. Although we first had to limit our problematic to purely methodological considerations, at this point the problem of demonstrating the relations

---

[9][Chapters 1 and 2 of *Die Grenzen*, not included in this translation.]

between our methodological results and general questions of weltanschauung remains open. This can take place only on the basis of a more penetrating and comprehensive epistemological development of the results established thus far. In particular, we still have to clarify the role played by metaempirical elements in every science, that is, in natural science as well as in historical science.

In turning to these problems, much of what we established in the foregoing must again be placed in question. From this new perspective, it is especially the objectivity of historical science that can seem quite problematic to many people. Thus if anyone is so convinced of the illegitimacy of metaempirical elements in science that he regards their discussion as absurd and anachronistic, it would perhaps be best for him to read no further but rather to be satisfied with the results established thus far. In any case, for the really *consistent* empiricist, we have done our work. Indeed, it is important to note that for *every* thinker who does not employ undemonstrable metaphysical-rationalistic dogmas, historical life must qualify as the limit to all concept formation in natural science, regardless of the philosophical views he may otherwise hold. Under all circumstances, *natural scientific, generalizing knowledge of the historical remains logically impossible.* Whoever proposes to acquire knowledge of the past in its unique and individual development can grasp it only by means of concepts that have an individual content, and whose elements are consolidated with respect to a value to form a unity. It is precisely empiricism that can never contest the objectivity of this sort of concept formation. This is because, for empiricism, there simply is no higher level of objectivity. This holds true under all conditions, regardless of how the soundness of the following line of thought may be judged. Thus as long as the issue concerns only the *empirical* objectivity of historical science, it is not legitimate to introduce the ideas developed in the ensuing into the discussion.

For a more penetrating epistemology, however, the sort of objectivity that natural science and history attempt to achieve cannot be understood on the basis of pure experience. As regards natural science, we no longer need to show why it is obliged to repudiate any demand that, in principle, it be limited to purely empirical generalizations. At this point, we do not yet have in mind the most general epistemological presuppositions that are also indispensable to history, such as the assumption of an objective temporal and spatial order, the principle of causality, and so on. On the contrary, we are thinking of methodological presuppositions that are distinctive to natural science. Whoever claims that laws of nature are valid goes beyond experience, whether he is aware of this or not. That is because he makes an assertion about objects that lie outside his experience. This should not be understood as the claim that the *content* of laws is not always inferred from experience. On the contrary, it means that an indefinitely large, incalculable number of unobserved objects are legitimately subsumed under a concept formed on the basis of a determinate number of observed objects, possibly on the basis of a single object. Nor does it mean that the unconditionally general validity of a law of nature could be derived from its content with indubitable certainty. On the contrary, it means only that a more or less substantial degree of probability can be claimed for unconditionally valid judgments as such, for there is already a metaempirical element in the concept of the probability of an unconditionally general law. The point at stake here presupposes that *some* unconditionally general judgments hold validly independent of cognitive subjects. The only remaining question is whether these judgments have in fact already been incorporated into human knowledge. Without the presupposition that we can go beyond experience in this manner, it makes no sense to claim that what holds true for one thousand observed cases will also be "probable" for the one thousand and first unobserved case. This presupposition implies that *some* laws hold *unconditionally*, even if we are not acquainted with a single one of them.

Not infrequently, of course, this is an issue that empiricism ignores in an unreflective fashion, or that it believes it can resolve with theories that only confuse the matter. In many cases, our subjective *conviction* concerning the validity of a law is indeed the result of a large number of observations, and thus the "psychological" analysis of the real scientific thought process can place concepts such as habit in the foreground in order to explain the conviction of the subject. But this has absolutely nothing to do with our problem. Our belief or the subjective state of certitude (also called "obviousness" ["Evidenz"]) may arise on the basis of thousands of observations. However, not even the probability of the unconditional *validity* of a law can ever be justified in this way. On the contrary, if the search for laws of nature is to have a logical sense, both the validity of *some* laws and the possibility of establishing knowledge of what has not been experienced on the basis of what has been, must lie beyond doubt *prior* to any observation of the specific material. Obviously, such a presupposition remains just as formal as it is metaempirical. It is possible that one day natural science may declare that all the substantively complete and unconditionally general laws it formerly believed it had discovered are false. However, as long as natural science is carried on at all, the validity of unconditionally general laws as such and the possibility of at least approximating knowledge of them can never be placed in question.

Let us assume that the legitimacy of these assumptions is settled. What are the corresponding assumptions that *history* must make if its objectivity is not to be found wanting in comparison with that of a nomological science? Does history require metaempirical assumptions at all? We now turn to the resolution of this question.

In natural science, there are concepts whose content more or less approximates what holds true in an absolutely general fashion. Such concepts do not appear in historical science itself. If historical science includes metaempirical constituents, they can lie only in the governing *perspectives* of concept formation or in the *principle for the selection of what is essential*. Nevertheless, the *content* of its governing value perspectives is also based on experience. This is because, in principle, the "normative" universality of values can also be established for a particular society by means of experience. Thus historical science will surely never come to the point of invalidating all its representations on the grounds that the values it has employed as principles of selection are no longer regarded as normatively general. In other words, history will never find it necessary to form its concepts on the basis of completely *new* cultural values. That is because it must understand the human life of the past "on its own terms," that is, on the basis of the meaning in which the historical centers really lived. And it must relate every individual to the values that were normatively general in his community. Thus the validity of unconditionally general values and the possibility of at least approximating their knowledge seems only to be a requirement for a "*philosophy* of history" that inquires into the objective "progress" of humanity or something of that sort, but not for the empirical science of history.

Therefore, what do we mean when we speak of metaempirical presuppositions of history? Perhaps the possibility that in confirming values by observing certain cultural spheres, we obtain knowledge of the values of cultural spheres that have not been observed? It is obvious that this has nothing to do with the distinctive features of concept formation in history. That is because the difficulties this issue poses for the historian are not, in principle, irresolvable on the basis of pure experience. Thus the metaempirical presuppositions of history must have a completely different locus.

Suppose natural science with its concepts can approximate unconditionally general laws. In that case, it is freed from all human caprice in which, according to the empiricist view, it would otherwise inevitably be trapped. History, on the other hand, remains committed to purely human value positions – even though the values may be acknowledged by many millions – as the ultimate criterion for the selection of what is essential in the formation of its concepts. Thus it could be claimed that from the purely scientific standpoint, the entire development of human culture may be regarded as a completely indifferent and meaningless chaos of individual events, the representation of which must be far inferior in scientific importance to the search for general laws. In general, the relating of reality to values is always a matter of human caprice. The consensus of many or of all makes no difference. Thus if historical science claims that its problem is a scientific necessity, it must assume that in the domain of value as well, it is not *only* a question of the caprice of many or all persons. This, in fact, implies the metaempirical presupposition that *some* values are *unconditionally* valid and that all human value positions stand in a more or less proximate *relation* to them that is defined as more than capricious. If this were not so, purely scientific history with a value-relevant, individualizing concept formation could never be written.

A presupposition such as the one that is indispensable here is again obviously formal. In other words, it makes no assertions about whether a cultural value with which we are acquainted has a substantive claim to unconditionally general validity. On this basis too, the empirical objectivity of the history that employs de facto recognized values remains intact. At the same time, the formal presupposition is perfectly sufficient for the objectivity of history in the highest sense. For suppose that at least *some* values or other are absolutely valid. And suppose that, in consequence, substantively embodied and normatively general human values objectively approximate them more or less closely. Then human cultural development also has a necessary relation to unconditionally valid values. As a result, the attempt to establish knowledge of the unique process of history with reference to normatively general values can no longer be regarded as a product of mere caprice.

Thus we see that history also requires a metaempirical element if its forms of comprehension – that is, the concepts of the historical, value-relevant individual, the historical, value-relevant nexus, and historical, value-relevant development – are not to be inferior in scientific significance to the forms natural science requires so that its endeavor to arrive at laws of nature does not become senseless. Suppose we investigate the unique development of human culture in a value-relevant and individualizing fashion. And suppose we regard this as a necessary problem of science that transcends human caprice. If we reflect on the epistemological basis of our endeavor, we must be permitted the following assumption. Consider all normatively general nonreal values whose substantive definitiveness governs a representation and that are recognized on the basis of valuations that can be confirmed. We do not have to assume that these values themselves are unconditionally valid. But we must be allowed to assume that they are more or less closely related to *some* values that are unconditionally valid, or whose validity is independent of every de facto recognition. Thus we must be allowed to assume that human culture possesses some objective meaning or other – perhaps still completely unknown to us – with reference to unconditionally and generally valid values. Only then is it logically unavoidable to theoretically relate the historical process to values in general. And from a purely scientific standpoint, only then does it hold true that there are no conditions under which the unique development of history is an absurd chaos of transitory and meaningless events.

It should not be necessary to prove that this presupposition of history is at least implicitly made in "practical" life – in other words, by the willing and acting person. I can, of course, believe that I am always in error about the objectives I set for myself and strive for as valuable. I can also have the fear that every act of my life has been a failure because it has produced no good to which a value is attached that is more than individually subjective. However, such a fear presupposes the unconditional validity of *some* values or other and the obligation to produce goods to which these values are attached, just as this presupposition holds for the conviction that I have always attained what has genuinely positive value. So if the presupposition of unconditionally valid values cannot be contested for the domain of the active life, the following point is also clear: For the willing and acting person, the world also presents itself as a process of development that with reference to values, falls into essential and inessential individual components. In other words, in this sense the practical person must always think in a value-relevant, "historical" fashion, and not only in a generalizing fashion, regardless of how limited the spatiotemporal segment of the real world may be to which his interest in the unique, individual process of things is restricted. Thus as soon as he brings himself to explicit awareness concerning that on which the meaning of his life rests, a representation of this segment by means of value-relevant, individualizing concept formation acquires a necessity for him that transcends all caprice.

The standpoint of the practical or the active life is not that of science, however. This poses the question of whether the presupposition of unconditionally valid values is also indispensable from the scientific standpoint of mere contemplation and purely theoretical value relevance, and thus whether historical science qualifies as logically necessary in the same sense as natural science. This problem – the solution to which cannot even be attempted on the basis of a consistent empiricism – must still be posed in the present context if we want to reach ultimate clarity concerning the nature of objectivity in historical science.

3. METAPHYSICAL OBJECTIVITY

Before turning to this new question, suppose we take an explicit stand on a view we have repeatedly mentioned in passing but thus far have not considered thoroughly. On this view, the foregoing discussions can appear as a superfluous pursuit of self-fabricated difficulties that spring only from a false assumption about the nature of scientific knowledge. We attempted to understand all scientific activity as the working up and reshaping of contents that are drawn from reality as immediately given. Can the issue be left to stand in this way? On the basis of this presupposition, can scientific objectivity be understood at all? In the first place, does it make sense to designate this reshaping as the problem of natural science? Does not the essence of all knowledge of natural science rather rest on the consideration that it advances to an *absolutely* real being that is not immediately given, and that it has to form the content of its concepts in such a way that they reproduce this being as it really exists? Must not all concept formation that reshapes given existence be regarded solely as a means to this end? But in that event, does the criterion for the objectivity of concept formation not consist in correspondence with *absolute* reality? And so is it not the case that the validity of principles of selection is justified when their use produces the requisite correspondence of thought with absolute real being?

As long as we were concerned only with the *methodological* structure of scientific concept formation, it was irrelevant how the resolution of this far-reaching question turned out. It was sufficient if we could show how science advances by reshaping and simplifying the imme-diately *given*. Consider the concept of truth as the substantive corre-spondence of a concept with the real object it is supposed to apprehend. It was, of course, necessary for us to give up this concept because science cannot reproduce *empirical* reality, and also because, in fact, no formation of concepts even exhibits the tendency to approximate this objective. Thus if we regard empirical or given reality as the only real world, we will never be able to claim more than the following: Although scientific concepts have to *hold validly for* reality, they do not have to *contain* reality itself. In fact, however, the problem of objectivity is formed in a completely different way if we assume there are *two* realities: an empirical "world of appearance" and an absolute, transcendent, or metaphysical reality that lies behind the world of appearance as its "essence." Then it can be said that concepts in natural science, which are formed by reshaping and working up empirical reality, have the purpose of reproducing the absolutely real being of things, and that the measure of their validity depends on the extent to which they approximate this objective. In that case, the pictorial correspondence of the content of the concept with the absolute content of reality becomes the criterion for objectivity.

In particular, the most *general* natural scientific theory of the physical would have to represent true physical reality as it really exists, and the most general psychological theory would have to represent the true being of mental life as it really exists. Thus the natural sciences would succeed in penetrating the many-colored veil of appearance that conceals genuine reality from the unscientific eye. Bodies really consist of immutable atoms that move according to immutable laws. This is the basis on which natural science decomposes the content of qualitatively heterogeneous things. In other words, it reduces them to relational concepts until it ultimately arrives at concepts of simple things that have reciprocal relationships that can be mathematically represented. In the same way that the objectivity of the concept of the atom rests on the real being of the atom, so in psychology *that* theory alone is justified that tells us, or will tell us, what the metaphysical being of mental life consists in and what the laws are that govern the association and disjunction of its absolutely real elements. If an indubitable metaphysical objectivity has been produced in this way for the most general physical and psychological theories, this objectivity can easily be transposed onto more specific natural scientific investigations that take corporeal or mental existence as their objects. Therefore, are we not obliged to accept a metaphysical objectivity if objective science is to come about by means of our concept formations?

It may seem self-evident to many people that this is the only way to give a correct account of the nature of truth in natural science, and at most there will perhaps be opposition to the expression "metaphysical" objectivity. However, as long as the "ultimate things" or the "elements of the psyche" have not been made accessible to immediate experience, it may be advisable to distinguish, even in principle, the mode of their real existence from observable empirical reality. Thus we will call *every* view "metaphysical" that presupposes *two modes of the real*: one empirical and the other absolute, which "lies behind" the former. Accordingly, we will speak of metaphysical objectivity if the validity of scientific concepts is held to depend on the extent to which their content reproduces absolutely real being. In any case, it is necessary for us to take a critical position concerning this "realistic" concept of knowledge, for by its means the relation of history to natural science once more becomes completely different from the way it previously appeared. The fundamental equivalence of objectivity in history and natural science, the result of the standpoint of pure experience, is again suspended in a way that is quite prejudicial to history.

The reason is obvious. Whereas natural science advances from appearance to metaphysical reality, history, with its individualizing formations of concepts, remains in opposition to this position and explicitly limited to the world of appearance. It was precisely the character of history as an empirical science that was responsible for this limitation. Of course, it could be said that history and natural science *divide* knowledge of the world in such a way that the former is concerned with genuinely real, unchanging being and the latter with variable, constantly changing phenomena that are always in a state of becoming. On the basis of this assumption, however, the objectivity of historical science is quite deficient in relation to that of natural science. Its concepts would be products *only* of the subject who reshapes and works up the given world of appearance. For historical science, there would be no absolute reality to which it could conform. Thus regardless of how generally acknowledged its governing perspectives might be, they lack the relation to a real "object" of knowledge that exists as an autonomous fact. In comparison with natural science, history becomes an "empirics" ["*Empirie*"] in the pejorative sense of the word, in other words, a science that not only remains completely attached to appearances but also never provides more than incomplete knowledge, limited to a small part of the phenomenal world. As the determination of facts of the past ordered on the basis of value relevance, it is mere "chronicle." In all respects, however, natural science abandons everything that is merely factual and merely historical to reach what is timeless in reality.

On the basis of such assumptions, nevertheless, another view also remains conceivable. In spite of these considerations, the prospects for the objectivity of history are not hopeless, even from a metaphysical standpoint. This is because the preceding consequences follow only if the concept of historical knowledge as we have expounded it is maintained. But is not this concept perhaps just as open to criticism as the view that natural science amounts to nothing more than a reshaping and working up of empirical reality, without an absolutely real object? If concept formation in natural science possesses the firm

standard for its endeavors and the foundation of its scientific significance in an absolutely real being, is it not possible that history can
enjoy a metaphysical objectivity as well?

In fact, a way seems to be open whereby history and natural science
are again placed on the same level of scientific objectivity. It is only
necessary to show that history can also be based on a metaphysics in
the sense in which the natural science of the corporeal world is based
on the metaphysics of atomism. It would be necessary to establish the
following: Cultural values are linked to the metaphysical "essence" of
the world in such a way that temporal reality can be grasped as a
process of development by means of which this essence appears in the
phenomena or is temporally manifested in empirical existence. Then
history would also have its objective standard in an absolute reality,
and it would no longer need to be intimidated by the comparison with
natural science.

Attempts of this sort have actually been made, and Hegel can again
qualify as the prototype for this sort of undertaking. In his work,
"spirit" comes to itself – that is, it comes to freedom – in history. Here
the principle for the selection of the essential seems to coincide with
the metaphysical essence of reality. Should this metaphysics prove
sound, therefore, the objective validity of this principle would lie
beyond doubt. In the Introduction, we already pointed out the
significance that such a philosophy can have for historical comprehension. Suppose this philosophy can be scientifically grounded.
Then it seems that with reference to the metaphysical principle,
reality is divided in an absolutely objective fashion into a sequence of
developmental stages, each of which is objectively significant in its
distinctiveness. Even the singular and the individual acquire an
eminently scientific interest as a result of the position they occupy in
the gradual manifestation of the metaphysical essence in the sensual
or phenomenal world. From this perspective, therefore, a historical
representation of reality would be free of all caprice, because its
governing principles would no longer be taken from value positions
that are merely human. Historical representation would make it
possible for human beings to transcend themselves, just as natural
science achieves this by teaching us to discern absolutely real existence
and its timeless laws.

Therefore, must not the philosophy of history also attempt to
penetrate appearance in order to reach the most profound essence of
the world, and in this way obtain objective perspectives for concept
formation in history? It is true that thus far we see no way it could
reach this goal, but that does not prove the goal unattainable. In
consequence, it seems that if we want to retain our concept of history

and at the same time arrive at a fundamental decision about the ultimate question in the philosophy of history, we are confronted with the problem of proving the unattainability of this goal; in other words, the problem of showing that there is no metaphysical reality on which historical science can base the objectivity of its governing principles and its concept formation.

But this is not feasible for us either. It might be possible, of course, to show that the perspectives that are supposed to govern historical representations cannot be taken from metaphysical realities, since that would require deducing the known from the unknown. Perhaps the view could also be made plausible that the metaphysical essences we thought we had discovered are nothing more than metaphysically reified *value* concepts that were already at hand before the construction of a metaphysics was begun. In that case metaphysics would, at best, rest on objective values. But the converse relationship – the derivation of the objectivity of values from a metaphysics – would never be possible. Nevertheless, as soon as metaphysical realities come into question, all the means that stand at the disposal of logical or epistemological inquiry prove ineffectual, regardless of whether it is an issue of positive construction or negative arguments. And precisely those who draw the consequences of the view that at least on the ground of the theory of science, *nothing* can be claimed with certainty, except with regard to immanent, empirical *realities*, must give up the possibility of proving that there *can* be no absolutely real world that appears in the empirical, sensual world in the course of history.

Nevertheless, we need not conclude our discussion of this problem with a question mark, at least insofar as the issue still concerns a problem in the *philosophy of history*. Suppose there were two different realities: an absolute, metaphysical reality and an empirical reality that is the manifestation of the former. And suppose we also knew precisely what the essence of the metaphysical world consists in. Under these conditions, could we even *conceive* a science on the basis of which it would be possible to endow *historical* science with the metaphysical objectivity that is wanted?

To resolve this problem, suppose we attempt to sketch the picture of such a science. Then, in the first place, it is clear that this science cannot see the absolute essence of the world in a timeless, invariable, and *unchanging* reality, as practically all metaphysics does. That completely destroys the "objective" meaning of history, which is what this science requires. It makes every *development* represented in a historically individualizing fashion senseless. Schopenhauer already saw this. From his metaphysical standpoint, therefore, he was justified in denying any deeper significance to history. Rather, metaphysics, to do justice to the unique development of the historical, must itself become "evolutionary." In other words, it must shift the concepts of becoming and change into the metaphysical essence of the world itself. In addition, such a science cannot conceive this evolving essence as indifferent to positive or negative value, for in that case no governing principles for concept formation in history could be derived from it. Finally, and this is the decisive point, such a science must conceive both the metaphysical world in a completely *rational* or conceptually transparent fashion. In other words, it must discern the *law* according to which the metaphysical essence develops and becomes apparent. Only in this fashion would it be possible both to relate the empirical world to the metaphysical world in a way that is scientifically justifiable and logically completely unequivocal, and to confidently distinguish the essential from the inessential in historical life. An irrational or metascientific *faith*, such as a religious conviction, may be quite important from other perspectives, but it remains insignificant for the question of the *scientific* "objectivity" of history that is at stake here.

Suppose these conditions are satisfied. Let us consider what such a rationally prudent metaphysics would offer to the scientific activity of the historian. The answer is not difficult: To make a generally valid distinction between the essential and the inessential in the infinite experiential world, we need a principle of *selection* with reference to which the essential content of historical concepts is consolidated to form a unity, and everything else is left aside as inessential. Can a concept of the rationally comprehensible metaphysical essence of the world ever be the principle of selection for the representation of the reality that is the appearance of that metaphysical essence, and whose relationship to the metaphysical essence we have comprehended and made rational? Is it not precisely the rational knowledge of the relation between essence and appearance that destroys such a possibility? As soon as we knew the general metaphysical law acording to which the essence developed and manifested itself in the course of development, is it not true that for us, *all* empirical reality would be *equally* necessary for the manifestation of the essence in appearance? And would we not thereby immediately forfeit the possibility of *distinguishing* essential individuals from inessential individuals in the historical world of appearance, and thus the possibility of forming historical *concepts*?

Again, it is Hegelian metaphysics that exhibits this point most clearly. Of all metaphysical systems, it seems to be most compatible with a conception of history. In light of our earlier stress on its positive significance for history, it is now necessary for us to have a look at its tendency to assume a totally *antihistorical* character as soon as it is elaborated into a metaphysics of history in the sense at issue here. Suppose the concept of freedom were more than a *value* concept that makes it possible to distinguish the historically important from the unimportant. In that case, consider the highly controversial proposition: "What is rational is real, and what is real is rational." With reference to the gradual development of Spirit in the phenomenal world, this proposition would in fact have to take on the meaning that every empirical reality is *equally necessary*, and thus has *the same* meaning. But as soon as this claim is made – which is certainly not what Hegel wanted to say – history no longer exists. For in that event, *everything* in the world is either historical or unhistorical in the same fashion, and everything individual loses its *distinctive* meaning. It becomes an indifferent instance of a generic concept that represents the general essence of a certain stage in the nomological development of the World Spirit.

This can be generalized. The concept of progress in the metaphysics of idealism is just as antihistorical as the naturalistic concept of progress that some have tried to derive from the principle of adaptation according to natural selection. In the foregoing, we have already shown that historical individuality is destroyed by laws of progress no less than by laws of nature.[10] Thus we need not pursue the matter here. It is sufficient to point out that the concept of a rationally ascertainable metaphysical reality, to which empirical reality is related in a rationally ascertainable fashion, cannot provide precisely *that* which history requires: an "objective" principle of *selection*.

So we can say that a metaphysical idealism, which believes it has discerned the general developmental law of the world, must see the unique course of history as meaningless and superfluous in precisely the same way as a metaphysical naturalism, which regards absolute reality as a process of eternal recurrence. Hegel's significance for historical science was a consequence of the fact that freedom was an absolute *value* for him, and he followed its development in the historical process. But he could not *exhaustively* comprehend the essence of the temporally real world as a nomological progress toward freedom. This is precisely why the empirical reality of history – which remained *irrational* even for Hegel – could be organized into a sequence of developmental stages by means of the relation to the absolute value of freedom, in the same way that every historical

[10][*Die Grenzen*, pp. 426–7, which are not included in the translation. Here Rickert argues that when historical phenomena are regarded as nothing more than preliminary stages in a progressive sequence of development, their individuality as entities with a distinctive significance is destroyed.]

representation must arrange its material by means of value relevance. If Hegel had ever taken seriously the idea that *everything* that is historically real is "rational," his philosophy of history could not have been written. It exists only on the assumption that one configuration of empirical reality is *more* or *less* significant than another.

This very consideration, however, suggests still another idea. Perhaps the impossibility of metaphysically grounding a philosophy of history and thereby providing objective principles for historical concept formation holds only for a "monistic" metaphysics that knows no more than *one* principle. Does not a dualistic system – which sees the essence of the world in the conflict between a good metaphysical principle and an evil one – offer history more? Is it not true that empirical reality can be related to the conflict between the two transcendent cosmic forces? And in this way, does not what is illegitimately claimed in monistic conceptual schemes become possible?

Even on such assumptions, we could regard the temporal process as history only as long as neither the relationship between the two metaphysical principles nor their relationship to empirical reality had become *rational* for us, in other words, only as long as we had *not* yet *comprehended* the world metaphysically. But then it would still not be possible to represent the unique course of history with metaphysical objectivity. On the other hand, suppose we had knowledge of the general law according to which the two cosmic forces conflict with one another, and the necessity with which one or the other or both becomes apparent. Then *everything* in the world would again be *equally* essential. In other words, we would have to relate every reality whatsoever to the metaphysical opposition, and the possibility of historical *concept formation* would be destroyed.

In short, for an "optimistic" metaphysics, everything becomes essential. For a "pessimistic" metaphysics, everything becomes inessential. And for a dualistic metaphysics that presupposes the conflict between two principles of good and evil, *everything* also has a specific positive or negative significance for the cosmic metaphysical opposition. History remains possible only as long as we do not comprehend the world metaphysically, and empirical reality stands in an *irrational* relationship to values. Reality, which is irrational for theoretical knowledge, must also remain irrational with respect to its relation to *values*.

It is obvious that in this context, the word "irrational" cannot mean "*anti*rational." On the contrary, it can only be intended to express the indifference of the real to the concept and to value. Understood as metaphysical comprehension, all rationalization – regardless of whether it is naturalistic or idealistic – in fact destroys the significance that can be ascribed to things by virtue of their individuality. Historical thought – in quite the same way as moral volition – is tied to the resistance of the *insensible* world and to the *imperviousness* of reality with respect to both general concepts and values. Even the philosophy that thought historically in a way that was true of none other before it – namely, German idealism – failed to see this. In this respect, therefore, we must abandon its ground in principle.

In this context, however, we always have only one *kind* of metaphysics in view. As a *rational* science, it proceeds in a *logical* fashion in order to advance from empirical reality to absolute reality. Our sole purpose is to determine whether there can be a metaphysical objectivity for history that has the same status as objectivity in natural science. It is obviously far from our intention to deny *any* legitimacy at all to the *belief* in an absolute reality that lies beyond all experience, or to claim that this belief is incompatible with a historical conception. Consider the mere supposition of a *necessary* relation between empirical reality and formally general values, which we have come to know as the presupposition for a scientific necessity of history. Consider, moreover, the conviction that even from a scientific standpoint, no real human values can be regarded as indifferent. It might be supposed that these considerations already imply a metaphysical conviction. That is because what has absolute positive value could have a necessary relation to empirical reality only if there is some *real* connection between the two. And since this connection would always be removed from experience, it would have to be regarded as a metaphysical reality.

Be that as it may, the conviction that views of this sort are true can arise only when the unconditional validity of absolute values is no longer in doubt. Indeed, it must be *founded* on the belief in this validity. That is why a metaphysics "grounded" in this way would never be qualified to provide history with a foundation, since the metaphysics itself is supposed to ground the validity of values. It would simply not be the kind of metaphysics that has as its goal a rationalization of the cosmos, in other words, a logically judicious knowledge of the metaphysical essence. In this context, we wanted only to demonstrate the worthlessness of this *kind* of metaphysics for historical science. . . .

4. THE OBJECTIVITY OF VALUES

However, if neither empirical actuality [*Wirklichkeit*] nor a metaphysical reality [*Realität*] is qualified to endow concept formation in natural

science and history with objectivity, what way remains open on which
the foundations of a scientific validity of concepts can be understood?
A complete answer to this question obviously far exceeds the scope of
our inquiries. Here, as in the preceding account, we must restrict
ourselves to the relationship in which historical objectivity stands to
objectivity in natural science. However, even if we do no more than
clarify this relationship, suggestive remarks on some of the general,
fundamental concepts that determine our conception of the nature of
all knowledge as such cannot be avoided.

In view of the foregoing analyses, it is to be expected that our
epistemological standpoint will be called "subjective" in the pejorative
sense. Suppose we call the "object" of knowledge that with which
conceptual knowledge must conform in order to be "objective."
Then, in fact – since that object can be equivalent neither to an
absolutely real being nor to empirical reality – what we know is not
the actual [*wirkliche*] or really [*real*] existing "objects" of concepts in
natural science or history. For us it is only the factual material
reshaped in the concept that is actual [*wirklich*] or real [*real*].[11] For
this reason, the validity of concepts can depend only on the kind of
activity in which the cognitive subject engages in forming them. In
natural science as well as in history, this is decisive for the formation of
the material in the concept. In every case, it is a question of the
distinction between the essential and the inessential, and this
distinction is always made by the cognitive subject. Thus far,
therefore, we have taken a "subjectivistic" position, and at the outset
we again want to explicitly clarify the extent to which epistemology
must be "subjectivistic" in the sense indicated. For this purpose, we
will attempt to systematically order the different subjective factors of
scientific conceptual knowledge, which to some extent we have
already encountered here and there.

If we reflect on the different kinds of attitude the cognitive subject
exhibits, then two kinds of subjectivism can be distinguished. In part,
we can say that this subject perceives or "conceives"; that is, it merely
accepts something given. We can also say that it takes a *position* on what
it has perceived, conceived, or accepted. In other words, to "conception" in the broadest sense, we have to juxtapose a "*valuation*."
Accordingly, scientific knowledge may not only be dependent on a
conceiving subject. On the contrary, it must further be determined

<hr/>

[11] In this context we need not discuss any further the concept of methodologically
unanalyzed "objective reality" or the concept of empirical reality as consisting of
real things acting on one another, the reality that the individual scientist invariably
presupposes as his material. On this point, see my *Gegenstand der Erkenntnis*, 6th
ed., 1928, pp. 383 *seq.*

that it depends on a valuing subject, in which one would have to see an even "more subjective" subjectivism.

At the same time, it is clear how this possibility is connected with the question of the relation between objectivity in natural science and objectivity in history. Since values are its governing perspectives, it seems that historical science is dependent not only on the conceiving subject but also on the valuing subject. And thus again, it would seem that, prima facie, the objectivity of history is more problematic than that of natural science. Precisely for this reason, however, we propose to link the sketch of the different subjective factors of conceptual knowledge with the proof that natural science also must be regarded as dependent on the conceiving subject as well as on the valuing subject. In other words, at first we will bring natural science *down* to the subjectivistic level of history to see what scientific objectivity can still mean on the grounds of this epistemological subjectivism, and then we will see how the validity of concept formation in natural science is related to the validity of concept formation in history. In precisely this manner, it can be shown why the objectivity of natural science is in principle no greater than the objectivity of historical concepts, in other words, why an objectivity of scientific concept formation in general would not exist without the recognition of some valid *values*.

To gain an overview of all the subjective elements that appear in all scientific knowledge obtained by means of concepts, suppose we explicitly differentiate – in addition to the conceiving and the valuing subject – the subjective factors contained in knowledge of the *material* from those that lie in scientific knowledge of the material, or in its conceptual *reshaping* by means of specific *forms* of concept formation. In that case, *four* different possibilities result. First, the *conceiving* subject necessarily belongs to the form of science; second, it belongs to the material *and* the form; third, the *valuing* subject also belongs to the form of science; and fourth, neither the form *nor* the material knowledge can ultimately be conceived without a relation to a valuing subject as well. Ordered in this way, the four possibilities represent a sequence in which the subjective factors present in science progressively increase, so that in the final analysis the highest conceivable degree of the subjectivism of knowledge is reached.

In view of the foregoing exposition, it will not be doubted that the forms of all scientific concept formation are at least related to a *conceiving* subject. If we assume that empirical reality is the only material of science, and if empirical reality forms an infinite manifold whose purely factual rendition can never be provided by science, it is self-evident that science is possible only by means of the reshaping undertaken by the subject. In the same way, we know that without presupposing a metaphysically real existence, the material of the empirical sciences in its pure facticity must also be related to a conceiving subject. In that case, there is only one reality: the one that is given to the conceiving subject, or "immanent" reality. Thus we need not detain ourselves with a more detailed justification of the standpoint according to which both the form and the content of empirical knowledge are related to the *conceiving* subject in the same way.

However, the relation of knowledge to a *valuing* subject probably requires explicit discussion. In the first place, as regards the form of concept formation, it seems, as we have already indicated, that although the valuing subject is of decisive importance for history, this does not hold true for natural science; for we have shown that disregarding all values attached to real objects is even a necessary presupposition of natural science. In spite of this, should its form also be related to a valuing subject?

In fact, it can be proved that this is necessary. Of course, it obviously remains true that only historical objects are brought under a *historical* concept by means of theoretical value relevance. The essence of natural science, on the other hand, requires abstraction, even abstraction from the theoretical relation of objects to values. It does not follow, however, that concept formation in natural science could exist in *every* respect without a valuing subject. In the foregoing, we disregarded the values indispensable to *all* scientific concept formation. We did this only to stress as clearly as possible the theoretical relation to values that is distinctive for history alone. Now, however, it is also important to clarify the extent to which *all* scientific concept formation is valuative, or the extent to which *every* cognitive subject must take a position on values. In that case, it can be shown that the real *objects* of the natural sciences are detached from theoretical value relevance just as they are detached from practical valuation. But natural science is possible only if the forms by means of which it subsumes these objects under a system of general concepts are necessarily acknowledged by a subject as valid values, for it is only with reference to such acknowledged values that the subject can *distinguish* the essential from the inessential. In the final analysis, therefore, the form of every empirical science must also be conceived as valuated by a subject that acknowledges values. Indeed, we can actually claim that even the abstraction from all value relations that are attached to individual objects – which becomes necessary with respect to generalization in natural science – can be understood only as an act of a subject that valuates the forms of concept formation in natural science. To this extent, an act of valuation cannot be eliminated from *any* formation of concepts.

Finally, it remains only to discuss the fourth possibility: the question of whether not only the form but also the material of science – in the sense of the mere "factual material" – must be related to a valuing subject. Or was this possibility mentioned only in the interest of systematic completeness? This seems to be the case, for what could it mean to claim that the given facts or empirical realities are necessarily connected with a valuation in order to be known? With this question we arrive at the point on the understanding of which insight into the consistency of the following line of thought depends. Here too, however, our specific purpose requires only that we set out explicitly what we have already repeatedly touched upon.[12]

A "fact" is relevant for science only insofar as it is known, that is, insofar as the judgment, which as a fact it states, can be considered *true*. Consider, however, the idea that what is called "true" is what has theoretical value for the cognitive subject. On no account is this idea to be detached from the concept of a true judgment. So the statement of every fact in a judgment that makes a claim to truth already implies as a necessary presupposition to the commitment to the value of truth and its recognition by the cognitive subject. Thus the "subjectivism" of knowledge in fact extends to the point where not only the forms but also the material of all science – namely, the "facts" that are held to be true, or more precisely, the purely factual judgments – must be related to a valuing subject. If it is legitimate to characterize something as "real," the cognitive subject must *necessarily* designate a content as real, or ascribe the form of reality to this content. And this necessity – which is always what is at issue here – can only be the necessity of a theoretical value, the necessity of an *imperative*.

Thus there is *no* knowledge at all that is not the product of a valuing subject who *acknowledges* the intimate *connection* of form and content. It surely does not need to be established in detail that this does not once more place in question the fundamental distinction between value-free concept formation in natural science and value-relevant concept formation in history. First, the individuality of the objects of knowledge in natural science remains independent of every relation to values. In other words, the cognitive subject of natural science values only to the extent that in the formation of concepts, the value of truth that his judgments have must be implicitly acknowledged. Moreover, this acknowledgment differs in principle from the histor-

---

[12]For the detailed development of the concept of knowledge of real existence that provides the basis for this discussion, see my book *Der Gegenstand der Erkenntnis* (1892; 6th ed., 1928).

ical relation of objects to values and the formation of in-dividuals. This is because the former represents not a mere value *relation*, but a direct *valuation* on the part of the subject, an acknowledgment of the intimate connection of form and content.

This may suffice to demonstrate the extent to which the concept of *all* knowledge includes the idea of a valuing subject. If we have become clear on this point, we also know what – from exclusively epistemological perspectives – the question of the objectivity of scientific concept formation can still mean. It depends solely on the *validity of the values* on which the cognitive subject takes a position in the process of knowledge. If these values are valid, the concepts that are formed with reference to them are scientifically objective. Indeed, they possess the utmost objectivity that can be required of them. On the other hand, if the values are not valid, we can no longer speak of scientific objectivity at all.

This will seem paradoxical on the ground of every "realism." That is why we should again note the following: We are obviously not claiming that the individual scientist always becomes explicitly aware of the validity of his concepts or the necessity of his judgments as the necessity and validity of a value. In empirical science it will be easy for him to come to terms with the idea that things really "are" just as they are judged to be, completely independent of the cognitive subject. In epistemology, however, we cannot act on this presupposition. On its basis we would never understand what the objectivity of scientific knowledge means. This is because there simply is no "real" world that is reproduced as it actually is by the content of our concepts, or at least we have no knowledge of such a world. Thus, consider the supposition that an independently existing reality is the criterion for scientific concept formation. As we have already seen, it is precisely this supposition that would produce skeptical consequences. In that case we would have to call in question the objectivity of all scientific concept formation. This objectivity can be grounded only on the validity of theoretical values, but never on the existence of a mere reality.

As regards the values concerning which we can show that the cognitive subject always acknowledges them whenever it asserts something as true, it will, of course, be supposed that their validity can be called in question. As a basis for scientific objectivity, therefore, they are too uncertain. Such a doubt, however, if carried out consistently for *all* values, would destroy the concept of truth itself. The result would be a logical absurdity. We know why *every* judgment that can make a claim to truth must presuppose the absolute validity of truth value. Thus there are no conditions under which the acknowledgment of the validity of *some* values can be avoided. On the other hand, it should be admitted that we have thereby obtained no more than the *general* principle. In other words, we do not yet know which specific values can be presupposed as valid. Nor in this connection do we intend to develop and defend a general system of theoretical values whose validity provides the basis for the objectivity of scientific concept formation. By means of an example, however, we propose to clarify the principle with whose help we can show the extent to which the validity of certain value presuppositions is absolutely necessary or indubitable. This will suffice to determine the relationship between historical objectivity and objectivity in natural science.

Those who attempt to discover laws of nature presuppose that some unconditionally general judgments are valid. For them, therefore, the form of unconditional generality is necessarily a valid theoretical value. Of course, it might possibly be claimed that unconditionally general judgments are not valid. This does not seem to imply a contradiction in the sense in which one is implied by the judgment that contests the unconditional validity of *all* theoretical values as such. But this depends on what meaning we connect with the claim that unconditionally general judgments are not valid. Suppose it holds true only for a special case. In other words, it asserts that this particular individual cognitive subject at this particular time and place could form no unconditionally general judgment about this particular cognitive material. In that event the claim is indeed unobjectionable. But then it is not inconsistent with the epistemological presupposition on which the objectivity of concept formation in natural science depends. On the contrary, it comprises only a purely factual statement that has no significance for the problems of epistemology, and it is obvious that the mere accumulation of purely factual statements of this sort would in principle make no further difference. Only if the unconditionally general validity of *all* natural laws and *every* possibility of making any unconditionally general judgments are contested, do we find the *attempt* to deny what is a formal, logical presupposition of nomological concepts in natural science, and thus what must also hold valid as a theoretical value. Such an attempt itself, however, necessarily has the form of an *unconditionally general* judgment. Therefore, it already implies the acknowledgment of the formal presupposition it would like to deny. In other words, it asserts that it will contest the basis of its own validity. As a result it must invalidate itself as a logical absurdity.

Of course, advocates of radical empiricism are in the habit of calling arguments of this sort "sophistical." But this involves a minor confusion. In Plato's dialogues, it is precisely the sophistical theories that are *repudiated* in the manner popularly called sophistical today. In such cases, therefore, one ought to be somewhat more cautious with the reproach of sophistry and not throw stones when one finds oneself in the glass house of relativism. The absolute relativism of the Sophists and the modern empiricists can easily be repudiated by exhibiting its *inner contradictions*. By following out its own consequences, this position is reduced to absurdity. The presuppositions that lie at the foundations of *all* knowledge cannot be demonstrated in any other way. It is necessary to show that any attack on their validity is circular, because the assailant – to carry out his own proof – must ground himself on precisely what he wants to attack. For this reason, psychologism also necessarily becomes circular in this way whenever it attempts to arrive at judgments about the validity of cognitive presuppositions by means of a natural scientific explanation of cognitive processes. Consider, for example, the analyses of Hume, which in principle remain unsurpassed to this day. They contain many epistemological infractions of this sort, thereby proving that they are also implicated in this circle. Notice how little the explanation of the genesis of the causal concept would tell us if Hume had not already invariably *presupposed* the *validity* of the principle of causality and of causal laws. It is only on the basis of the causal concept that he succeeds in showing how recurrent succession in *all* cases necessarily *produces* that association of ideas on which the causal concept allegedly rests. Theories of this sort can indeed be useful if they explain how belief in the soundness of the formal presuppositions of knowledge gradually comes about. However, they can never have anything to say about the validity of these presuppositions as theoretical values.

A more detailed inquiry into the problem of the objectivity of concept formation in natural science does not lie within our plan. Suppose the validity of its presuppositions can be contested only by propositions that already imply these very presuppositions. In that case, the circumstance that it is only the cognitive subject that forms the material of knowledge on the basis of these presuppositions can no longer constitute an objection to the objectivity of concept formation in natural science. At this point, moreover, we are interested only in the question of the relationship between the objectivity of concept formation in history and the objectivity of concept formation in natural science, assuming that generalization and the establishment of laws are not possible without the acknowledgment of valid theoretical values either.

We already know that there is one respect in which historical representations approximate the statement of mere facts more closely than do the representations of natural science. Thus purely factual knowledge can already be called "historical" in the broadest sense of the word. To this extent, therefore, it seems that historical science makes fewer assumptions than natural science. But this concerns only the concept of history we obtained in Chapter 3 as a *problem* of methodology. For this reason, the scientific objectivity of historical concept formation, which proposes to be more than purely empirical, remains problematic at this point. As we have seen, historical science must be allowed to assume that the unique development of reality stands in a necessary relationship to some unconditionally and generally valid values. Is this also the sort of presupposition that does not in any way reduce the objectivity of history below the level of the objectivity of natural science?

To answer this question, let us reflect on an aspect of knowledge that we did not consider in the foregoing. Because science is not possible without concepts, all *purely* "intuitive" knowledge is denied it. As this is put, science must always proceed "discursively," and this is also connected with the fact that the real process of knowledge fills a certain span of time or reaches its goal only by means of a sequence of changes. Because this goal possesses absolute value for the cognitive subject, it seems indispensable to conceive the sequence of changes that leads to knowledge as a value-relevant development, in the sense of the fourth concept of development discussed earlier.[13] Finally, since the value to which the development is related in this case is an unconditionally general value, in this way we already see that all the presuppositions we have come to know as the condition for an objective historical concept formation are in principle fulfilled. In other words, as soon as we treat the real process of knowledge itself as the object of knowledge, we can never consider it solely in a natural scientific fashion; on the contrary, we must consider it historically as well. And since the concept of the historically value-relevant development includes the other forms of historical thought, in principle we have thereby obtained everything we need. Every new real act of cognition becomes a historical in-dividual with respect to the value of knowledge. The totality of cognitive acts is consolidated to form a historical development, and because this development is necessarily a link in the "most general" – that is, most comprehensive – totality of reality, the value perspective, which cannot be viewed as purely individual and arbitrary, is necessarily transposed onto the historical

---

[13][*Die Grenzen*, pp. 422 and 430–1, which are not included in the translation. In this fourth concept of development, a unique process is constituted as a teleological unity by virtue of the fact that its distinctiveness and individuality are related to a value in a purely theoretical fashion.]

nexus. In other words, the nexus itself assumes the form of a historical and value-relevant development.

In short, now there is no longer any sense in which we can doubt that even the conception of reality as history in the forms indicated – at least insofar as the real process of knowledge is at issue – also possesses a transindividual, or objective, validity. The forms on which this objectivity rests can be understood as necessary on the basis of the nature of knowledge, which can reach its goal only by means of a sequence of changes. As a result, these forms themselves are no less objective than the presuppositions that hold for the search for natural laws of unconditionally general validity.

In *principle*, naturalism is thereby breached. Even for the natural scientist, that on which he himself works exists as a reality only in the real thoughts of individual persons who have either formed or understood the concepts of natural science. From a situation in which no one pursued natural scientific reflections, a natural scientific investigation of the world has gradually developed as a result of the work of many individuals. This unique developmental sequence must be represented with scientific necessity in such a way that its individuality is related to the cultural value of natural science. But it is precisely the advocate of naturalism who must acknowledge this cultural value, which governs concept formation, as unconditionally valid. And since the historical development of natural science cannot be isolated but, rather, stands in a historical-causal connection with the total cultural development of humanity – indeed, the distinctiveness of this total development must also have had an essential influence on the distinctiveness of the development of natural science – the objective historical value is necessarily transposed onto the total development of human culture.

Suppose that in this way naturalism acknowledges the most general presupposition on which the scientific objectivity of the representation of a unique, individual, developmental process rests. Then the only possibility that remains open for naturalism is again to place human beings and human conduct in the *center* of historical reality, regardless of how it may conceive their spatial location in the universe. In other words, as soon as naturalism reflects on *its own* history, it must grant the historical standpoint its complete scientific justification. Consider the quite fashionable view mentioned earlier, which holds that although human history may have had scientific significance for the ancient and the medieval world, for science the objective value of all goals posited by human beings has disappeared with the displacement of the arena of all history from the focal point into any remote recess of the cosmos whatsoever. This view in particular now seems senseless. What destroyed those earlier weltanschauungen that held that the earth as the arena of world history forms the center of the universe? Natural science. And what is natural science in reality, if not a work of human beings who live on an insignificant particle of the cosmos? Because of the insignificance of the planet earth, should all human works lose their objective meaning and necessary value relevance from the standpoint of science? In that case, why do we ascribe any objective value to the human discovery that the earth is not the center of the universe?

Such questions need only be posed for the following point to become clear: If *every* historical perspective is repudiated as lacking scientific objectivity, naturalistic standpoints, like all other philosophical standpoints, would become self-defeating. In a certain sense, it is in science itself that we can never go beyond history. Thus, those who think in a consciously historical fashion, think "without presuppositions." Not even a radical skepticism can be consistently pursued if the skeptic reflects on the history of intellectual development and compares his skeptical posture with the thought of other times and other persons in order to juxtapose it to his own position as that which is more justified.

Indeed, we must still take one further step. The most general presupposition on which an objective conception of the world in historical science is based includes even fewer metaempirical elements than the presuppositions of natural science. And at the same time, the former must be regarded as more comprehensive than the latter. That is, whoever thinks historically needs only to assume that the temporal development of reality is related to *some* absolutely valid values, which may be completely unknown to him. Nomological science, on the other hand, must make the much more specific assumptions that the discovery of unconditionally general judgments or laws of nature embodies an absolute theoretical value and that in the course of history an approach to the realization of this distinctive, substantively defined value is possible by means of science. From this perspective, therefore, the "a priori" of natural science may be represented as a special case of the historical a priori. Accordingly, the historical, value-relevant perspective proves to take precedence over the natural scientific, value-free perspective. In other words, history can be pursued without making the metaempirical assumptions of natural science; but without the metaempirical assumptions of history, natural science loses its meaning. This is because every natural scientist has implicitly set the unique historical development of natural science in relation to a value that is absolutely valid.

In any case, as certainly as we want scientific knowledge, just as certainly are we obliged to acknowledge an objective, historical value-relevant concept formation as valid, a formation of concepts that represents the history of real knowledge and thus ascribes an objective significance to culture in general. From philosophical standpoints, "nature" itself – in other words, the conception of reality with respect to the general, or the nomological nexus – becomes a product of the historical *work of culture* [*Kulturarbeit*]. In principle, this is already sufficient to resolve the question of the relation between history and natural science. It is not only the case that historical objectivity occupies its own status, completely equal to the objectivity of natural science. In addition, suppose natural science proposes to reflect on its own objectivity. Then, in the first place, it implicitly makes all the assumptions on which an objectively valid individualizing formation of concepts in the cultural science rests. Moreover, to these it adds other, more specific assumptions about the substantively defined, theoretical validity of values.

On the other hand, precisely this consideration shows that we cannot yet conclude with such a result. We have reached our conclusion by a purely logical path, and it seems that in this way we have bought it at a high price. In one respect, of course, we have obtained even more than we need. We can define the governing value, whose transindividual and unconditionally general validity is beyond doubt, with reference to its *content* as well, namely, as the value of natural scientific truth or knowledge. As a result, however, it also seems as if we had gained less than is necessary for our purposes. We could point *only* to the intellectual perfection of concepts in natural science as an unconditionally general value. This seems to bring us straight to the philosophy of history we rejected earlier, which gives way to a pseudonaturalistic basis when the gradual perfection of the intellect – or even the progressive realization of the absolute sovereignty of the natural scientific method – is made into an "evolutionary law" of history.

Thus we are still not finished with our work, even though in general, the precedence of the historical, value-relevant standpoint over the generalizing standpoint is already established. It seems that the history of the intellect can make a higher claim to objectivity than the history of the other cultural processes. This is all the more problematic since it is necessarily connected with the essence of our argument. In our deduction we had to limit ourselves to logical values. This preference for a specific cultural value that debases the others would be unsatisfactory not merely from general philosophical perspectives; it would also fail to agree with historical science as it actually exists. At this point, therefore, we will have to demonstrate the grounds on which the appearance of a preference for the intellectualistic conception of history had to develop in a philosophical investigation. Then we will have to show how a more exact view of the matter demonstrates that in spite of this, intellectual values can be linked with the other values of culture in such a way that the contradiction between our view and historical science as it actually exists disappears. As regards what we have gained in the foregoing, it is obvious that we are not thereby abandoning anything in principle. By this point, the objectivity of a certain concept of value-relevant, individualizing concept formation has already been established beyond any doubt. But the concept of history that we have obtained in this way proves too narrow. For this reason, it must be extended in the requisite fashion, without thereby diminishing the objectivity of history.

First of all, given the path we have taken thus far, it is clear why we could not arrive at any other result. It was necessary for us to proceed in a purely logical fashion. In our attempt to develop a logical deduction of the metaempirical presuppositions of science, the only criterion absolutely compelling for the intellect is the demonstration of the contradiction that lies in every denial of these presuppositions. So it seems that as regards the issue of the theoretical justification of absolute values, a compelling criterion is available *only* for the proof of logical values. In other words, for the purely theoretical person, what lies beyond doubt becomes not only the highest but also the only absolutely valuable good.

In fact, this must be the case, and there is a certain respect in which we will never advance beyond this point with a logical investigation. It is only the denial of logical values that can be proven to be logically contradictory. Once we have seen this, we can also understand why so many philosophical systems that attempt not only to obtain the ultimate principles of real being but also to ascertain the nonreal *meaning* of life have made the intellect into a universal principle and regarded intellectual perfection as the absolutely valid value, in comparison with which all other values either became secondary or lost their validity altogether. Whoever pursues science can, of course, doubt the validity of other values, but he can never doubt the validity of the value of science. For such a person, therefore, the world of science turns into a scientific world. This does not mean only that the world takes on scientific *forms*. No objections could be raised against this. On the contrary, the world also receives a purely scientific *content*.

This holds true of all cases. Materialism does not stand alone when it makes the methodological principles for the working up of its material – principles that result in quantification – into true reality and thereby produces atomism as the metaphysical reification of its conceptual apparatus. For Plato as well, the general *concept*, the *logos*, becomes genuinely real being. For Aristotle the highest ideal of scientific knowledge is transformed into the concept of the divinity and the concept of the one consummate reality. As a result things form a realm of graduated levels. They become all the more real the more the principle of knowledge, logical form, has penetrated matter, which is not actually real. For Spinoza the meaning of the world is the *amor intellectualis dei*, which again coincides with *cognitio intuitiva*, the highest ideal of knowledge. Thus human beings can do no better than immerse themselves in the pure contemplation of God, the most comprehensive general concept conceivable. Even for Kant, who otherwise advanced far beyond intellectualism, the purely problematic counterpart of the highest intellectual perfection or of the *intellectus archetypus*, the noumenon, becomes the thing in itself. Even for this thinker all human striving at least occasionally seems deficient because it is not able to grasp the meaning of the world by means of knowledge of that purely problematic indefinable entity.

In short, we see that in the work of many philosophers, intellectual values are placed at the pinnacle of all values, as if this were self-evident. As a result the most serious difficulties must arise if other aspects of human beings and other values are to find their legitimate place in philosophical systems. The religious, ethical, and aesthetic life and the values on which its meaning rests are either degraded or become so thoroughly intellectualized that they threaten to lose their own distinctive significance. In particular, a conflict arises between the "practical" person who *wills* and the theoretical person who *knows*. As a science, philosophy unintentionally comes to favor theoretical or logical values. Thus philosophy is usually disposed to resolve the conflict in favor of the theoretical person, thereby attenuating the legitimate claims of the practical person.

Is it a distinctive characteristic that necessarily attaches to philosophy that it separates the intellectual side of persons from their other activities and then favors this side because of its logical transparency? In its character as theory, must philosophy always rank theoretical values above all others and reduce the remaining values to a status of insignificance in comparison with them? Or is there a way that the nonintellectual aspects of human beings and values that are not exclusively logical can also occupy their legitimate place in a comprehensive theory of weltanschauung? In other words, can the domain of alogical values be correlated with intellectual values? Or in part, can the former perhaps even take precedence over the latter? The issue of whether we can understand the objectivity of a comprehensive historical science depends on the answer to this question.

A "voluntarism" in opposition to intellectualism is now on the scene. In other words, there is an emphasis on how the will is invariably the decisive factor in practical life, also holding that its right to influence our convictions about the totality of the world and the meaning of life cannot be contested. By means of such a voluntarism it also seems possible to override a preference for intellectual values and the completeness that is merely scientific. However, if our *scientific* convictions are at stake, then this way of "surmounting" intellectualism seems highly questionable. That is because, in principle, it opens the door to all wishes and every sort of whim, and this must evoke the opposition of the scientist. A scientifically grounded theory of weltanschauung can come about only in a purely theoretical way by means of logical thought. So as long as theoretical thought is conceived in such a way that, in every respect, it stands in a fundamental opposition to volition and action, logical values will always claim primacy in relation to other values, and philosophy will not be in the position of juxtaposing any other value to the theoretical as having a validity that is equally legitimate. In that event, the practical side and the theoretical side of human beings necessarily remain in conflict. On the one hand, the theoretical person must reject as unjustified all claims made on behalf of the validity of extratheoretical values. On the other hand, not only will the person of volition and sentiment perceive the claims of science as an outrage; in addition, the sciences in which nonintellectual values play a decisive role, as holds true for most of the historical sciences, must apparently lose their purely theoretical character – and that means their scientific character as well.

Thus consider the manner in which we proclaim the primacy of the will on the basis of its quantitative preponderance in practical life. In other words, we attempt to ascribe primacy to the will, not on the basis of logical reasons but by means of an act of will that stands in opposition to logical thought. We will not be able to advance scientifically in this way. On the contrary, this would only once more place in doubt the validity of theoretical values as well. Thus *everything* would be reduced to the level of an unlimited relativism or skepticism.

But perhaps it is possible for the epistemology that proceeds in a purely logical fashion to overcome the opposition between intellectual and nonintellectual values in a different way, or at least resolve it to the extent that, precisely from the epistemological perspectives with the fewest presuppositions, the appearance of a preeminence of the scientific objectivity of an intellectualistic philosophy of history disappears. To show this, we need only make explicit a consequence that follows from what we have established concerning the nature of all real knowledge, and especially of all real *judgment*.

In all knowledge as judgment – and this is the only sort of knowledge relevant to scientific concept formation – the object of knowledge and the cognitive subject are necessarily correlated. In other words, the concept of knowledge loses its sense if, on the one hand, an "object" is not assumed as a *standard* that *holds validly* as a value independent of the real cognitive act. On the other hand, a real cognitive *act* is also presupposed that *appropriates* this object, either through recognition or through valuation. In this context, we propose to disregard the "objective" aspect of the concept of knowledge. We will only ask, What can be said about knowledge if we consider not the objective validity of the value but the real act of the subject that is indispensable for the realization of truth value, the act that appropriates the valid value? How does it present itself for a historical conception?

In the present context, this question is of decisive importance. For if it is the *history* of intellectual completeness that is at stake, then *only* real cognitive acts in which the development of scientific concept formation takes place are relevant. They are the indispensable conditions for the realization of science in its gradual historical development. And since, as we have seen, they consist of judgments as theoretical valuations, the realization of science necessarily includes the concept of a *valuing cognitive subject*.

As the real condition for all historical realization of truth, this cognitive subject must awaken our interest. Insofar as it has to orient itself to values when it wants to acquire knowledge, this cognitive subject encounters a norm that demands recognition. Moreover, this recognition is not relative or "hypothetical" but absolute, for it concerns the recognition of an absolutely valid value. Thus we can say that for the cognitive subject, theoretical value appears as a "categorical imperative." This can be expressed in the following way: On the basis of the standpoint with the fewest presuppositions, as long as the historical development of truth or the perfection of science is at stake, there is under all circumstances also an objectively valid "duty" that holds for the person whose only aspiration is the truth. We use the word here in the broadest sense conceivable. In other words, we want to do more than characterize the manner in which normatively general values are juxtaposed to the will of the subject as obligatory. Or we speak of a consciousness of duty when we acknowledge a value simply because it is a value. At this point, we will try to show that such an "autonomous" or "free" recognition of values – in which we usually

see only the nature of the *morally* volitional or the practical person –
also cannot be thought away as the basis for the realization of value,
assuming that a development of scientific truth by *cognitive* subjects is
to be possible. In other words, every real cognitive act whatsoever is
preceded by a *will* that desires what it should, an "autonomous" will
that ordains its own law on the basis of an imperative.

Once this is clear, then in *history* we can no longer oppose the
volitional to the cognitive person, as if the two had nothing at all in
common. Rather, the two aspects of the person, the theoretical and
the practical, now seem to be two different modes in which an
autonomous will expresses itself. In consequence, an investigation of
the real process of knowledge as it gradually develops in history forces
us to see that the presupposition of the realization of even the values
of truth in science lies in the autonomous will that acknowledges a
norm. In other words, in the volitional subject that freely acknowledges values, we have to recognize – if the expression is allowed – a
metalogical real "basis" for the realization of logical values in historical
development as well.

This should not be misunderstood in a "voluntaristic" manner.
There is no sense in which the foregoing calls into question the
autonomy of the theoretical, how it is "objectively" *valid* on its own
terms. As long as we are concerned only with logical values themselves, we can – indeed, we must – disregard every will that takes a
position on them. To this extent, it is correct that the will, or indeed,
the primacy of volition, does not exist for *pure* logic.[14] But if the
historical realization of value – in other words, the *real genesis of science
by real subjects* – is at stake, the concept of an autonomous will that is
no longer logical but metalogical, and that recognizes theoretical
values as objectively valid values, becomes a necessary presupposition.

The paradox that is perhaps connected with the concept of the
metalogical that is obtained in a logical fashion is only apparent. Here,
logical thought on the basis of which we arrive at this metalogical good
merely becomes aware of the fact that the pure *validity* of the
theoretical as a value does not yet qualify as the realization of the
value in a *real* good. In consequence, an act of will is required in order
to realize the theoretical value in the good of science. Science can arise
only on the basis of a will to truth. This will, therefore, is no longer
logical but metalogical. The value of truth does not rest on a will. But
since truth is a value that demands recognition, real science rests on
a will that wills values as such. For this reason, only in the will that

---

[14]On this point, see E. Lask, "Gibt es einen Primat der praktischen Vernunft in der
Logik?" *Bericht über den III. internationalen Kongress für Philosophie zu Heidelberg*,
1909, pp. 67 *seq.*

acknowledges the norm for its own sake do we have the basis of real knowledge, even if not, of course, the basis of the validity of values. From this perspective, the judgment that stands in the service of scientific knowledge is a special kind of value-oriented *action*. It follows from this that the absolute valuation of the autonomous will is a necessity for the theoretical person as well.

Thus we can show that an autonomous will that "freely" wills what it should is a good whose value, precisely from the theoretical standpoint, can never be placed in doubt. Theoretical thought that pursues knowledge has to qualify as a special case of the "practical" endeavor that realizes values as such in goods. Consider the obvious objection that intellectualism still has not been surmounted, since in this connection the will appears only as a good that has an intellectual value. In other words, the will has unconditional value only *to the extent* that it constitutes the presupposition of logical goods or scientific knowledge. This objection is not sound. In the investigation of the logical indubitability of the value attached to science, we of course advance to the point where we also compel the theoretical person to acknowledge the autonomous, value-conscious will as an absolute value. Because of this disposition of our thoughts, which is unavoidable in a logical investigation, it can appear as if we had grounded the unconditional value of the autonomous will only in the unconditional value attached to the good of science. This appearance, however, arises only from the course of the investigation. The absolute value of the autonomous will rests on the consideration that it is the presupposition of every realization of unconditional values *whatsoever*. This was the only reason why we had to begin with the logical to show that *even* the purely theoretical person has to acknowledge as valid the unconditional value of this will.

But what follows from this as regards the question of the objectivity of historical science? We have added nothing concerning the *substantive* definition of the values that we may presuppose as absolutely valid. On the contrary, we have shown only how the value of the autonomous will that acknowledges values for their own sake also lies beyond all doubt. So it seems that we have obtained only a good whose value is *even more* formal – and thus also *even more* devoid of content – than the value we already had. As a result, are we now faced with the problem of finding, through a more precise substantive definition, a sequence of distinctive cultural values that are related to the most general formal value of the value-conscious will in the same way that holds true for the value of truth and the value of science? And do we then also have to exhibit their objectivity and general validity with reference to their content in such a way that with reference to their validity, they can be made either equivalent to scientific values or correlated with them?

The answer to these questions follows obviously from the foregoing considerations. Suppose that historical development is not represented in a theoretical and value-relevant fashion but is positively or negatively valuated in a practical fashion. In that case, derivation of specific substantively defined cultural values to serve as a standard for valuation would, indeed, be necessary. In quite the same way, a philosophy of history that proposes to define and articulate the uniform "meaning" of the total development of humanity would not manage without substantively defined values. Indeed, even a universal history or a world history can be written in a *uniform* fashion only on the basis of a system of cultural values, and to this extent it presupposes a material philosophy of history. For the rest, however, the knowledge of a substantively defined value system is irrelevant to the question of the scientific objectivity of purely *empirical* historical representations. Accordingly, at this point we have already attained everything necessary for the foundation of historical concept formation and its objectivity.

The cultural value of science offers history *more* than it needs, and this surplus is precisely what distinguishes the cultural value of science from the most general, purely formal value of the value-conscious will: Truth value makes possible a direct value judgment concerning volitional processes of history. Such a judgment, however, is not the problem of a purely scientific history. Further, the historian proceeds all the more objectively the more he takes the *content* of his governing value perspectives from the historical material itself that he represents, namely, the "meaning" in which the historical centers have really lived. For these reasons the metaempirical presupposition of the empirical science of history lies exclusively in the consideration that from a purely theoretical, scientific standpoint as well, the relationship of real valuing and willing subjects to *some* absolutely valid values or other remains *necessary*.

In other words, science can never regard the commitment of persons to normatively general values and real life in the service of the realization of value and meaning as something that is merely "individual," in the sense of being *arbitrary*. The presupposition is already guaranteed by the unconditional validity of *that* value that an autonomous will really has. For just as the value attached to this will holds necessarily, so the relation of reality to it is also necessary. In this context, we should keep in mind only the sense in which we use the word "autonomy." We do not mean that we would thereby arrive at a philosophy of history that employs "ethical standards," or at some sort

of moralistic weltanschauung. Consider the most general and comprehensive concept of culture conceivable. With respect to its gradual
realization in history, this concept also presupposes an autonomous,
value-conscious will, in the sense we have in mind here. This is
because we know that culture exists only in a community whose
members regard certain values as a common concern – that is, as
normatively general values – and, therefore, freely or autonomously
take a value position on them.

In consequence, we see that what we need is precisely the purely
formal value concept we have obtained from the concept of a will that
as such freely acknowledges values. The contradiction between our
results and existing historical science was based on what seemed to be
a necessary preference for intellectual values. Now, on the other
hand, the relation of unique and individual reality to *all* values that
are autonomously acknowledged as normative by persons who will
becomes just as necessary as the relation to the value of science. In
other words, wherever social individuals regard the cultivation of
goods as a common concern – and thus wherever their individual
volition and action are essential to the social values of culture that are
attached to these goods – something takes place to which we must
ascribe an objective significance for the unconditionally valid, especially from the standpoint that employs the fewest presuppositions,
the standpoint of the formal affirmation of values by the autonomous
will.

Further, we now know that persons who will and who take a
position on the normatively general values of their community stand
in the center of every historical representation. As a result we are
especially obliged to ascribe objective significance to the individuality
of these historical acts of will. They stand in a necessary relation to
what should unconditionally be the case, regardless of whether they
advance or inhibit it. This is because the presupposition of practical
life – according to which every such action is more or less proximate
to, or remote from, what should be done – remains untouched for the
purely contemplative theoretical relation of reality to values. For the
reasons already given, this relation is then transposed onto the other
primary historical individuals, and onto the secondary material of
history as well. In consequence, the representation of the total
historical nexus in terms of absolutely or relatively historical concepts
is a theoretically unconditional or scientific necessity.

Of course, we do not know which *substantively* defined "meaning"
the development of human cultural life has; and since in this respect
we will always remain historically conditioned beings, we will never
know it in absolute completeness. But as long as we are concerned

with the objectivity of an empirical science of history, this is not the issue. The historian is always guided by substantively defined values that he has to take from the historical, cultural life itself with which he is concerned. It is important only that the development of human cultural life in general possesses some objective meaning or other. In other words, there are some values to which this development must be related that hold unconditionally. But we can already be certain of this as soon as the value of the autonomous will – which wills the realization of values in goods generally – is established. Further, that is logically or theoretically certain, for we have seen why the validity of this value is the presupposition of the meaning of real knowledge as well. So, although it is only a relation between reality and some unconditionally valid values or other that remains – in which case the assumption we are permitted to make is purely formal – nevertheless, this relation is sufficient in order to regard the historical conception of the world as having the same necessity as the natural scientific conception. As regards the objectivity of the establishment of natural laws, we needed no metaempirical factors except the formal presupposition that some unconditionally general judgments or other are absolutely valid. All content was taken from the specifics of experience. Correspondingly, as the sole metaempirical factor in empirical history, we can also stop with the purely formal presuppusitic that some values or other are absolutely valid. In that case, every substantively defined, specific, normatively general cultural value we know of is more or less proximate to, or remote from, the absolute values whose content we do not know. Thus the individuality of all cultural life has a relation to absolute values that is more than arbitrary.

Suppose we proposed to forge beyond the empirical science of history to a philosophy of history that undertakes to provide a substantive interpretation of the meaning of historical life in its totality. Only then would it be necessary for us to have knowledge of the *content* of the absolute values to which reality must be related in order to maintain that its historical development has an objective significance. Because that cannot be a problem for empirical history – the objectivity of which is our sole interest here – the question of the objectivity of the historical disciplines may now be regarded as resolved, insofar as this is possible on the basis of epistemological perspectives. Consider the formation of concepts whose components are consolidated with reference to a normatively general value to constitute an absolutely or relatively individual and value-relevant whole, and which represent in their entirety the individual totality of a unique developmental sequence. There is no further philosophical standpoint from which it would be justified to claim that this formation of concepts has a more modest claim to the status of scientific legitimacy than the formation of concepts that comprise what is common to a plurality of things and processes or express unconditionally valid judgments about reality in the form of natural laws. An intellectualistic definition of the content of general, valid values includes not fewer presuppositions but more. Moreover, it has also proved itself to be a completely unjustified and dogmatic foreshortening of the horizon of history. It is precisely the "emptiness" of the formal values presupposed as valid that gives history the freedom and latitude in the substantive determination of its governing perspectives that are indispensable to its status as an empirical science.

Index

abstraction (*see also* concept formation; natural science), x, 36, 146, 218
Aristotle, 228
Austin, J. L., xxx

Baden school (*see* Southwest German school)
Baer, K. E. von, 189
Bauch, Bruno, xxx
Bergson, Henri, 14
Boeckh, P. A., 77
Buckle, H. T., 4

Cohn, Jonas, xxx
Comte, Auguste: on philosophy of history, 12–13, 22–5, 181–4; on sociology, 9, 182–4
concept formation: abstraction and, xiv–xvi, xx–xxiv, 46; analytic theory of, xiv–xvi; emanationist theory of, viii, xiv–xvi; generalizing, 44, 51, 62, 74, 119, 152, 154; historical, viii, xxiii, xxvii, 8, 135, 172, 174; individualizing, xiv, xxiii, 51, 62, 74, 87, 119, 148–9, 152, 154, 157, 205, 226–7; Lask's theory of, viii, xiv–xvi; natural scientific, xx, 33–4, 36–45, 51; representation and, xix, 27; teleological, 62, 101–2; value-relevant, 62, 99–106, 205, 219
concepts, 27, 32, 73–4, 79; elements of, 79–80; general, 40–1, 47, 79; historical, xxvii, 31, 61–2, 68, 73–4, 86–7; natural scientific, xx, xxii–xxiii, 37, 40, 47, 60, 79; science of, xxii–xxiii, 73
culture, 134–5; content of concept of history and, xxvi, 64–5, 135–8; historical reality and, 141–3; material of historical science and, 36, 136–8, 141; nonreal configurations of meaning and, 139–43; objective

meaning and, 235; science of, 8–9; valuing subject and, 234–6

Darwin, Charles, 186
demarcation of historical science and natural science, xxi–xxiii, 146, 148
Descartes, René, 14
Dilthey, Wilhelm, xxinn9–10, xxii, xxviii, xxx, 159n29; and theory of historical understanding, 158n28; and theory of human sciences, 146–7
Droysen, J. G., 59, 66

empiricism, 77–8, 195, 221; cultural values and, 199; difference from naturalism, 196; distinction between valuation and value relevance and, 200–1; objectivity of historical science and, 197–200, 202; objectivity of natural science and, 196–9; unconditional validity of values and, 199
epistemology, xixn24, 19–22, 65–7, 202, 220–1, 229; empiricist, 196; in relation to science, 75
explanation: historical understanding and, 29, 140, 156–61; in natural science, 29

Fichte, J. G., viii, xiv, xvi, 13, 182–3
Fischer, Kuno, viiin3
folk soul, 150–2, 154
Frege, Gottlob, xxx

generality: of concepts, xiv; fifth, of history, 149–55; first, of history, 79–80, 90; fourth, of history, 115–16; normative, 130–1, 135–8, 196–7, 199, 204–5, 234; second, of history, 90;